C000252404

Excavations at Thames Valley Park, Reading, Berkshire, 1986–88:

Prehistoric and Romano-British Occupation of the Floodplain and a Terrace of the River Thames

by I. Barnes, C.A. Butterworth, John W. Hawkes, and L. Smith

with contributions from

W.J. Carruthers, Rosamund M.J. Cleal, I. Fenwick,
A.P. Fitzpatrick, R. Gale, P.A. Harding, M. Iles, A.V. Jenkins,
M. Keith-Lucas, S.J. Lobb, Jacqueline I. McKinley, M. Maltby,
Lorraine Mepham, Quita Mould, Rachael Seager Smith,
and Sarah F. Wyles

illustrations by
Julian Cross

Wessex Archaeology Report No. 14

Wessex Archaeology 1997

Published 1997 by the Trust for Wessex Archaeology Ltd
Portway House, Old Sarum Park, Salisbury, England SP4 6EB

British Library Cataloguing in Publication Data
A catalogue record for this book is available from the British Library

ISBN 1–874350–22–1
ISSN 0965–5778

Produced by Wessex Archaeology
Printed by: Derry Print Ltd, St Ervan Rd, Wilford, Nottingham, NG11 7AZ

Editor: Melanie Gauden
Series Editor: Julie Gardiner

The publishers wish to acknowledge with gratitude a grant from English Heritage for the publication
of this report

*Front cover: Thames Valley Park under development in 1988, looking west along the River Thames towards Reading
(© Aerofilms of Borehamwood)*

Back cover: Palaeolithic handaxe from the 1986 evaluation (photo: Elaine A. Wakefield)

Excavations at Thames Valley Park, Reading, Berkshire, 1986–88:
Prehistoric and Romano-British Occupation of the Floodplain and a Terrace of the River Thames

by I. Barnes, C.A. Butterworth, John W. Hawkes, and L. Smith

Contents

List of Figures

List of Tables

Acknowledgements

This report is the culmination of several different phases of fieldwork and report production and the acknowledgements duly reflect this.

The funding for all fieldwork, and the majority of post-excavation analysis, was supplied by Thames Valley Park Ltd, who should be applauded for their wholehearted support for the project. The latter stages of post-excavation analysis and the report production were funded by English Heritage.

The 1986 evaluation fieldwork was managed by Sue Lobb and directed in the field by Ian Barnes with the assistance of Mark Fletcher and Lorraine Mepham (finds). A geophysical survey, conducted in early 1987 as part of a second phase of evaluation, was undertaken by John Gater, now of Geophysical Surveys of Bradford.

The strategy for the 1987 excavations was devised for Wessex Archaeology by Sue Lobb whilst the work was managed by Chris Gingell. The fieldwork was directed in the field by Ian Barnes (Trenches 47 and 48) and Linda Smith (Trench 49), assisted by Vince Jenkins, Phil Mason, Lorraine Mepham (finds), Brett Scaife (planning), Jim Spey (planning), Henry Stevens (publicity) and Sarah Wyles (environmental).

The 1988 excavations were managed by Chris Gingell and directed in the field by Christine Butterworth, assisted by Lee Martin, Catrina Saunders, John Wilson, and Sarah Wyles.

Many thanks are due to the numerous site assistants, volunteers, and work experience students who helped during the three phases of fieldwork, especially to those hardy souls who managed to work on all three, and also to those who helped during post-excavation.

The post-excavation was managed in turn by Chris Gingell, John Hawkes, and Ian Barnes. In addition to the named contributors, to whom we are grateful for their efforts, Phil Mason should be thanked for his contribution during the initial post-excavation work. The illustrations were prepared for publication by Julian Cross. Earlier working illustrations were prepared by Elizabeth James, Karen Nichols, Hans Rashbrook, Rob Read and Laura Templeton.

The information for the archaeological background was supplied by the Sites and Monuments Record maintained by Berkshire County Council, and thanks are due to Paul Chadwick (then County Archaeologist) for his help and support.

In due course, with the permission of the landowners, the archive will be deposited with Reading Museum and Art Gallery.

Abstract

Between 1986 and 1988 Wessex Archaeology undertook an archaeological evaluation and series of excavations on behalf of Thames Valley Business Park Ltd, a subsidiary of Speyhawk Plc, on the site of a proposed 47 ha business park development (centred on SU 7450 7420), 2.75 km to the east of Reading. The site encompassed areas of floodplain and the associated terrace south of the River Thames.

The evaluation, undertaken in 1986 and covering both the floodplain and terrace, confirmed the presence on the terrace of an Iron Age/Romano-British sub-rectangular enclosure previously known from aerial photographs. In addition, possible Mesolithic/Neolithic activity was identified on the terrace.

A series of trenches, with a total area of approximately 6 ha was opened over the terrace portion of the development site in 1987 (W164). The earliest recorded remains comprised a Mesolithic flint scatter associated with a stream channel. The flint scatter appeared to be in situ but to have been disturbed by geological movements. Both knapping waste and tools were present on the site and it was concluded that the site represented an 'industrial' base with limited domestic activity. The remains of a probable Late Neolithic/Early Bronze Age burial were found, from which artefacts, including sherds from a comb-decorated Beaker, a flint knife, and 18 barbed and tanged flint arrowheads were recovered. The sub-rectangular enclosure, identified during the evaluation, was excavated and pottery recovered from the boundary ditch showed that it was founded in the Middle Iron Age and utilised, intermittently, into the late Romano-British period. It would appear to have functioned primarily as a centre of agricultural production rather than consumption. No settlement structures were found within the enclosure, and an associated element of small-scale industrial activity, including possible pottery manufacture, was also recorded. Outside the enclosure there was evidence of land divisions and burial rites; three separate cremation groups were found.

The excavations conducted in 1988 (W244) examined the area of the development on the floodplain, where approximately 7 ha of trenches were opened. As on the terrace, a Mesolithic flint scatter was identified, in this instance associated with a shallow, rectangular hollow of uncertain origin; here, flint knapping had been undertaken on the site. A single pit dated to the Late Neolithic was discovered, pottery from this comprising at least three Peterborough Ware vessels of the Mortlake or Ebbsfleet sub-styles. A cluster of features which could be dated to the Late Iron Age/Romano-British period was found. These features included a number of post-holes which may have represented a rectangular structure, and a series of pits, one of which was timber-lined and was interpreted as having a possible industrial function. Other features were found which remained undated; many of these may have been of natural origin, but others probably related to the activity represented by the dated features.

During the floodplain excavations a number of palaeo-channels was encountered, amongst which was a major channel, running from south-west to north-east, which was filled with a substantial peat deposit. A single trench was hand excavated across the channel at a point where it was 35 m wide and 3.3 m deep. A wealth of palaeo-environmental information was recovered from the channel, including a pollen column recording vegetation changes from the Late Devensian period to the present day. As well as plant macrofossils, a significant number of animal bones were recovered from the channel deposits. These include the semi-articulated skeleton of a Bos sp., several bones of which displayed cut-marks, and which could be dated by comparison with the pollen column to the Mesolithic period.

The results have been published by excavation season, the report being divided into the 1986 evaluation, the 1987 terrace excavations and the 1988 floodplain excavations, and by period within each excavation season. A short overview of the whole project is included at the end of the report.

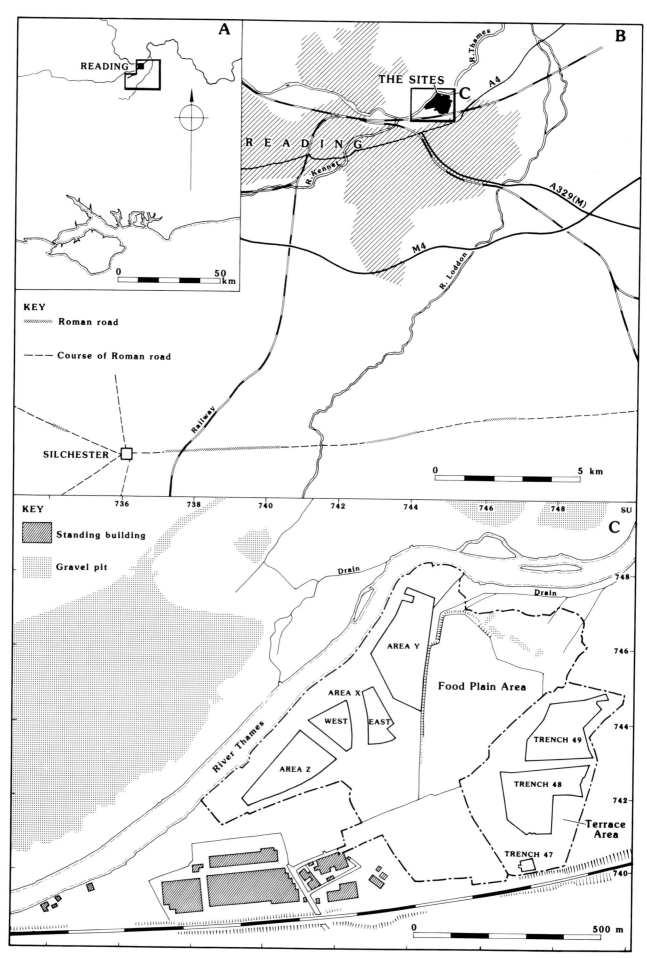

Figure 1   Site location

1. Introduction

The site of Thames Valley Park lies 2.75 km east of the centre of Reading, and occupies an area of approximately 47 ha, centred on SU 7450 7420, between the main Reading–Paddington railway line and the River Thames, less than 1 km downstream from the confluence of the Thames with the River Kennet (Fig. 1).

The development straddles the junction of the Thames floodplain with a low terrace to the south which has a complex drift geology (Fig. 2). The gentle slopes of the terrace are formed from outcrops of Upper Chalk with overlying loam. Areas of valley gravel, plateau gravel, and Reading Beds clays all occur elsewhere on the terrace within the development site. The alluvium-covered valley floor occupies some 21 ha. More detailed soil and geological descriptions based on observations of archaeological and contractors' trenches are presented elsewhere in this report (Fenwick, below).

Prior to the Thames Valley Park development, a large proportion of the terrace area was occupied by the redundant buildings of the Earley Power Station (Fig. 3), with extensive dumps of waste pulverised fuel ash (PFA) extending onto the floodplain. Other parts of the floodplain provided rough grazing in seasonally flooded water meadow.

At the time of the application for redevelopment in 1985, the only known archaeology within the site boundary was a rectilinear enclosure visible on aerial photographs and located on the terrace in the south-eastern corner of the proposed development (Berkshire Sites and Monuments Record (SMR) 1120), with a further series of cropmarks showing trackways and field systems beyond the site to the east (Fig. 3). The more general archaeological setting is discussed below; this section will demonstrate that finds of all periods have been made in the immediate vicinity of the development area.

Development of the Archaeological Response

An application to develop the site into a business park containing low density warehousing and light industrial units was made in 1985. The scheme included the provision of improved road access by means of an extension to the existing A329M and construction of a first stage of the proposed Reading cross-town route which was eventually to provide a direct link between the site and the town centre. The retention of the open character of the area was to be accommodated by developing part of the site as a country park, thus establishing a wildlife refuge, a public amenity, and an attractive setting for the development.

In view of the archaeological potential of the area, evaluation of the site prior to the determination of the planning application was required by Berkshire County Council, to whom the application was referred by the local planning authority, Wokingham District Council. Evaluation and field survey were undertaken in 1986 in two areas of the terrace and a small part of the floodplain, with a second phase of evaluation taking place in early 1987. As a result of these preliminary investigations proposals for further work were developed, with a general field survey preceding excavation of the cropmark enclosure and adjacent areas of the terrace later in 1987.

As the detailed development scheme was formulated, it became apparent that the removal off site of some 265,000 m^3 of PFA would cause considerable disruption to local traffic and to nearby residential areas if carried by lorry. An alternative approach was developed, whereby the PFA was to be disposed of on-site, backfilling areas on the floodplain from which gravel would be extracted and then reinstating the land beneath a sealing layer of redeposited alluvium. Although a more environmentally acceptable solution, on-site disposal would involve the disturbance of a much larger area of the floodplain than had originally been envisaged. A watching brief previously agreed with the developer was augmented by a series of machine stripped trial trenches in advance of gravel extraction, and through much of 1988 a programme of investigation and recording was undertaken both in advance of and during contractors' operations. During operations on the floodplain, a watching brief was also maintained on the construction of the new roundabout required for the Reading cross-town route and Thames Valley Park access road. Access problems at that time prevented an evaluation from taking place immediately to the west of the roundabout, and these investigations were not undertaken until 1990 (Butterworth and Hawkes 1990). Post-excavation analysis has continued separately for each of these elements, and this report is organised in individual sections: 1, the evaluation of 1986; 2, the survey and terrace excavations of 1987, and 3, the floodplain excavations and watching brief of 1988. All aspects of the project, both the fieldwork and subsequent analysis, were funded by Speyhawk Plc (Thames Valley Business Park Ltd). The latter stages of post-excavation and the report production were funded by English Heritage.

Archaeological Background

The Sites and Monuments Records of Berkshire and Oxfordshire were examined for the area within 15 km of the site, a distance chosen because it includes two major prehistoric settlements which may be considered to have been social, political, or economic centres of influence over the site in earlier times. The Iron Age hillfort of Caesar's Camp lies at the south-eastern boundary of the area, the Roman town of *Calleva Atrebatum* (Silchester) at the south-west limit, and the

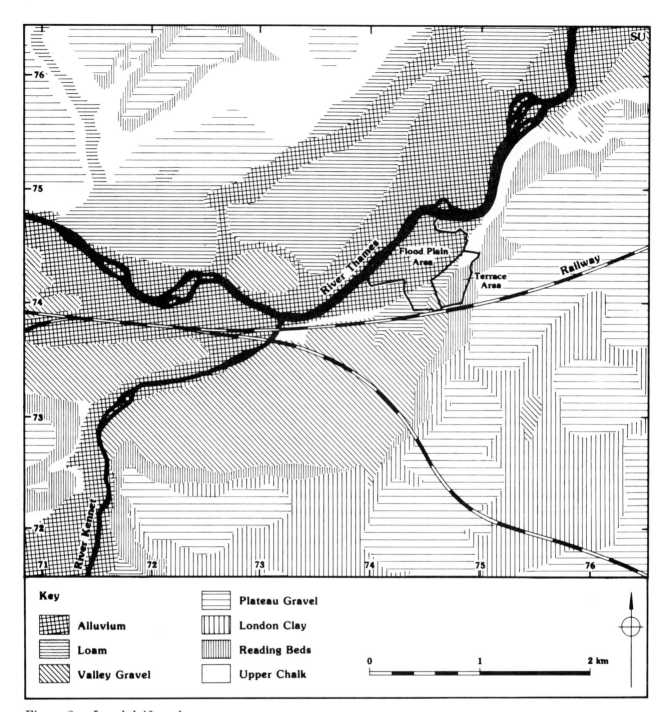

Figure 2   Local drift geology

post-Roman Grim's Ditch just beyond the northern limit. An appraisal of this evidence is held in archive.

Figure 3 shows sites and find spots immediately bordering the development area (record numbers are from the Berkshire SMR):

Palaeolithic

- SMR 970 (SU 733737) Dubious hand-axe and unspecified faunal remains from the Kennet Mouth gravel pit.

Mesolithic

- SMR 877 (SU 750750) Group of 7 tranchet adze/axes from the general area.
- SMR 988 (SU 731739) Group of 7 tranchet adze/axes and a pick from the river near Kennet Mouth.
- SMR 995 (SU 7340 7394) Tranchet adze/axe and flint core of Mesolithic type.

Neolithic

- SMR 2032 (SU 731739) Arrowhead from same location as SMR 988 (above).

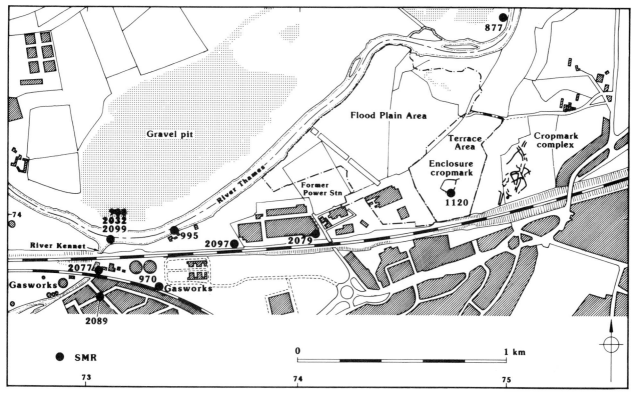

Figure 3   Previous find spots and known sites in the immediate area

Romano-British

- SMR 2077 (SU 73057376) Various finds from dredging and bridging works at Kennet Mouth: layer containing Romano-British pottery, including a sherd of Nene Valley Ware; bronze coin of Tacitus; worked bone, and antler needles of unspecified date.
- SMR 2079 (SU 74067396) Sestertius of ?Vespasian.
- SMR 2089 (SU 73047358) Coin of Domitian.

Post-Roman

- SMR 2097 (SU 73657385) Mixed inhumation and cremation cemetery of 5th–6th century AD date from gravel digging adjacent to railway line.

- SMR 2099 (SU 731739) Saxon battle-axe and 11th century Viking sword from River Kennet.
- Other less well-provenanced finds are also known from the general area, in particular collections of later Bronze Age metalwork dredged from Sonning not far to the east of the Thames/Kennet confluence (Ehrenberg 1980). In addition, a complex of un-dated cropmarks is known on the terrace to the south of the River Thames, including an enclosure (SMR 1120) which lay within the development area.
- The relationship of the evidence recovered from the Thames Valley Park sites to the wider archae-ological and environmental patterns is discussed in the concluding sections of this volume.

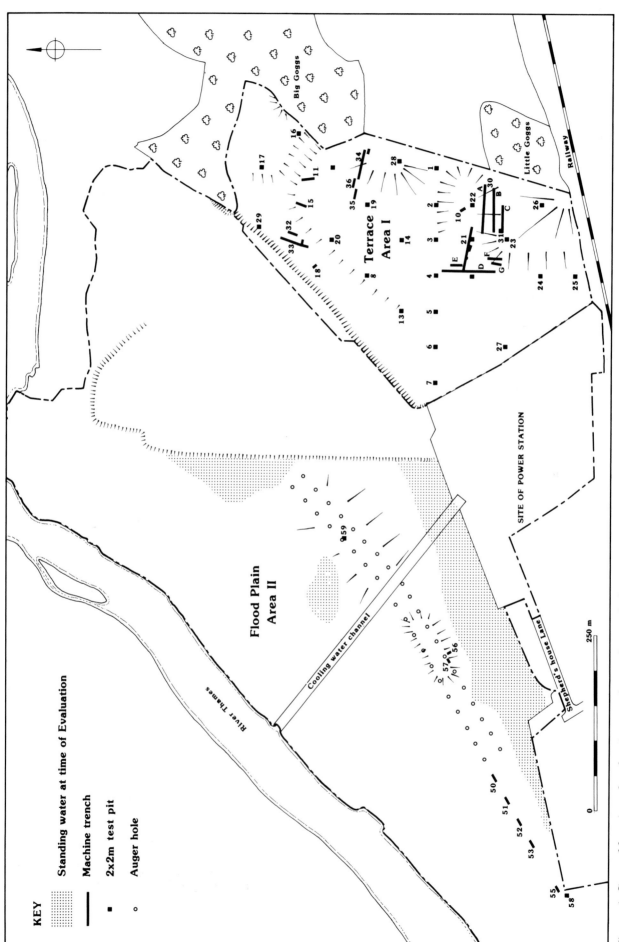

Figure 4 General location of evaluation trenches and auger holes

2. The Archaeological Evaluation

by I. Barnes and S.J. Lobb

Introduction

An application, submitted by Speyhawk Plc (Thames Valley Business Park Ltd), for planning permission to construct a Business and Country Riverside park on the site of the former Earley Power Station and surrounding land was approved, subject to legal agreement and conditions, by Wokingham District Council in April 1986.

The concentration of known archaeological sites and findspots in the immediate area of the proposed development identified it as a site of high archaeological potential. Policy EN26 of the *Review of Berkshire Structure Plans* (1985) made provision for the evaluation of such sites prior to the final determination of development proposals and an archaeological strategy for the evaluation of the site was accordingly commissioned by the applicants and devised by the Trust for Wessex Archaeology. Two levels of evaluation were suggested:

• A broad assessment of the nature and distribution of archaeological deposits over the whole site in order to identify areas of past human activity.

• A more detailed evaluation of specific features, in particular the previously identified cropmark enclosure. Any additional areas of investigation were to be selected following the results of the broad assessment.

The assessment and preliminary investigations of the cropmark enclosure were carried out in November and December 1986. The location of trenches and auger holes is shown in Figure 4.

Area I

Within Area I (Figs 4 and 5), hand-excavated 2 m^2 test pits were laid out at c. 100 m intervals. In the area of the cropmark enclosure, the spacing was reduced to 50 m to try to define more closely areas of activity. Some test pits could not be dug because of underground services, but a total of 28 pits was excavated by hand. A further 17 trenches were subsequently opened by machine. Trenches A to G were intended to identify and define the enclosure; trenches 10, 11, and 18 were located to examine various topographical features; and trenches 14, 15, 32, 33, 34, 35, and 36 to investigate further features found in the test pits previously dug. The ploughsoil across Area I had an average depth of 0.25 m, overlying silty loam subsoil which increased in thickness down the slope to the north-west. In places, where the Reading Beds were closer to the surface, the silty loam had a higher clay element. Elsewhere (trenches 2 and 14), occasional sand pockets were encountered. The test pits suggested that the Reading Beds dipped away to the west of the site, where they were covered by colluvium. A possible remnant of river gravel terrace was found to the west of the enclosure, aligned north–south along the contours.

Unstratified Artefacts

The distribution of finds from the test pits is shown in Figure 5. In all, 143 artefacts were recovered from the topsoil, from the interface between the topsoil and the subsoil, and from the subsoil to a maximum overall depth of 0.4 m.

In general, there were small quantities of worked flint dating to the early prehistoric period found in the northern part of the area, with a Palaeolithic hand-axe coming from the topsoil in test pit 13. Burnt flint, often associated with prehistoric activities, was found in moderate quantities over the whole area. Some sherds of Bronze Age, Iron Age, and Romano-British pottery were also found across the evaluation area, but most especially in the area of the enclosure. Post-medieval material was also collected. These finds are all described with those from the 1987 excavations, with the exception of the hand-axe which is described below.

Palaeolithic hand-axe, by P.A. Harding
The oldest implement found at the site was a derived hand-axe from the base of the ploughsoil in trench 13 (Fig. 6). It is a sub-cordate of Wymer's Type G (1968, 55): wide-butted pointed hand-axes with curved sides and heavy butts. It measures 102 mm in length, 74 mm in breadth and is 39 mm thick. It is in a rolled condition (*cf.* Wymer 1968, pl. xi), although some upstanding ridges are very rolled, being over 3 mm wide. The edges are heavily battered, which has removed most of the detail of manufacture. Light-blue patinated flake scars up to 16 mm long have removed the original surface, which is stained yellow. The hand-axe is also crisscrossed by incipient thermal fractures.

This implement is undoubtedly derived from the Lynch Hill Gravels which mark the former course of the Thames through Earley and Sonning (Wymer 1968, 180). These gravels are one of the richest sources of Palaeolithic implements in England. The condition of this example is typical of many which have been derived from these deposits during subsequent down-cutting and solifluction.

6

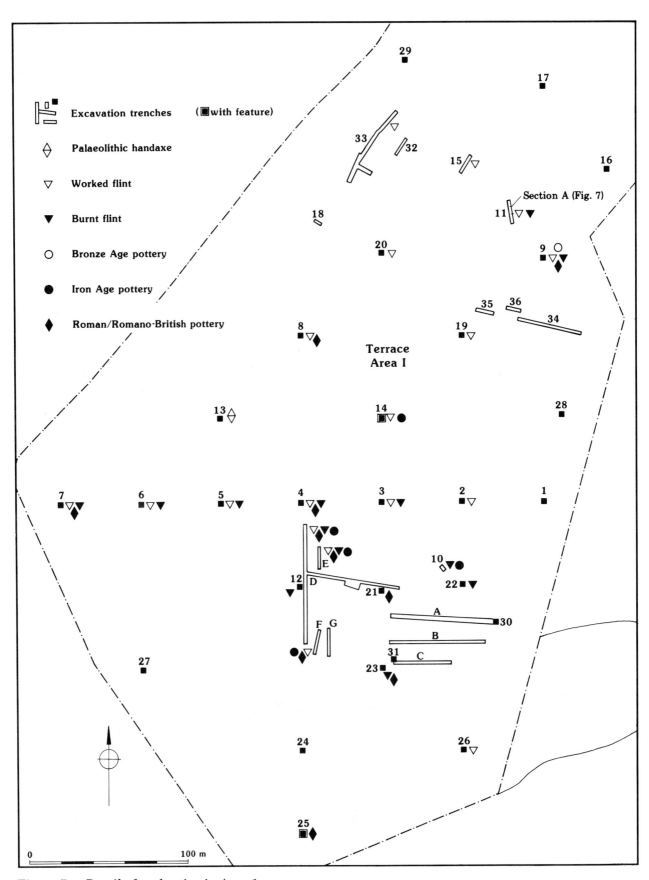

Figure 5   Detail of evaluation in Area 1

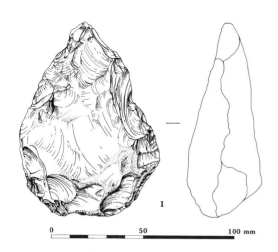

Figure 6   Palaeolithic hand-axe

A fragment of a second hand-axe was found in the main terrace area excavations in an unstratified context in trench 49 (XII).

Enclosure Ditch and Internal Features

Seven trenches, A–G, were excavated by machine to define the rectangular enclosure (Fig. 5). Trenches D, E, F, and G all revealed the course of the ditch, but only in trench G was it fully excavated to show a complete profile. Here the ditch was 'V'-shaped, with a maximum width of 3 m and a maximum depth of 1.6 m. Pottery from the lower fills was dated to the Late Iron Age (*c.* 50 BC–AD 50), with the upper layers containing Romano-British pottery of 2nd century AD date.

Within the enclosure, two pits and one shallow slot were investigated. Pit 9 was beehive-shaped and contained quantities of Late Iron Age pottery. Pottery of a similar date was also found in pit 11, which had a less well-defined profile. The terminal of a shallow north–south slot (4) produced no finds.

Subsequent excavation provided a better context for the interpretation of these features, their stratigraphy, and associated finds and these are considered in more detail in later sections of this report.

River Channel/Ditch

During the excavation of test pit 9 and machine trench 11, it became apparent that a linear feature, at that time thought to be man-made, crossed the northern part of the evaluation area on a curving but approximately east–west alignment. Further evidence for the course of this feature was recovered from trenches 15, 32, 33, 34, 35, and 36, supplementing the profile revealed by total excavation in trench 11 (Fig. 7).

Finds within the fill were confined to the upper levels, with 54 pieces of worked flint and quantities of burnt flint being recovered. The flintwork (considered in more detail below) was characterised by long thin blades, flakes, and tools, including two scrapers, all of which can be compared with Late Mesolithic or Early Neolithic assemblages. The ditch section in trench 11 was capped with a buried soil containing fragments of Romano-British pottery, which in turn was sealed by some 0.5 m of ploughsoil.

An attempt to map the course of the feature in more detail and over a wider area by means of geophysical survey did not produce positive results. Likewise, an additional series of machine evaluation trenches dug in April 1987 failed to define it further.

On the basis of the evidence available from the evaluation, it was not possible to establish firmly whether the ditch was of deliberate, man-made, construction or a natural stream channel. Further excavation in 1987 (described below) suggested the latter interpretation to be more likely.

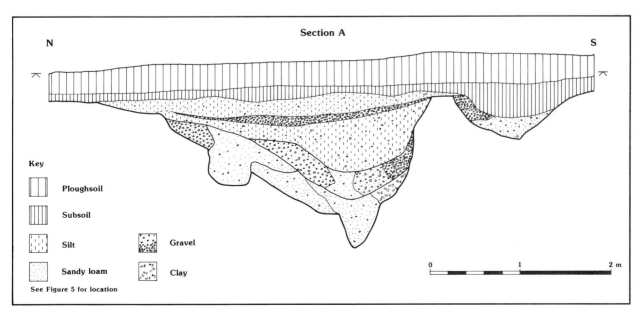

Figure 7   Section of river channel/ditch in trench 11

Other Features

Other archaeological features were identified in only two trenches/test pits. In trench 14 a shallow scoop (context 95), of unknown function, was associated with Iron Age pottery and a fragment of rotary quern. This feature was sealed by topsoil only. Three sherds of Romano-British pottery were found in a post- hole (context 187) in test pit 25.

A second trial excavation, on a much smaller scale than the first, was carried out in April 1987 in a further effort to clarify the course and nature of the channel/ditch. No additional information was recovered on the channel, but some insubstantial and largely undated features were found. A cremation burial with a single vessel of Late Iron Age or early Romano-British date was discovered (1409; Fig. 32), but was left *in situ*.

Area II

Within the area of the floodplain it was decided to limit the amount of hand-excavation because of the high water table. Two hand-excavated test pits, 58 and 59, and seven machine-excavated trenches, 50–53 and 55–57, were dug on higher ground to investigate the nature of the alluvial soils and examine the possibility of settlement or other activity in the area (Fig. 4). An auger hole transect was also undertaken. The excavation trenches and auger bores revealed depths of alluvium varying between 0.2 m and 1.5 m, although later excavation demonstrated considerably greater depths closer to the present course of the Thames. The underlying gravel undulated and appeared to have been cut by channels in a number of places. No archaeological levels were encountered, although a few pieces of worked flint and burnt flint were recovered from the alluvial silts. The only subsoil feature was from trench 51, a shallow scoop of probable recent date.

3. Terrace Area Excavations (W64), 1987
by L. Smith and I. Barnes

Introduction, by A.V. Jenkins

Following the earlier evaluation, a series of surveys designed to further investigate the archaeological content of the terrace area was undertaken in the summer of 1987.

The whole area was contour surveyed and a series of phosphate analyses was undertaken at 25 m intervals, supplemented by three transects sampled at 5 m intervals (Fig. 8). Two of the phosphate transects, at 90° to each other, crossed the sub-rectangular enclosure, and the third ran from east to west across the line of the ditch/channel examined during the evaluation. The survey produced no significant results, revealing no concentrations notably higher than the norm, with the exception of an area near the field entrance on the northern boundary of the field, which was taken to result from modern farm animal activity.

A further series of 62 hand-excavated test pits was dug, completing the work started during the earlier evaluation. In order to test and compare with previous artefact recovery levels, the spoil from eight of the test pits was dry-sieved through a 25 mm mesh, and from five through a 50 mm mesh. The recovery of finds through sieving was not significantly higher than that from unsieved test pits.

Excavation Strategy

The evaluations suggested that archaeologically significant deposits might occur extensively within the development area. It was thus decided to machine strip as large an area as possible and to define priorities on the basis of features revealed. The storage of spoil on site restricted the area which could be examined, and trenching was further constrained by the need to avoid underground services and to include the whole of the cropmark enclosure and the early channel/ditch recorded during the evaluation. The excavation area was divided into three main trenches, 47, 48, and 49 (Fig. 9), so numbered to avoid confusion with trench numbers allocated during the evaluation. Sub-trenches in trench 49 were assigned Roman numerals.

Trench 47 lay towards the southern end of the site, in an area which had produced Romano-British material during the evaluation.

Trench 48 was over the enclosure. A grid of 10 m squares tied in to the National Grid was laid within the trench and alternate squares were cleaned and excavated to assess the density of internal features. It soon became clear that the enclosure contained only a low density of severely truncated features, and it was decided to excavate the whole of the interior, together with a number of sections across the enclosure ditch.

Trench 49 was laid out over the course of the previously observed channel/ditch. In the absence of obvious features or stratigraphy, a series of 5 m squares (Fig. 10) was laid out where flint scatters were noted and were excavated in 50 mm or 100 mm spits. Additionally, and overlapping with the 5 m squares within trench 49, a line of sub-trenches running north-westwards, I–IV and X–XI, was laid out to trace channel 5121. Colluvial and underlying deposits below a shoulder of higher ground separating trench 49 from trench 48 were investigated in trenches VIa and VI–VIII. Sub-trenches V, XII, and XVII–XXI explored the nature of the silts and associated flint scatters elsewhere within trench 49 (Fig. 9).

A watching brief was maintained during topsoil stripping to define further areas of interest. This produced large numbers of finds, but very few features. Only one area of possible archaeological activity, trench 48H, at the top of the slope in the north-east corner of trench 48 was noted.

Mesolithic, by L. Smith

Stream Channel 5121

After the topsoil was stripped from trench 49, the line of the channel identified in trial trenches 9 and 11 could be seen as an irregular band of light grey, sandy material (5027) running in a roughly westerly direction. The alignment was more accurately defined by hoeing across the surface. The channel, 5121, cut tertiary deposits of the Reading Beds series: clays, sands and gravels. These deposits were present over the whole of trench 49 and were partly overlain by a thin deposit of silt (5082) which had developed over the clay on a slight terrace between the 40 m and 41 m contours. A scatter of worked flint (discussed below) was present within the silt but was only rarely found on the surface of the Reading Beds deposits.

Where the fill (5027) of channel 5121 could not be seen on the surface, machine sub-trenches IV, X, and XI were cut across the projected line to trace its course (Fig. 9). These showed that there were two curvilinear features running roughly parallel with each other, both containing leached sandy, gravelly fills and quantities of worked flint. Sections through the southernmost of the two features (Fig. 12) showed an irregular profile, up to 6 m in width and with a depth in excess of 2 m. This variation, which was not consistent with the section observed in the evaluation, suggested that the feature was more likely to have been a stream channel of natural formation rather than a deliberately excavated ditch, despite the presence of quantities of

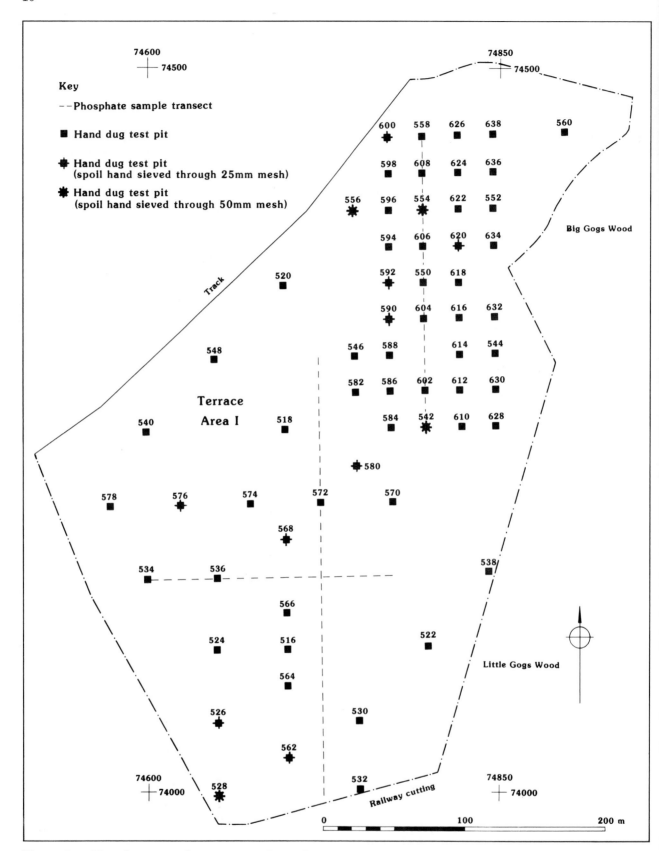

Figure 8   Phosphate sample transect and supplementary test pits over terrace area

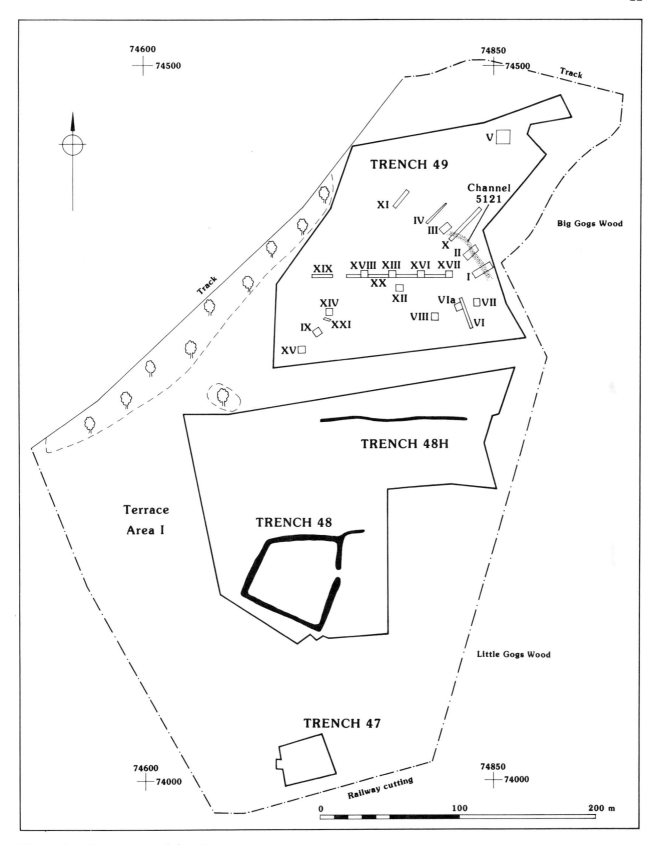

Figure 9   Terrace trench locations

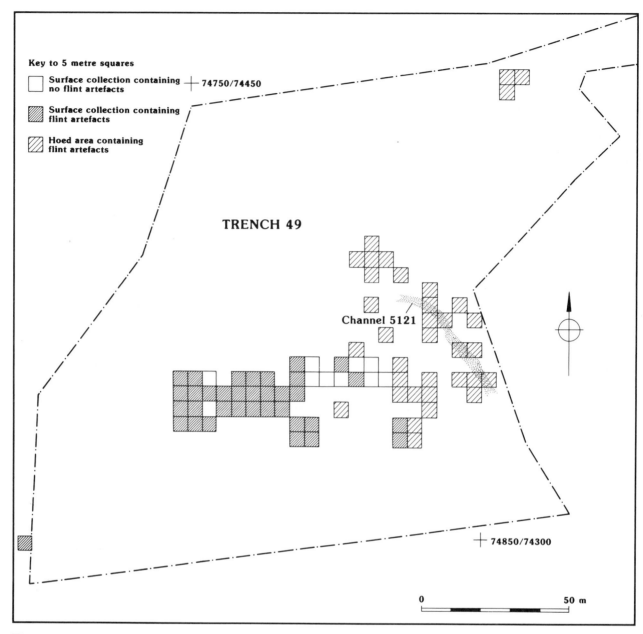

Key to 5 metre squares

☐ Surface collection containing no flint artefacts   + 74750/74450

▨ Surface collection containing flint artefacts

▨ Hoed area containing flint artefacts

TRENCH 49

Channel 5121

+ 74850/74300

0   50 m

Figure 10   Location of 5 x 5 m sample squares within trench 49

worked flint within the fills (*see* below). This interpretation was supported by an appraisal of the sediments visible within the excavated section. In view of the limitations on available time and of other priorities, no further sections were excavated, nor was the northern channel examined.

Sediments within channel 5121,
by I. Fenwick

Sections across feature 5121 were observed in trenches II (Fig. 12) and X. The channel was lined (in trench X) with small, sub-rounded flint pebbles, whilst in trench II, the Reading Beds clay was armoured on its western side with flint gravel. The bulk of the fill of the feature was a pale grey, virtually stonefree, clayey sand. A natural (non-anthropogenic) origin is suggested by the sinuous form of the feature and the sandy texture of the

fill. The surrounding materials were loams or clay loams. The only likely explanation of the feature is that it was an infilled channel, probably fed with sediment from the sandy terrace deposits upslope. Either the sandy material of the fill had been preferentially podsolized after deposition, or the channel was filled with material which had already been depleted of iron. There is little evidence in support of the first hypothesis, which should have been accompanied by a zone of iron enrichment at some point in the profile. However, it is also difficult to account for the depletion of iron prior to the deposition of the sand. If the stream had been sluggish, then conditions could have been anaerobic, so releasing the iron from the sediment and resulting in the ashen coloration of the fill. There is a substantial gradient to the channel at the point of observation, however, which might have been expected to promote sufficient flow of water to prevent this process from occurring.

Flint Scatters

A scatter of worked flint at a significant density was found during cleaning to define the course of channel 5121 and, once this was recognised, the flints were plotted within 5 x 5 m squares (Fig. 10). The scatter continued further to the west and a surface collection programme, again with 5 x 5 m units, sought to define its extent and density. In order to achieve near total collection and to investigate the vertical distribution of worked material, a series of 5 x 5 m trenches (XIII, XVI, XVII, and XVIII) was laid out at 20 m intervals along the 74350 (Fig. 9) northing. The trenches were trowelled down in 50 mm or 100 mm spits. Each trench was divided into 25 1 x 1 m squares, and from three of the squares, selected at random, 20 litres of spoil from each spit was wet-sieved for artefact retrieval. Additional trenches (VIa, VII, VIII, and IX) were subsequently examined by the same method.

These investigations established that the struck flint was almost completely confined to a layer of colluvial silt, variously numbered as sub-divisions of 5082: elsewhere along the transect, the clay, sand, and gravel deposits produced only isolated finds of flint or pottery. However, the greatest number of flints per metre square within a 50 mm spit was only 25 (including 1 core) plus a quantity of chips. The densest scatter was sealed by colluvium (5072) on the hill slope in VI/VIa (Fig. 9) within sandy clay (5073) disturbed by gravel flares.

A further flint scatter was examined by the same method in the north-east corner of trench 49 (trench V), within a layer of silt (5049) overlying clay, almost certainly identical to 5082. This had been disturbed then the material was scraped up to form a mound over a postulated Beaker burial (see below). In the south-east corner of trench 49, approximately between the 43 m and 46 m contours, colluvium was found to be approximately 1.2 m deep.

The trenches dug to examine the flint scatter in the south-eastern part of trench 49 are briefly described below. Table 1 gives a broad outline of the quantities of material recovered from contexts not including uppermost cleaning levels. More detailed analysis of the flintwork and the post-Mesolithic finds are to be found elsewhere in this volume.

Trenches on the Terrace Slope

In the south-eastern corner of trench 49 trenches VI, VIa, VII, and VIII (Fig. 9) were intended to examine possible preserved old ground surfaces or a branch of the linear feature (5017, 5074, and 5121) below the shoulder of high ground between trenches 49 and 48. A section through the Reading Beds clays (which were exposed at the top) and the silts which included the flint scatters would also be obtained.

Trench VI/VIa

The trench (c. 23 m long by 2 m wide) was excavated to a depth of c. 1.5 m. The stratigraphy was very simple (Fig. 13): (5072), a firm yellowish–brown sandy loam 0.2–0.4 m deep overlay 5073, a firm brownish–yellow clay loam, on average 0.5 m deep, which had been dis-

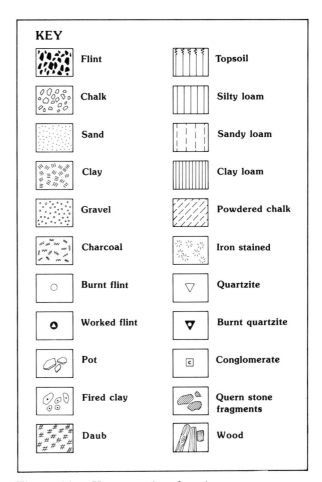

Figure 11   Key to section drawings

torted under periglacial conditions by gravel flares of the underlying Reading Beds (see the detailed description of the geological sequence below). Worked flints (68 in number) were recovered from the spoil but could not be assigned to either context with certainty. The section showed flints lying within a discrete area in 5073 but not within a feature. Trench VIa was offset from the western side of the north end of trench VI so that the stratigraphy of the two trenches could be compared. Trench VIa was excavated by hand in five 100 mm spits to explore the nature of the scatter, with finds recorded within 1 x 1 m squares. The stratigraphic sequence was identical to that in trench VI, ie 5072 above 5073. The boundary between these contexts was not sharp, and consequently spit 3 contained elements of both layers.

Trench VII

A slightly deeper sequence was present here, and comprised a yellowish–brown silty loam (5042) which varied in thickness between 0.4 m and 0.7 m and contained a 0.1–0.15 m thick lens of sub-angular shattered chalk lumps, a 0.5 m thick layer of well-sorted dark yellowish–brown friable sandy loam (5077), a mottled brown/grey/red friable silty loam 0.2–0.25 m thick (5088), distinguished from 5077 by the mottling and its fineness. Almost continuous with 5088 was a silty clay with the same mottled appearance (5106); the edges between the two were not easy to distinguish since they tended to merge with each other. Layer 5106 thickened to the south and east, thinning to the north and west. Cut into

14

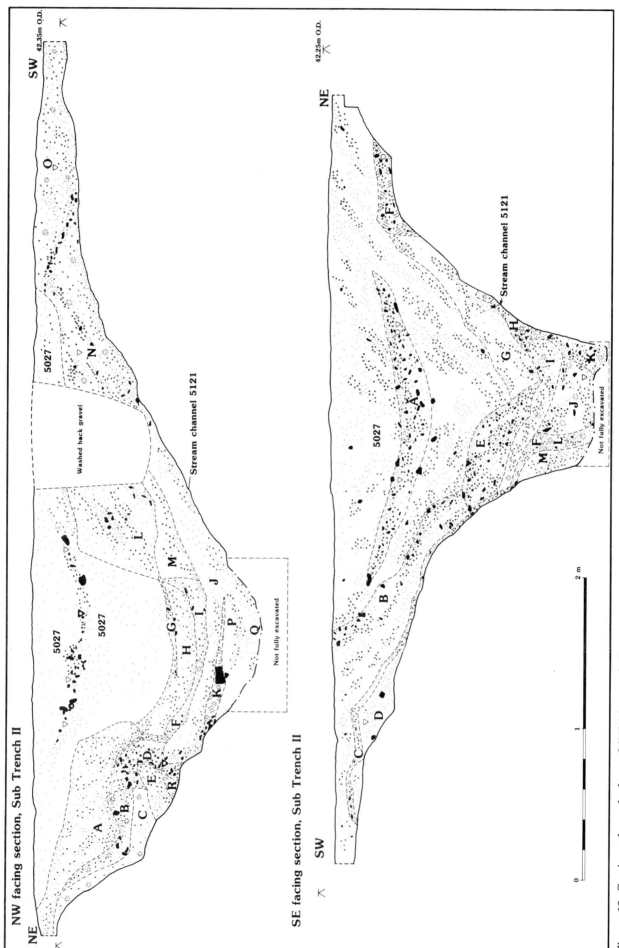

NE ⟰ 42.35m O.D.

SW

NW facing section, Sub Trench II

5027

5027

5027

Washed back gravel

Stream channel 5121

Not fully excavated

A B C E D R F G H I J K P Q M L N O

NE ⟰ 42.25m O.D.

SE facing section, Sub Trench II

SW ⟰

5027

Stream channel 5121

Not fully excavated

C D B E A G H F M J L K I F

0 1 2 m

Figure 12 Sections through channel 5121 in trench II

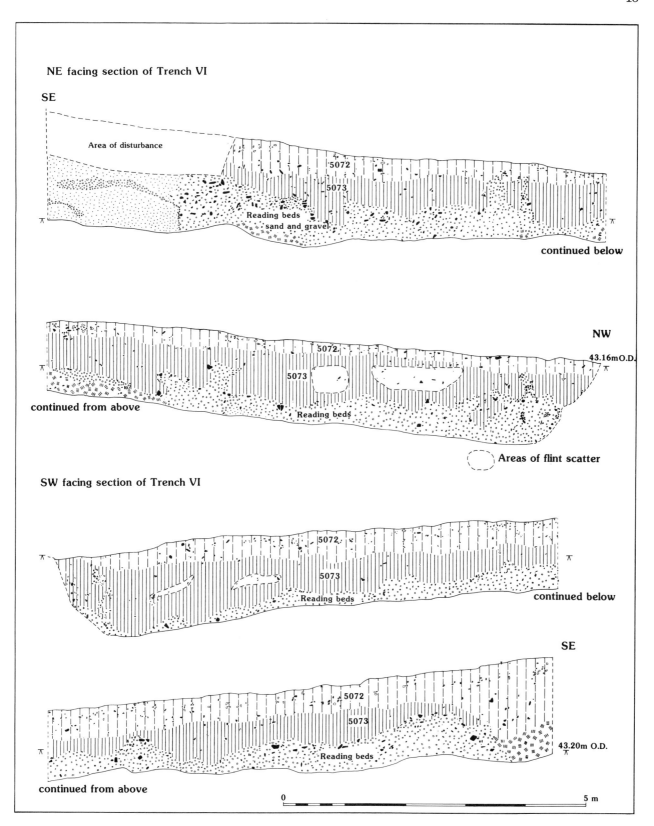

NE facing section of Trench VI

SE

Area of disturbance

5072

5073

Reading beds
sand and gravel

continued below

NW

43.16m O.D.

5072

5073

Reading beds

continued from above

Areas of flint scatter

SW facing section of Trench VI

5072

5073

Reading beds

continued below

SE

5072

5073

Reading beds

43.20m O.D.

continued from above

0   5 m

Figure 13   Sections along trench VI

the surface of 5106 was an irregular scoop (5113) 1.7 m long by 1.4 m wide with an uneven base up to 0.35 m deep filled with 5112 which was the same as 5088. Layer 5106 was not fully excavated for reasons of safety. It was excavated in 19 spits each of c. 50 mm.

Trench VIII

Firm yellowish–brown silty loam (5043) overlay friable brownish–yellow sandy loam (5078) which infilled a shallow scoop 0.12 m deep on the western side of the trench, with solid clay (Reading Beds) below it. Solid clay was not reached in trench VIII.

Trenches along Northing 74350

Trench XIII

This trench (Fig. 9) was important since it lay on the edge of a flint scatter which also occurred in trench XII and so provided a useful comparison with the other trenches along the grid line. The major context within XIII was friable yellowish–brown silty loam 5081, very similar to 5082 in XII but here much disturbed by gravel flares (5104). It was excavated to a depth of 0.15 m in three 50 mm spits.

Trench XVI

Only one context was present (5097). It was excavated by mattock in two 100 mm spits until it became apparent that it was a purely natural layer with lenses of sand and clay through which gravel flares had been thrust. It was a strong brown, loamy sand containing some gravel.

Trench XVII

The sequence here was the same as in XVI, context numbers 5107–5111 and 5118–5120 being assigned to a number of gravel flares thrust through sand and clay.

Trench XVIII

This trench was not fully excavated but contained a modern field drain slot 5114 and a burnt feature 5116.

The trenches along the transect were united via a long machine trench, XX, 0.15 m deep, in order to link them stratigraphically. The line of trench XX was continued further to the west by trench XIX.

Geological Sequence, by I. Fenwick

In an attempt to clarify the origins and post-depositional processes responsible for the formation of the observed deposits, the sections of two of the excavated trenches were recorded in some detail.

Trench VI

In trench VI (Fig. 12), the bedrock was represented by a sandy facies of the Reading Beds. This was mantled by a poorly-sorted deposit of sandy clay and gravel. The clasts mainly comprised rolled flints and sub-rounded flints with the occasional rounded quartz pebble. This material would appear to have been derived, probably by solifluction, from the plateau deposits and the clay facies of the Reading Beds which outcrop upslope. Over-

lying this was a quite different unit. This was a well-sorted clay loam up to 0.1 m thick which was virtually devoid of stones. This unit was disturbed by 'flares' of the gravely sandy clay from below. The fine texture of this material suggests that it had been moved by very modest forces such as would be represented by slope wash in an environment cleared of trees and shrubs. A slight change in the energy of the slope processes was reflected in the appearance of flint and Bunter clasts in the overlying unit, which was of loam texture. It seems likely that both these units represented a continuous period of deposition, in the course of which the horizon of Mesolithic flint artefacts was laid down.

At a relatively late stage, the surface layers of the existing soil had been disturbed by marling and ploughing. Whether this activity also involved the movement of more material downslope could not be ascertained. However, sufficient time had elapsed to permit the dissolution of much of the chalk which was added in the marling process. Accordingly, some 0.35 m of topsoil had either been decalcified or represented a later, non-calcareous addition. That it may be the latter is indicated by the fact that this unit wedged out along the southernmost face of trench VII. At the eastern end the horizon was 0.35 m thick, while at the western limit, only 0.05 m of non-calcareous material was found.

Trench X

The trench was opened by machine to a depth of 2 m and was described but not drawn. The lower (older) part of the sequence was revealed at the base of the slope and comprised a basal unit of Reading Beds clayey sand through which a rubbly and pastey unit derived from the chalk appeared to have been thrust. The diapiric forms of this latter unit suggested that it had been emplaced as a result of periglacial processes. This chalky paste also penetrated the overlying unit (a reddish brown pebbly sandy clay). This deposit contained numerous rounded flints and, especially, Bunter pebbles, suggesting that it must have been derived from the terrace materials. Cold climate solifluction processes would seem to have been the most likely vehicle for this emplacement.

The deposition of all of theses units would seem to have been completed by the beginning of the present Flandrian warm stage some 10,000 years ago. Likewise, the injection of the chalk diapers must have occurred prior to this.

Flint, by P.A. Harding

Total quantities of flint are listed in Table 1. Chips from sieved soil samples are shown present by an asterisk, but are uncounted. This section discusses the Mesolithic industry, together with one Early Neolithic arrowhead; the Bronze Age material is considered later in the volume. The Palaeolithic hand-axe from the evaluation and a second, fragmentary example from trench 49 have been previously considered (above). A spread of blades (length = twice width) and bladelets (width less than 12 mm) was found across trench 49. This industry will henceforth be referred to as the blade industry. It occurred in trench V in the east, was negligible in the west

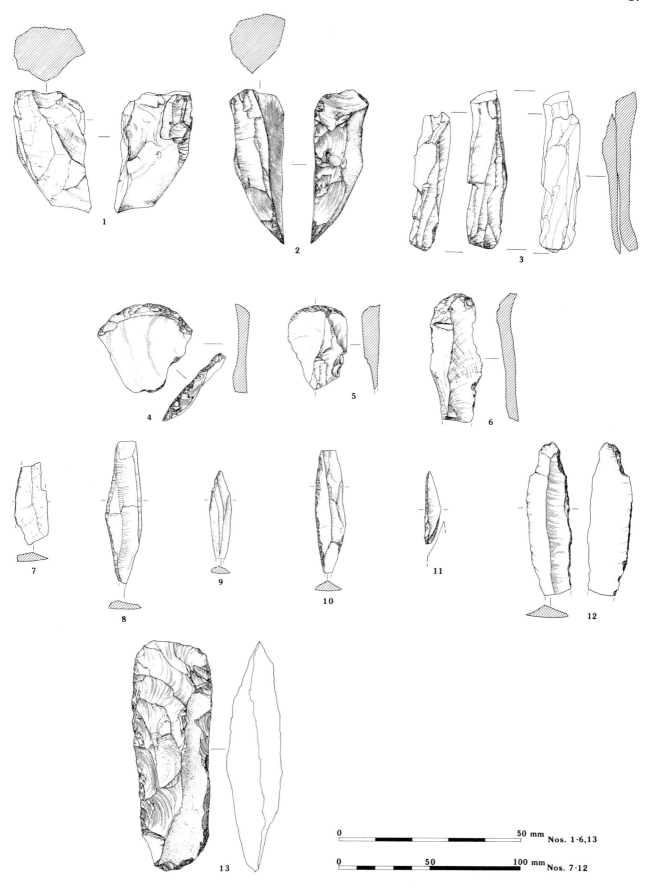

0   50 mm Nos. 1-6,13

0   50   100 mm Nos. 7-12

Figure 14   Selection of Mesolithic worked flint

Table 1 quantification of flint from the terrace area

Trench	Cores	Core Frags	Debit.	Flakes		Blades		Bladelets		Burnt	Ret. Tools	Chips	Total
				C	B	C	B	C	B				
I	–	–	–	4	1	1	3	–	–	–	1	–	10
II	58	6	14	327	274	114	115	52	69	52	34	*	1115
IV	–	–	–	1	–	–	1	–	2	–	1	–	5
V	3	1	1	54	42	8	10	2	20	4	27	*	172
VI	8	1	7	74	73	24	10	10	14	11	2	*	234
VIa sp. 3–5	13	3	12	196	208	64	51	53	43	88	11	*	742
VII	3	1	–	49	48	18	9	2	13	2	4	*	149
VIII	1	–	–	8	14	2	4	1	2	1	2	*	35
IX	6	–	–	23	38	5	7	1	10	2	6	*	98
X	–	–	–	5	5	6	–	1	–	2	2	–	21
XII	28	3	10	166	145	52	45	32	84	35	32	*	632
XIII	5	–	2	29	30	6	6	3	10	–	–	*	91
XIV	1	–	–	6	2	–	–	–	3	3	–	*	15
XV	–	–	–	–	1	–	1	1	–	–	–	–	3
XVI	–	–	–	–	–	–	1	–	1	–	–	–	2
XVII	–	–	–	–	3	–	–	–	–	–	–	–	3
XVIII	1	–	–	1	1	1	1	–	–	1	1	–	7
XX	–	–	–	5	5	6	–	1	–	2	2	–	21
Total	127	15	46	948	890	307	264	159	271	203	125	–	3355

B = broken; C = complete; * = presence of chips

(trenches XIV and XV), and absent from the surface of the Reading Beds to the south. Individual concentrations associated with silt pockets in the natural clay were identified around trenches XII, XIII, and VI/VIa. This second group was amalgamated with the blades and cores from trench II to form the basis of the technological analysis. Flint occurred throughout the fill of trench II. The origin of this material, particularly the cores, is uncertain. Solution may have winnowed out the chips and allowed heavier material to migrate into channel 5121. Most pieces are in mint condition and two pairs of artefacts refit; however, four patinated blades and others with damaged edges indicate mixing. Three of the patinated pieces have broad (4–6 mm) butts, two of which are faceted. An additional unpatinated blade from spit 5 is made from reused patinated raw material. This suggests that at least two phases of blade production may be represented, although the amount of contamination appears to be insignificant.

Trench VI/VIa also contained flint throughout the fill. Disturbed blade material overlay a concentration of waste from core preparation and blade production in the machine excavated section of trench VI. Conjoining pieces from this concentration were found over 1 m apart in the subsequent controlled excavation. This horizontal distribution, the absence of abrasion chips and the rarity of the refits, suggests that the material has been moved or represents a dump. *In situ* knapping is unlikely to have produced such a large spread, unless flaking was done from a standing position (cf. Newcomer and Sieveking 1980). Finds were distributed through spits 3–5, of which larger pieces were found in spit 5. This indicates some vertical movement within the silt. Industrial activity is represented in both trenches. Microburins in trench II, spits 16 and 17, and a Krukowski microburin (Fig. 14: 11) from trench VIa, spit 3, indicate the conversion of blades into tools. Non-industrial activity is also represented in trench VIa/spit 5 by two burnt microliths,

Table 2 flint: core rejection (in percentages) from the terrace area

Sub-Trench	Exhausted	Hinge Fracture	Abandoned	Raw Material	Flaking Angle	Others
II (58 cores)	37	44	31	14	17	37
VI/VIa (21 cores)	39	39	55	22	5	17
Total (79 cores)	38	42	38	17	14	32

Table 3 flint: flake and blade dimensions from the terrace area

		Trench II Blades	Trench VI/VIa Blades	Trench VI/VIa Flakes
Sample size		136	148	268
		%	%	%
Hammer*:	Hard	3	1	12
	Soft	30	40	30
	Indet.	67	59	58
Butts	Plain	40	28	47
	Punctiform	20	25	10
	Linear	34	41	20
	Others	6	6	23
Percussion angle*:	<60	3	3	6
	60–64	3	1	8
	65–69	5	3	16
	70–74	12	3	14
	75–79	10	14	12
	80–84	14	9	8
	85+	4	3	4
	N/R	49	64	32
Planform:	Convergent	37	35	23
(Issac 1977)	Intermediate	40	42	61
	Divergent	12	9	14
	Parallel	11	14	2
Flake class:	1A	85	92	30
(Gingell and	1B	7	5	19
Harding 1979)				
	2	1	1	6
	3	–	–	23
	Misc.	7	2	22
Flake scar pattern*:	Angled	9	9	9
	Right angle	29	27	29
	Parallel	90	92	69
	Opposed	12	12	12
	Thermal	28	20	21
Cortex:	0	65	68	36
	25	26	23	35
	50	8	8	17
	75	1	–	7
	100	–	1	5
Length:	0–9	–	–	–
	10–19	3	7	13
	20–29	15	17	24
	30–39	23	19	17
	40–49	20	22	17
	50–59	20	13	16
	60–69	12	7	5
	70+	7	15	8
Breadth:	0–9	11	15	1
	10–19	58	53	23
	20–29	27	26	24
	30–39	4	5	16
	40–49	–	1	13
	50–59	–	–	9
	60–69	–	–	7

Table 3 continued

		Trench II Blades	Trench VI/VIa Blades	Trench VI/VIa Flakes
Sample size		136	148	268
		%	%	%
Breadth contd:	70+	–	–	7
Breadth: length	1.5:5	32	22	–
	2.5:5	68	78	–
	3.5:5	–	–	32
	4.5:5	–	–	29
	5.5:5	–	–	19
	6.5:5	–	–	8
	6.6+:5	–	–	12
Thickness:	0–3	23	34	17
	4–6	40	32	28
	7–9	20	15	14
	10–12	9	9	13
	13–15	4	7	8
	16–18	2	1	5
	19+	2	2	15
Butt width*:	0–1	59	75	37
	2–3	30	17	19
	4–5	7	5	16
	6–7	2	1	13
	8–9	1	1	5
	10+	1	1	10

*Trench II blades sample size = 167 ie including 31 broken blades with proximal ends intact

one of which is broken by an impact fracture. A tranchet adze/axe was found in trench VIa/spit 3; however, there was no evidence of core tool manufacturing or resharpening on the site. No environmental or faunal remains were present and no hearths were found, although burnt flint was associated with the industry.

Sub-trench VIa, spit 3 also yielded a flint arrowhead of the characteristically Neolithic leaf-shaped form.

Aims

This report aims to describe the technology of the blade industry and to examine the wider relationships. Refitting has assisted interpretation by indicating post-depositional movement and by providing technological information.

The analysis has recorded details of raw material, platform preparation, blank production, and causes of rejection for all complete cores. Flakes and blades have been examined for hammer mode, butt width and type, percussion angle, platform preparation, and details of the dorsal surface. Comparisons between cores, flakes, and blades have then been possible. Relevant results are shown in Tables 2 and 3; details are retained in archive. A limited number of examples are illustrated (Fig. 14).

Condition and raw material

Most flint is in mint condition with a brown to orange–brown staining. The patinated material from trench II is derived from a calcareous source. Nodules of flint eroded from the underlying chalk were primarily used for raw material. The Mesolithic industry occurs where the chalk outcrops close to the surface from below the Reading Beds. The flint is of good knapping quality but internal thermal fractures caused by weathering result in nodules breaking. Refitting pieces from trench VIa suggest that accidental or deliberate breakage of nodules was an acceptable method of obtaining blanks for blade/bladelet cores. The flint is naturally dark grey/black in colour with cherty inclusions, particularly near the centre of the nodule. Most cortex, which can be up to 5 mm thick, has been weathered to a thin rind.

Flint from the local gravel, including Tertiary nodules and Bullhead flint, with its distinctive green-stained cortex over an orange rind, was also used.

Mode

Blade production was probably by direct percussion using a soft hammer. These conclusions were made on the presence of vague 'points of percussion, diffuse bulbs and lipped butts' (Ohnuma and Bergman 1984, 169). It is unclear whether this was an organic material or soft stone, although a hammer which permitted a precise point of aim was beneficial. This point was sometimes located on the edge of the striking platform, but off-centre to the main guiding ridge. The microburins, including the Krukowski microburin (Fig. 14: 11), and backed points, indicate that direct percussion on an anvil was also used for retouching.

Cores

Fifty-eight cores were recovered from sub-trench II and 21 from trenches VI/VIa (Fig.14: 1–2). The differential ratio of cores to waste (1:16 in trench II; 1:47 in trench VIa) has been explained as the result of small material having been winnowed out of the channel, the fill of which also contains a high proportion of coarse gravel. The cores from trench VI/VIa are probably more representative of the proportions of cores to waste which were produced by this industry.

The precise number of nodules represented in trench VI/VIa is unknown; however, at least three cores appear to have come from one nodule. Refitting has demonstrated that nodules were quartered or used after they had broken along thermal fractures. Eight cores from trench II and one from trench VIa are made on flakes. A Janus flake from trench VIa/spit 4 probably originates from trimming a core of this type. Most cores have a single striking platform and were prepared for the production of blades/bladelets. Additional cores have an opposed striking platform, often for core rejuvenation. Striking platforms were usually prepared by a single blow from the flaking surface to the back of the core (59% in trench II); less frequently (16%), the blow was directed from the side of the core, or an unprepared thermal surface (12%) was used. Additional trimming or shaping which preceded blade production, involved narrowing the base of the core by unifacial cresting to guide the initial blade, or by thinning the side if this was necessary. This technique can be demonstrated by a flake which refits to a failed core from trench II. The flake was designed to narrow the side of the core but plunged, removing the base of the core which had been prepared by unifacial cresting. Most cores, however, are unmodified around the back, sides and base, as Figure 14 (1–2) shows, and natural crests often made cresting unnecessary.

The exhausted cores, which account for 37% of those analysed, retain most of the features of cores in their production stages. They show that blades were predetermined end products and that the cores could be controlled to produce them. Blades were produced down the long axis of the core. The rejected cores suggest that the flaking angle round the edge of the striking platform averaged 70°–84°. This angle was normally strengthened by abrading the edge of the core to remove overhang. The failed core, noted above, indicates that some striking platforms were abraded during core preparation. Faceting to modify the flaking angle is absent from the cores and also from the core rejuvenation tablets. The patinated blades with faceted butts have been regarded as a separate industry for this reason. It is difficult to identify platform rejuvenation on the cores as the entire striking platform was removed by the tablet. The flaking surface could be rejuvenated or modified from an opposed striking platform or by cresting.

Table 2 shows the main categories of assessed core rejection from both trenches. Some cores were included in more than one category if this was thought to apply. The results indicate that a higher proportion were abandoned from trench VI/VIa than trench II, presumably during core preparation; however, the exhausted cores illustrate that trench VI/VIa was not restricted to core preparation. The remaining figures show that hinge fractures, often just below the striking platform, also contributed to core rejection. Some of the flakes and blades indicate that hinge fractures were occasionally removed from an opposed platform or by cresting, although it is not clear how often this occurred. The relatively small proportion of cores on which the flaking angle is too high, testifies to the care which was taken to control this angle throughout blade production.

Some cores were still capable of producing functional bladelets when they had been reduced to a very small size; however, most cores from both trenches (46% in trench II; 39% in trench VI/VIa) were rejected when they weighed 50–99 g. Some 39% of cores from sub-trench VI/VIa, which weighed over 150 g, undoubtedly represent failed cores.

Flakes and blades

There is no evidence for the deliberate production of flake blanks from this industry. The 404 flakes and broken flakes from trench VIa, spits 3–5, must represent by-products from core preparation and trimming of the blade industry (Fig. 14:3). The results of blades analysed from trench II and of blades and flakes from trench VI/VIa are shown in Table 3. From trench II, 31 broken blades with complete proximal ends were added to the complete pieces to maximise the recorded sample. Most blades and flakes were measured with length and breadth perpendicular and parallel to the butt; however, it was necessary to measure some blades along the axis of morphology when an undulating striking platform caused the butt to be off-set to the longest axis of the blade.

The results show that the two groups of blades are similar, but the flakes, which have a different function and method of production, contrast markedly. Plain butts predominate throughout, which is in accord with the evidence of the striking platforms; however, punctiform and linear butts are more prevalent amongst the blades than the flakes. This results from the frequent use of platform abrasion during blade production (69%; flakes 28%), which allows a blow near the core edge. This is confirmed by analysis of planform width. The blades have proportionally steeper percussion angles which result from the increased control that platform preparation allowed. This distribution might have been more marked if punctiform and linear butts could have been recorded. Most blades have a central guiding ridge (flake class 1A; Gingell and Harding 1979) and convex edges (intermediate planform). Blades with a convergent planform (Issac 1977) result from narrowing the base of the core during preparation. Flake scars on the dorsal surface are usually parallel to the axis of percussion and typify the use of single platform cores; scars at right-angles probably result from cresting.

The flakes by comparison are flatter, less well-ridged, and less likely to show parallel flake scars. They exhibit less platform abrasion, are more cortical and can be confirmed as products of core preparation, including cresting and trimming.

Chips

The use of platform abrasion during blade production is under represented by chips. It is likely that they must have been dispersed by post-depositional activity.

Retouched tools from trenches II and VI/VIa

Scrapers

Twelve end scrapers made on flakes and one made on a broken blade were found, of which four are from trench VIa/spits 3–5 (Fig. 14: 4–6). They measure 35–50 mm long, 30–40 mm wide and are 8–11 mm thick. The blanks include a rejuvenation tablet, broken pieces, and core preparation flakes, which represent by-products of the blade industry. Most were selected for their divergent platform, which provided a broad working edge, and for their dipping profile. They were all modified by direct, continuous, regular/irregular, semi-abrupt retouch at the distal end. Scraping edges vary from 26–53 mm (average 37 mm) long.

Microliths

Ten microliths were found, of which three, all burnt, are from trench VIa/spits 3–5 (Fig. 14: 7–10 and 12). Seven are obliquely blunted points (Clark 1934), with direct, abrupt retouch at the proximal end, which occasionally extends along the ridge. Two geometric microliths (trench VIa/spit 5, trench II/spit 1), one of which is unfinished, are also present. Evidence for use is restricted to a burnt microlith from trench VIa/spit 5. This has a burin-like break at the tip, resulting from impact (Barton and Bergman 1982, fig. 1g, h).

Tranchet adze / axe

A tranchet adze/axe, made from a thermal fragment of nodular flint, possibly a large pot lid, was found in trench VIa/spit 3 (Fig. 14: 13). It has straight edges, which were probably reshaped by hard hammer percussion. The blade has been sharpened from both edges. Length 120 mm, width 44 mm, thickness 30 mm. SF 3186.

Arrowhead

A leaf-shaped arrowhead from trench VIa, spit 3 was probably broken in manufacture. It was made on a flake with unifacial covering retouch on the dorsal surface. Length 32 mm; width 14 mm; thickness 2 mm. SF 3446.

Conclusions

This is the first Mesolithic assemblage to be excavated between the Thames/Kennet confluence and the Loddon valley. Mesolithic material is, however, common within a radius of 20–30 km of the site. Most discoveries have been made close to the river on the first terrace or near the bottom of hill slopes as at North Stoke, Oxfordshire (Ford 1987a, 118), Bray (Ames 1991–3), or Whistley, Berkshire (Harding and Richards 1991–93).

The recovery of 15,500 pieces of flint from Bray, 15 km to the east of Thames Valley Park, suggests a site of considerable size. Sites of this type probably form the main centres of occupation; however, additional find spots, mainly tranchet adzes/axes, indicate widespread Mesolithic activity on the higher ground. Intensive field walking by the East Berkshire Archaeological Survey (Ford 1987b, 59–61) confirmed that small scale sites existed on the Reading Beds and Bagshot Beds with larger centres in the valleys. Sites in this area can also be related to other published excavations, particularly the Late Mesolithic sites to the west in the Kennet valley (Wawcott III: Froom 1976), and to the south through the Loddon valley on the Hampshire/Surrey Greensand (Oakhanger: Rankine and Dimbleby 1961; Farnham: Clark and Rankine 1939).

Thames Valley Park continues the pattern of river valley occupation, although the scale is probably small. There is nothing to indicate the duration of occupation or its frequency. Insufficient material was found *in situ* and concentrations in individual trenches could not be related stratigraphically.

The primary function of the site was probably industrial, using flint from the chalk; however, scrapers and microliths with impact fractures indicate domestic activity. Barton and Bergman (1982, 242) have commented that impacted microliths were probably carried back to camp in the carcasses of dead animals.

The microliths include obliquely blunted points and geometric forms. The obliquely blunted points characterise most phases of the Mesolithic, but the geometric forms suggest that a Late Mesolithic date is more likely. Microdenticulates, tranchet adzes/axes, and microburins, which are found throughout the Mesolithic, are also present at Thames Valley Park. The tranchet adze/axe from trench VIa was found in a disturbed context; the relationship of the leaf arrowhead from the same context is uncertain. Radiocarbon dates from the Kennet valley provide sufficient overlap between the Late Mesolithic (Wawcott I: 5260±130 BP (BM-449; 4350–3780 cal. BC), Froom 1972), and the Early Neolithic (Lambourn long barrow: 5355±180 BP (GX 1178; 4580–3780 cal. BC), Wymer 1966, 4) for this arrowhead to be contemporaneous. (Radiocarbon determinations have been calibrated using CALIB 2; Pearson *et al.* 1986.)

Carbonised Plant Remains, by W.J. Carruthers

Forty bulk samples were taken from the silty loams and gravel deposits excavated in 5 x 5 x 100 mm spits across the site, five of which produced results (Table 25); for the methodology of processing and analysis see below. These produced large numbers of hazel (*Corylus avellana* L.) nut shell fragments and a few cereal caryopses (emmer/spelt, barley). Two carbonised rose (*Rosa* sp.) seeds were also recovered. The predominating evidence of wild foods, such as might be gathered from open woodland or scrub, is consistent with the Mesolithic date that has been suggested for these deposits. The 12 cereal grains, therefore, are likely to be contaminants from later activity on the site.

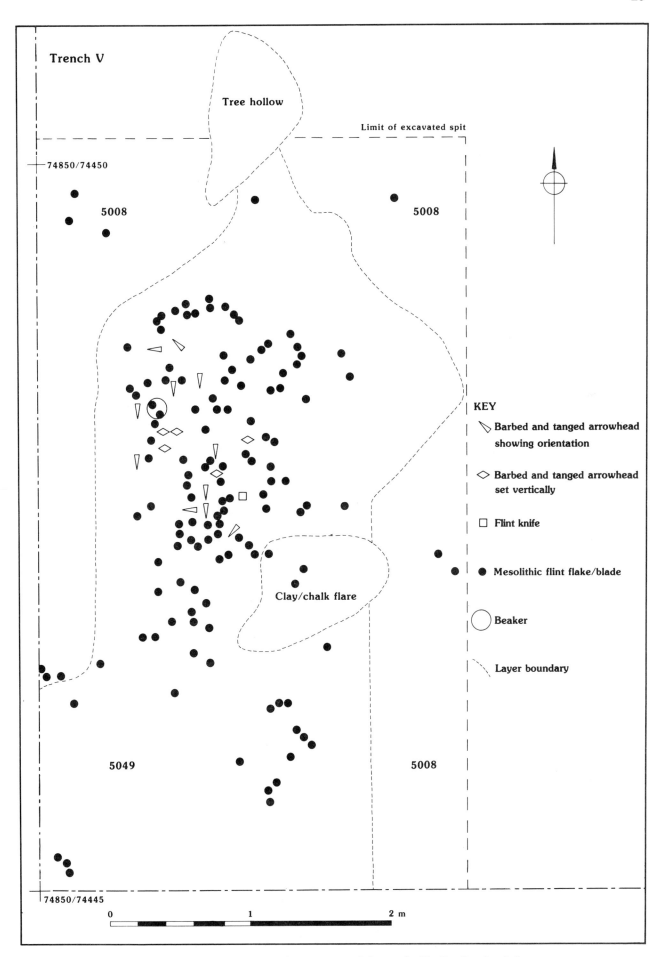

Figure 15   Distribution of worked flint in the vicinity of the probable Beaker burial

Bronze Age, by L. Smith

Probable Beaker Burial

Close to the northern limit of excavation, in trench V within trench 49 (Fig. 9), an incomplete and fragmented Beaker was uncovered in silt (5049) immediately below the topsoil. There was no evidence for any cut feature. Clustered around the Beaker fragments, within a relatively compact area measuring *c.* 1.6 m north to south and 1 m east to west, were 16 barbed and tanged arrowheads and a flint knife; a further barbed and tanged arrowhead lay approximately 2 m to the northwest and another was recovered during sieving. Figure 15 shows that the arrowheads lay within a larger spread of Mesolithic flints, which in turn was surrounded by an almost clear 'halo', *c.* 1 m wide, where few flints occurred. Slightly further afield was a sparse scatter of Mesolithic flints. This pattern suggests that the halo may have been a result of the construction of a small earth mound over the artefacts, although no such mound remained at the time of excavation, nor was there a ditch or any other evidence for the construction of a barrow.

The nature and grouping of the artefacts suggests a funerary context, but there was no evidence of human remains, whether cremated or otherwise. It is likely, however, that fragile bone would not have survived in the acidic soil conditions. Phosphate samples taken at 0.5 m intervals across the trench showed no significant concentrations.

Beaker pottery, by Lorraine Mepham

The 101 sherds (132 g) of a comb-decorated Beaker vessel (Fig. 16), recovered from the postulated burial, represent the earliest pottery recovered from the terrace area excavations. The fabric (C11) is described in the section on the Bronze Age pottery, below). The very fragmentary nature of the sherds precluded any reconstruction of the vessel form, although some idea of the decoration could be discerned: discrete zones of comb impressions in both horizontal bands and arcs or chevrons. The vessel appears to be in the Middle Beaker style of *c.* 1900–1700 bc, perhaps European Bell Beaker or Wessex/Middle Rhine (R. Cleal pers. comm.).

Associated flints, by P.A. Harding

Description and manufacture of arrowheads

Eighteen barbed and tanged arrowheads were found in trench V (Fig. 17). Two were broken (Fig. 17: 7 and 10) and a third had been damaged by an impact fracture (Fig. 17: 15). Twelve of the 16 complete examples are of Green's (1980, 117, fig. 45) Sutton b type, small miscellaneous arrowheads with 'unshaped' barbs. They range from 23–33 mm long and 20–24 mm wide; within the mean of this group of arrowheads (*ibid.*, table VIII.2). Most were 4–5 mm thick. They are of a consistent quality and technique of manufacture. Flakes with ridged and flat dorsal surfaces, which produce arrowheads with plano-convex and oval cross-sections, had been used as arrowhead blanks. The dorsal surface of most of the blanks had been removed by covering retouch, although areas of the ventral surface, which is often flaked by invasive retouch, remain visible. The arrowheads have slightly convex edges and reach maximum breadth at the top of the barbs. The base is usually flat or convex. Irregularities in the shape and size of the barbs often result from the production of the notches. Five of the arrowheads (Fig. 17: 1, 5, 9, 13, and 15) have a broken barb which can be associated with manufacture, use, or post-depositional activity. Nine of the tangs are squared in shape, which suggests that they were of more importance than the barbs. Two arrowheads are badly damaged; one (Fig. 17: 10) has no barbs or tang, while another (Fig. 17: 7) has a broken tip, barbs, and tang. One arrowhead (Fig. 17: 15) has a burin-like facet at the tip which is a characteristic form of impact fracture (Barton and Bergman 1982). Similar fractures have been found on barbed and tanged arrowheads at Stonehenge (Atkinson and Evans 1978), where three arrowheads, of which at least two had impact fractures, were found embedded in the skeleton of a young male.

Discussion

The Thames Valley arrowhead group is unusually large. Green (1980, table VIII.1) notes two graves with 13 barbed and tanged arrowheads, and only the hoard at Ballyclare, Co. Antrim (Flanagan 1970) is known to have contained more. The position of the arrowheads at Thames Valley provides uncertain information about how the objects were originally arranged in the putative grave. They were distributed randomly, although seven of the 16 tightly grouped examples found were aligned towards the south. Although it is possible that this alignment may have been the result of post-depositional disturbance, the pottery appears not to have been similarly moved. Scattered barbed and tanged arrowheads have been found in graves at Sutton, Glamorgan (Fox 1943), but the seven arrowheads lay in three groups, and at Mouse Low (Bateman 1861), where four

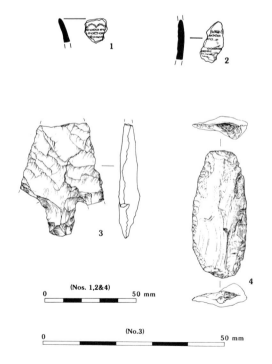

Figure 16   Beaker sherds and worked flint

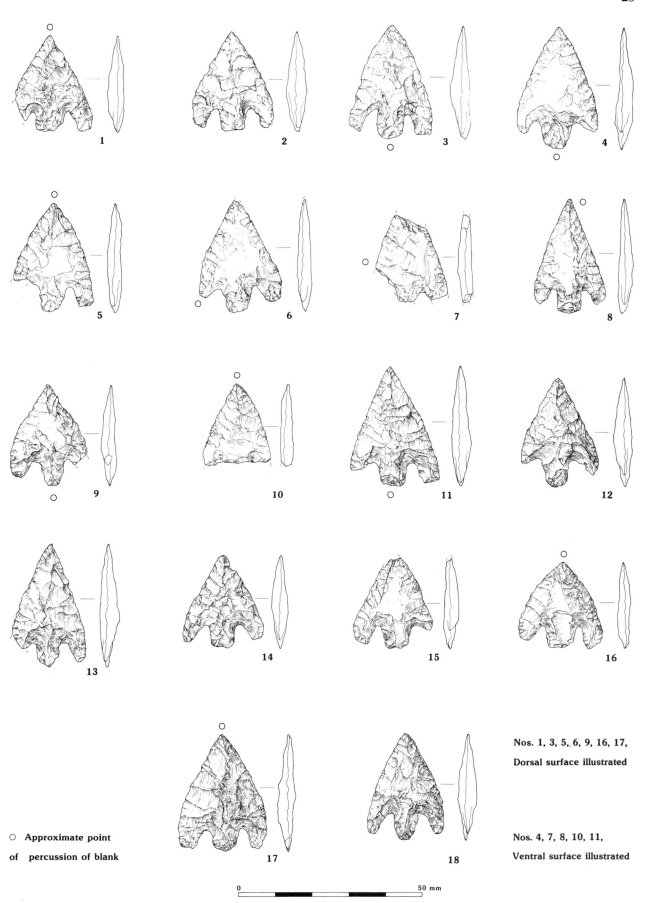

Nos. 1, 3, 5, 6, 9, 16, 17,
Dorsal surface illustrated

Nos. 4, 7, 8, 10, 11,
Ventral surface illustrated

○ Approximate point
of percussion of blank

0   50 mm

Figure 17   Barbed and tanged arrowheads

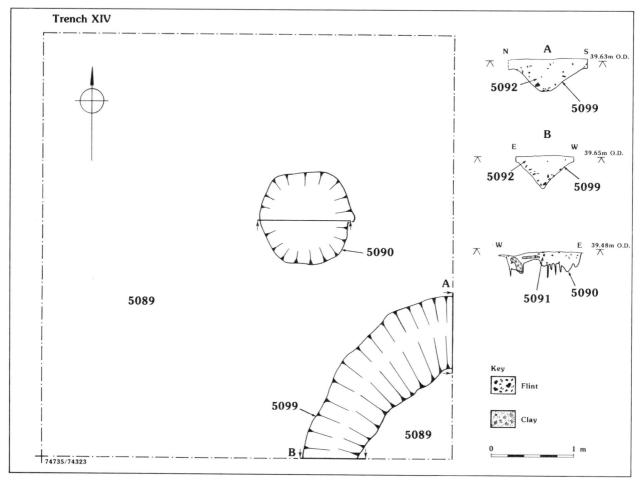

Figure 18   Plan and section of feature 5099 in trench XIV

occurred in two groups. Two of these arrowheads were found in a Beaker, which suggests that they were not hafted at the time of burial.

Sutton b arrowheads are the most common form of barbed and tanged arrowhead (Green 1980, 119). They occur with both inhumations and cremation burials and accompany all classes of Beaker, particularly those associated with archery equipment. Sutton b arrowheads have been found with European Bell Beakers in barrow 4a, Radley, Berkshire (Williams 1944), and also at Mucking, Essex (Jones and Jones 1975), where 11 arrowheads were found, nine of them Sutton b. The burial at Summertown, Oxfordshire (Abercromby 1912, pl. IX, no. 75) produced a Wessex/Middle Rhine Beaker associated with a Sutton c arrowhead. This type of arrowhead is also found with all other forms of Early Bronze Age pottery and therefore serves as a poor guide to date.

Knife

A knife made on a flake with a thermal dorsal surface was found associated with the arrowheads (Fig. 16). The circumference has been modified by continuous, direct, low angle/semi-abrupt retouch. A small area of rubbing is apparent at the distal end, similar to that found on fabricators. Knives and fabricators are both found in Beaker graves and this find is therefore not out of context.

Other Early Bronze Age Features

Early Bronze Age pottery was recovered from three widely separated features. The largest of these, gully 5099 found in trench XIV, had a 'V'-shaped profile, was about 0.35 m deep, measured 0.75 m wide at the top, and was traced for a length of 1.5 m (Fig. 18). It contained a silty loam (5092) from which 42 sherds of Early Bronze Age pottery (including a possible urn sherd) were recovered.

A small truncated pit 1243, near the southern limit of trench 48, produced 12 pieces of waste flint and 26 sherds of Early Bronze Age pottery. Five more sherds, almost certainly from the same vessel, were recovered from a root hole 2 m to the south. The base of a flint-tempered Middle Bronze Age vessel, 0.3 m in diameter, was revealed within the Iron Age enclosure by the topsoil stripping; no cut or distinctive fill was discerned around this vessel, yet the integrity of the surviving portion and its upright position can mean only that it was deliberately buried. There was no cultural material of any kind within the pot, nor any human remains; but since the very poor survival of bone on this site has been noted elsewhere in this report, the interpretation of this feature as a cremation burial cannot be entirely discounted. Other Bronze Age pottery was found in 5042, 5072, 5082, and 5088, all of which were disturbed contexts containing material of other periods.

Table 4 Bronze Age pottery fabric totals from the terrace area

Fabric	No. of Sherds	Weight (g)
C11 (Beaker)	107	145
C12 (EBA)	126	373
D9	67	1500
D10	17	103
D12	2	13
D13	9	23
D14	2	10
Total	330	2167

Bronze Age Pottery, by Lorraine Mepham

Three hundred and thirty sherds of pre-Iron Age pottery were recovered, with a total weight of 2167 g. The methods of analysis and recording were as those used for the later prehistoric and Romano-British pottery (*see* below).

Fabrics

Seven separate fabric types were identified on the basis of macroscopic inclusions. Terms used in the following fabric descriptions to describe the frequency of inclusions are defined as follows: rare (1–3%); sparse (3–10%); moderate (10–20%); common (20–30%). Fabric totals are given in Table 4.

C11. Iron-rich clay matrix with rare rounded quartz grains <0.5 mm; sparse to moderate grog <1 mm (rarely >1 mm); oxidised with unoxidised core. Most of this group comprises sherds of one vessel: a comb-decorated Beaker, described above.

C12. Iron-rich clay matrix with common, poorly sorted grog <2 mm; oxidised with unoxidised interior surface. This group has a general Early Bronze Age date. Some of the sherds have twisted cord decoration, characteristic of many Collared Urns (although this form of decoration also occurs on other forms of both Late Neolithic and Early Bronze Age pottery); while others have evidence of residues on internal surfaces which might suggest that they derive from Food Vessels. Only body sherds of this fabric type were recovered.

D9 Iron-rich clay matrix with common, poorly sorted crushed flint <2 mm; rare, red iron oxide <1 mm; oxidised throughout. Very similar fabrics have been found in the area, deriving from both Deverel-Rimbury type urns, eg Sulham, Berkshire (James 1982, 3), and from local later Bronze Age domestic vessels, eg Knight's Farm and Aldermaston Wharf (Bradley *et al.* 1980, 232, 266). Again, no diagnostic sherds in this fabric type were recovered from the site .

D10 A coarse, flint-tempered fabric very similar to D9, but the inclusions are generally sparser and coarser; very poorly sorted crushed flint <5 mm. Unoxidised. Probably of the same date as D9.

D12 Iron-rich clay matrix; moderate to common, poorly sorted crushed flint <2 mm; sparse grog <4 mm; spares black iron oxide <1 mm. Oxidised with unoxidised interior surfaces. Fabric types D12–D14

are all fairly similar; undiagnostic body sherds only were recovered, and a general date of Middle–Late Bronze Age is postulated on the basis of similarity with fabrics found on Bronze Age sites elsewhere in the local area, eg Field Farm, Burghfield (Mepham 1992).

D13 As D12, but with flint inclusions coarser (<4 mm), and sparser. Oxidised with unoxidised interior surfaces 81.1%).

D14 Iron-poor clay matrix with rare rounded quartz grains <1 mm; sparse to moderate crushed flint <1 mm; sparse to moderate iron oxide <2 mm. Oxidised with unoxidised interior surfaces.

Distribution

The four features (the possible Beaker burial complex, and contexts 5099, 1243, and 1237) account for 73.9% by weight of the total Bronze Age assemblage; other sherds, in all seven fabric types, were recovered from topsoil and subsoil contexts in trenches 48 and 49, although apart from a small group of sherds of fabric type C12 from trench 49/VIa (context 5072, spit 3), no significant concentrations could be discerned. The relatively small amount of Bronze Age pottery from the site, its generally dispersed nature and the very small number of features which could definitely be attributed to this period, suggest that any activity during this period was very sporadic.

Twenty-six sherds (71 g) of fabric type C12 were recovered, along with a small quantity of waste flint from feature 1243, with a further five sherds (4 g), which appear to belong to the same vessel, from a nearby root-hole. Residues observed on the interior surfaces of several of the sherds suggest that these sherds come from a Food Vessel rather than a Collared Urn.

Feature 5099 in trench 49, sub-trench XIV, produced 41 sherds (59 g) of fabric type C12, and a single sherd of type D10. No decorated or other diagnostic sherds were recovered.

The complete base of a coarse, hand-made vessel in the flint-tempered fabric type D9 from 1237 only survived to a maximum height of c.50 mm, and showed a heavy concentration of flint grits on the underside, a phenomenon frequently observed on Middle–Late Bronze Age vessels in the area, such as Aldermaston Wharf (Bradley *et al* 1980, 234). The base diameter (22.5–31 cm) suggests a fairly large vessel, such as a Deverel-Rimbury type urn, and the fabric is consistent with this, though no trace of any cremated remains survived.

Of the vessels identified, both the Beaker and the urn from 1237 were connected with the probable deposition of human remains, and other sherds may derive from burial urns of various types; the amount of definite domestic pottery recovered is therefore very small, suggesting that any occupation on the site was short-lived and/or non-intensive.

Bronze Age Flint, by P.A. Harding

In addition to the collection of flints associated with the presumed Beaker burial, a further barbed and tanged arrowhead (Fig. 16) was found 34 m south-west of this group in spit 2 of trench VIa. This broken example, with

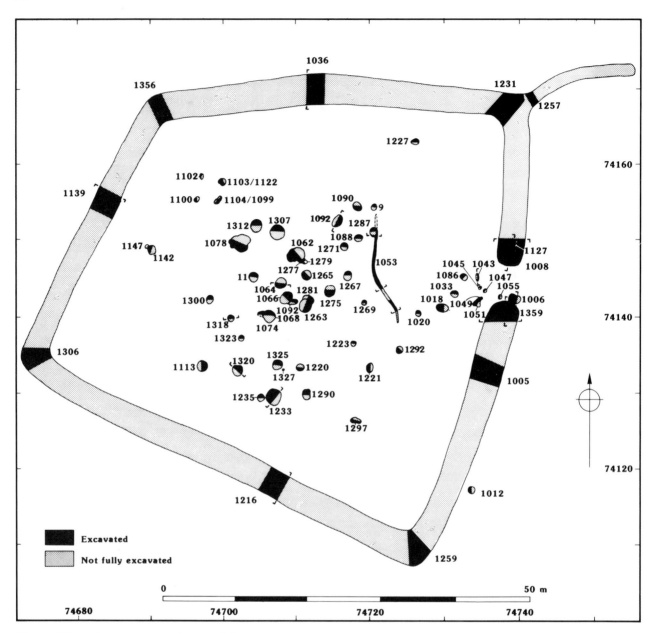

Figure 19   Enclosure and internal features

an elongated tang, was made on a flake with a plano-convex cross-section and has bifacial covering retouch. The tip and both barbs are missing. Length 30 mm; width 23 mm; thickness 6 mm. SF 3445.

Carbonised Plant Remains,
by W.J. Carruthers

Two contexts associated with a possible Food Vessel were examined from this phase (Table 25; *see* below for the methodology of processing and analysis). The presence of stinking mayweed (*Anthemis cotula* L.) seeds and an oat (*Avena* sp.) caryopsis amongst the few carbonised remains recovered, suggested contamination from later deposits. Neither of these taxa are common until the Iron Age, although Late Bronze Age sites sometimes produce oats. Since tree root disturbance was noted from this area, and Iron Age and Romano-British

artefacts were widespread across the site, contamination is quite likely to have occurred.

Iron Age and Romano-British,
by I. Barnes

Introduction

Evidence for later prehistoric to Romano-British occupation of the site was recovered principally from trench 48 (Fig. 9), which contained the cropmark enclosure. Four phases of activity are thought to have occurred during this period:

Phase 1: Middle to Late Iron Age (3rd Century BC–1st Century AD)
Construction of the enclosure, the primary filling of its ditch, and activities resulting in the majority of the internal occup-

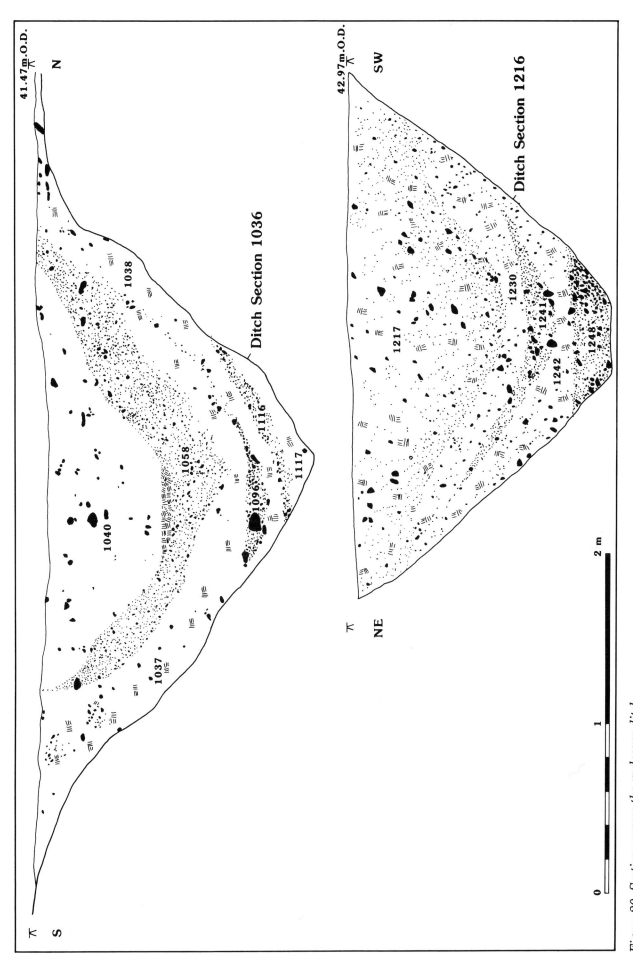

Figure 20 Sections across the enclosure ditch

ation features, and the origins of an associated field system may also date to this period.

Phase 2: Early Roman (1st to early 2nd century AD)
Continued use of the enclosure but with a broader range of activities over a wider area, including the construction of field boundaries.

Phase 3: Middle Roman (middle to late 2nd century AD)
Burial of cremations on the north side of the site after the abandonment of the enclosure.

Phase 4: Later Roman (3rd–4th century AD)
A diminishing level of activity represented only by finds in the upper fills of features.

The dating of the whole episode and its sub-divisions is based almost exclusively on the evidence of the associated pottery. Few other datable artefacts were recovered, and no other dating techniques were employed.

Sub-Rectangular Enclosure

The enclosure (Fig. 19), centred on SU 74710 74144, was situated on a slight shelf on the west facing valley side, with a fall of *c.* 4 m (5.6% gradient) from the south-east to the north-west corners. Overall, it measured 62 m north–south by 66 m west–east. An area of 2500 m² was contained by a total length of 209 m of ditch, which had a maximum width of 4.6 m. There was only one entrance, this being 5 m wide and in the centre of the eastern side, where it faced uphill and away from the river. A spur ditch, slightly curved and narrower than the main enclosure ditch, extended eastwards for approximately 13 m from the north-east corner of the enclosure. The underlying drift geology showed a change from sand and gravel on the eastern, upper third of the enclosure to clays and sands at the west.

Enclosure ditch 1367
Ten sections were excavated through the enclosure ditch, and another (1257) through a spur ditch to the north-east (Fig. 19). The ditch sections all displayed a 'V'-shaped profile; the dimensions of the sections are given in Table 5.

The widest excavated parts of the ditch were at the four corners of the enclosure (1231, 1259, 1306, and 1356). The sections through straight lengths of the ditch had a mean width of 3.06 m and a mean depth of 1.8 m. The pattern of silting and infilling (*see* Fig. 20) varied widely, and was dependent on the surrounding soil and the relationship of each area to the hill-slope. In general, the upper fills comprised clay sands up to 0.96 m thick with varying proportions of sand and charcoal flecks. These overlay further clay sand deposits up to 0.45 m thick, with varying amounts of gravel inclusions and ash and pebble lenses present. Below these colluvial and cultivation soils, the lower fills of the ditch comprised gravel-rich sandy clays, up to 0.5 m thick, eroded from the ditch sides at an early stage.

Of the eleven sections excavated through the enclosure ditch, only the two terminals (1008 and 1359)

Table 5   dimensions of excavated enclosure ditch sections

Section No.	Depth (m)	Width (m)
1005	2.00	3.00
1008*	2.00	3.00
1036^	1.65	3.00
1139	1.60	3.00
1216	1.59	3.05
1231	1.03	3.20
1257!	1.50	1.35
1259	1.40	4.50
1306	1.10	4.60
1356	1.40	3.50
1359*	2.00	3.00

* = ditch terminal; ^ = partially excavated as 0019 during the excavation; ! = north-eastern spur

showed features within their fills. The fills of the remaining nine sections showed no features and produced less pottery than did the two terminals (Table 15). The section through the south-east corner, 1259, produced a nearly complete pot within layer 1260; the vessel, dating from the 1st century AD, contained a fine copper alloy chain and a melon bead. No burnt bone was found with the vessel to indicate that it might have contained a cremation.

The pottery, 2,666 sherds of which (39,808 g) were recovered from the excavated sections, provided a datable sequence through the ditch fills. Middle Iron Age pottery was found in the primary fills and it is in this period that the enclosure was established. Small amounts of Late Iron Age wares are identifiable in the middle and upper fills, but the majority of the pottery from these layers dates to the 1st and 2nd centuries AD. A small amount of 3rd and 4th century AD material was found in the uppermost fills.

Features within the ditch fills
Two features assigned to phase 2 were recorded within the partially silted ditch terminals:

Feature 1127
A sub-rectangular double line of flint rubble had been constructed in the north terminal of enclosure ditch 1008 at a depth of 0.5 m (Figs. 21 and 22). The feature was not fully excavated, the excavated section measuring 0.78 m north–south and 0.6 m east–west. A lump of ferruginous sandstone and a large sherd of pottery were included amongst the flint rubble, which enclosed an area of burnt sand and clay 0.27 m in depth. The flint itself was not burnt, however, suggesting either that it had been protected by some form of lining (no indication of which was found) or that the fill had not been burnt *in situ*. Immediately overlying the feature was a deposit of pot sherds (1095), including eight near complete vessels all of the 1st century AD. One sherd from this deposit could be conjoined with the sherd incorporated in the rubble. Little pottery was found within the feature itself but the 14 sherds which were recovered were of a similar date to those from the overlying deposit.

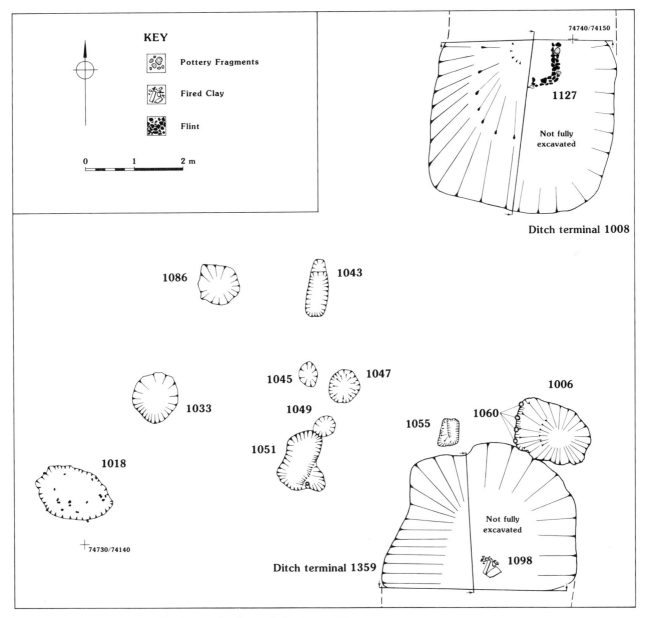

Figure 21   Plan of the ditch terminals and the immediate area

Feature 1098

At a depth of 0.55 m, near south terminal 1359 of the enclosure ditch, a 'basin' of burnt clay, 0.5 m in length and 0.3 m wide, was contained in a cut in the fill of the ditch. This feature was also filled with a spread of charcoal (Figs. 21 and 22) which contained at its centre a low-fired clay block or 'brick', 0.3 m in length, 0.24 m in width, and 0.12 m deep (see below). This deposit contained pottery dating to the 1st century AD.

Features 1127 and 1098, in the opposed ditch terminals, were at similar depths and contained pottery of the same date. It seems likely, therefore, that they were not only contemporaneous but may have shared a similar function. The shape and nature of 1098, and the presence of probable pottery wasters in overlying deposit 1360, suggest that the feature may have been a simple, short-lived kiln (see Fired Clay and Pottery below).

No positive indications of a bank were found. Some circumstantial evidence for the presence of an internal bank may be inferred from the fact that no features were found within 5 m of the inner edge of the ditch, except at the entrance, and few features lay within 10 m of it. This could be accounted for by an internal arrangement which avoided placing substantial structures or deep features near the perimeter. The majority of the pottery found in the ditches came from the two terminals (see Table 15) and it may thus have been that refuse disposal was elsewhere obstructed by a bank or barrier around the rest of the enclosure. No evidence survived of an internal palisade.

Internal features

A total of 64 features (Fig. 19) was excavated within the enclosure, 62 of which could be interpreted as either pits or post-holes. These two categories are discussed separately below, although there is almost certainly a degree of overlap because of the difficulty of interpretation in the variable subsoil. The remaining two

East facing section of northern terminal 1008

South facing section of northern terminal 1008

Figure 22   Sections across northern ditch terminal 1008

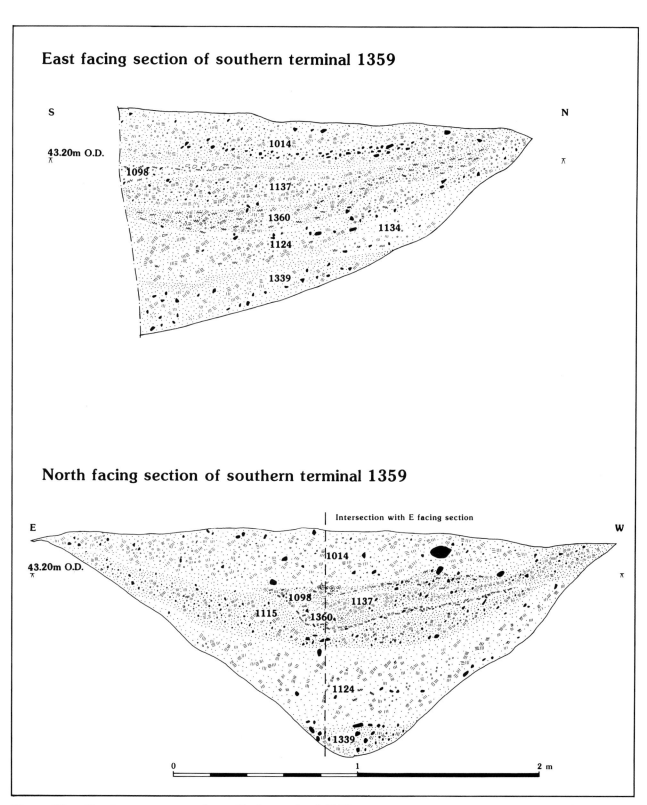

East facing section of southern terminal 1359

Figure 23   Sections across southern ditch terminal 1359

34

Table 6 summary of shapes and dimensions of pits within the enclosure

Pit	Shape	Profile	Length (m)	Width (m)	Diam(m)	Depth (m)
0009	round	belled	–	–	1.50	1.30
0011	round	'U'-shaped	–	–	1.30	0.45
1012	round	shallow 'U'	–	–	0.78	0.16
1020	round	flat bottom	–	–	0.90	0.45
1062	round	shallow 'U'	–	–	1.75	0.37
1064	round	belled	–	–	1.46	0.92
1066	round	belled	–	–	1.60	0.40
1068	oval	flat bottom	1.00	0.70	–	0.20
1074	round	belled	–	–	1.80	1.04
1078	round	belled	–	–	3.20	0.92
1092	oval	flat bottom	1.50	1.30	–	1.65
1113	round	belled	–	–	1.20	1.15
1142	square	'U'-shaped	1.30	1.30	–	0.37
1220	oval	belled	0.97	0.79	–	0.42
1227	oval	'U'-shaped	0.95	0.80	–	0.25
1233	round	flat bottom	–	–	2.00	1.65
1235	round	flat bottom	–	–	1.00	0.42
1263	round	shallow 'U'	–	–	1.10	0.07
1265	round	flat bottom	–	–	1.10	0.27
1267	round	flat bottom	–	–	1.10	0.35
1269	round	shallow 'U'	–	–	0.60	0.07
1271	round	flat bottom	–	–	0.90	0.28
1275	oval	flat bottom	1.40	1.20	–	0.26
1281	oval	shallow 'U'	1.30	0.95	–	0.20
1287	oval	flat bottom	1.90	1.00	–	0.55
1290	round	'U'-shaped	–	–	1.20	0.70
1292	round	flat bottom	–	–	1.20	0.15
1297	rectangular	flat bottom	1.65	0.84	–	0.32
1300	round	flat bottom	–	–	1.90	1.18
1307	round	flat bottom	–	–	1.50	0.50
1312	round	flat bottom	–	–	1.59	0.43
1318	round	flat bottom	–	–	1.10	1.05
1320	round	flat bottom	–	–	1.40	1.25
1323	round	shallow 'U'	–	–	1.10	0.12
1325	round	flat bottom	–	–	2.10	0.90

features are described separately at the end of this section.

Pits

A total of 35 pits was excavated, brief details of which are given in Table 6 and selected sections illustrated in Figure 24. Of these, 13 contained pottery of exclusively Middle–Late Iron Age date, either in the primary fill or throughout the whole sequence of fills; these are assigned to phase 1. Several of the phase 1 pits contained small amounts of Romano-British pottery in their upper fills, material considered to be intrusive. A single pit (1281) can be dated stratigraphically to phase 1. A further 20 pits contained a significant element of Romano-British pottery dating to the 1st to early 2nd century AD and are accordingly dated to phase 2. No pits were excavated

which could be considered to belong to phases 3 or 4. Only one pit (1325) remained unphased.

Pit form and dimensions: No significant differences between pits assigned to phase 1 and phase 2 could be discerned in terms of pit type or overall dimensions, nor was there any absolute correlation between surface plan and profile.

The details in Table 6 show that the most common type of pit found on the site was circular in plan with an average diameter of 1.4 m, an average depth of 0.64 m and a straight-sided, flat-bottomed profile. Depth was measured from the stripped surface of the trench and therefore may not be the original dimensions. The possibility that some features were substantially truncated has led to the inclusion of shallow features, the true

Table 7 summary of post-holes within the enclosure

Post-hole	Shape	Profile	Length (m)	Width (m)	Diam(m)	Depth (m)
1006	oval	'U'-shaped	1.55	–	–	0.32
1018	round	flat bottom	–	–	0.90	0.21
1033	round	flat bottom	–	–	0.90	0.13
1045	round	shallow 'U'	–	–	0.30	0.10
1047	round	shallow 'U'	–	–	0.40	0.09
1049	round	flat bottom	–	–	0.30	0.10
1051	oval	flat bottom	1.10	0.70	–	0.70
1055	rectangular	flat bottom	0.70	0.30	–	0.30
1060a	round	'U'-shaped	–	–	0.12	0.22
1060b	round	'U'-shaped	–	–	0.12	0.22
1060c	round	'U'-shaped	–	–	0.12	0.22
1060d	round	'U'-shaped	–	–	0.12	0.22
1086	round	shallow 'U'	–	–	0.85	0.10
1088	round	flat bottom	–	–	1.00	0.30
1090	round	flat bottom	–	–	1.10	0.25
1099	oval	shallow 'U'	0.74	0.46	–	0.20
1100	oval	shallow 'U'	0.74	0.50	–	0.31
1102	oval	'U'-shaped	0.71	0.55	–	0.38
1103	oval	'U'-shaped	0.73	0.68	–	0.43
1104	round	'U'-shaped	–	–	0.50	0.17
1122	oval	belled	0.70	0.49	–	0.25
1147	round	'U'-shaped	–	–	0.43	0.22
1221	round	flat bottom	–	–	0.60	0.17
1223	round	'U'-shaped	–	–	0.50	0.15
1277	round	flat bottom	–	–	0.40	0.30
1279	round	flat bottom	–	–	0.30	0.20
1327	round	'U'-shaped	–	–	0.10	0.10

depths of which may have been somewhat greater. Seven of the pits had bell-shaped profiles, despite the fact that the subsoil is not ideal for supporting undercutting. Other than circular examples, one square, one rectangular, and seven oval pits were also excavated. These had an average length/width of 1.16 m and an average depth of 0.47 m.

Only seven of the pits had surviving depths greater than 1 m. The ratio of depth to diameter for circular pits (Fig. 25) shows no distinction between phases of activity, nor did the distribution of pit volumes (Fig. 26), the average volume being 1.32 m³.

Pit fills and function: All of the pits had similar fills, clay/sands with varying proportions of gravel and charcoal components.

Three pits, one dating to phase 1 (1078) and two to phase 2 (1292 and 1318), had clay layers sealing them, although nothing survived of the original contents.

One pit, (1320) dated to phase 1, had a sealing layer of chalk rubble. The lowest of the pit's five fills contained the skeleton of a human foetus/neonate, and disarticulated bones representing at least four cattle, including the complete skull of a bull, fragments of at least three

sheep/goats, and the skeleton of a toad. In all, 12 sherds (36 g) of pottery, dating to the Middle–Late Iron Age, were found associated with the bones, as were two sherds of Late Bronze Age/Early Iron Age material. The nature of the cattle and sheep/goat bones, mostly skull and foot fragments, and the butchery marks they displayed, suggest that the pit was used for primary disposal of carcass waste.

The remainder of the pits had no noteworthy characteristics, only their internal volumes (see Fig. 25 and 26) hinting at former use; pits of larger volume are likely to have been storage pits related to an agricultural function. Artefactual evidence is scarce for the remaining pits and no specific function can be attributed.

Post-holes

Twenty-seven features excavated within the sub-rectangular enclosure were interpreted as post-holes; these are detailed in Table 7. The almost complete absence of finds within their fills makes any attempts at phasing tentative. On pottery and stratigraphic evidence, seven of the post-holes can be dated to phase 1, whilst eight date to phase 2 and one each to phases 3 and 4, the remainder are unphased.

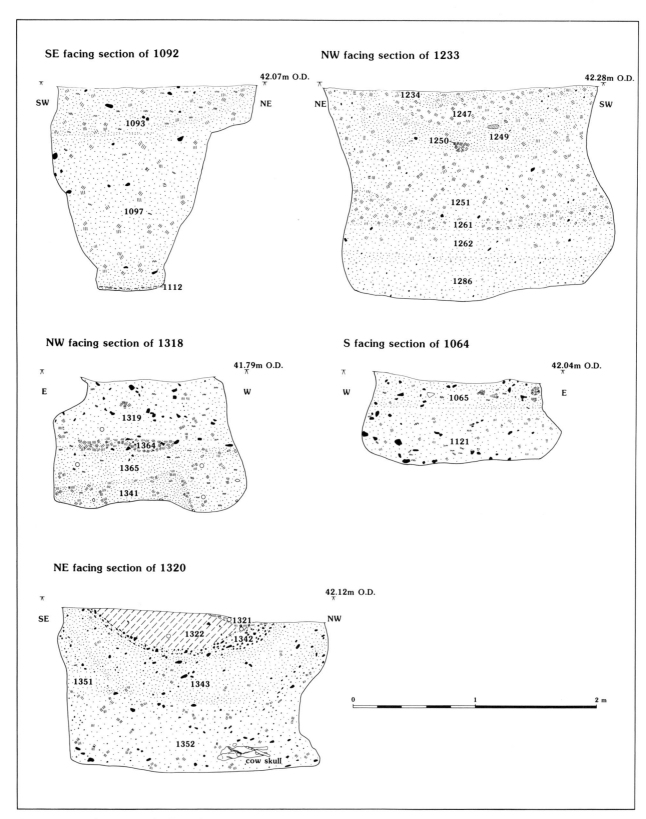

Figure 24   Sections of selected pits

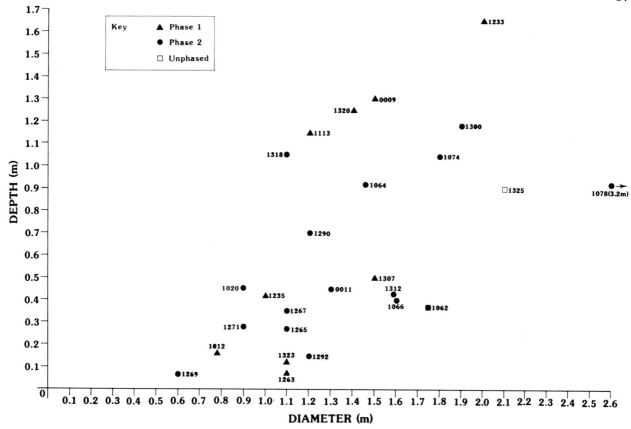

Figure 25   Plot of pit diameter against depth for circular pits

Nineteen of the post-holes were round, with an average diameter of 0.48 m. Seven others were oval and one was rectangular; these had an average length of 0.74 m. The post-holes had an overall average depth of 0.24 m. Only four post-holes contained any post packing, and only two displayed a post-pipe; these had both been dug into gravel and it thus seems likely that post-pipes did not survive on the clay/sand. The post-holes were filled with varying mixtures of clay/sand with gravel and charcoal components present.

Four-post structure 1410: A four-post structure, measuring 3 m square, made up of post-holes 1100, 1102, 1104, and 1122 was identified in the north-west corner of the enclosure (Fig. 27). Two of the post-holes were recut, suggesting a repair at some stage in the life of the structure.

A small amount (12 pieces, 51 g) of Iron Age pottery was recovered from two of the six post-hole and recut fills, as well as two sherds (6 g) of Romano-British pottery. It is therefore tentatively suggested that the structure dates to the first phase of occupation.

Post-hole 1006: Post-hole 1006 was immediately north of the southern terminal of the enclosure ditch, within the entrance (Figs. 21 and 28). Four small stake-holes (1060 a–d) were spaced evenly over 1 m along the inner edge of the post-hole. Packing, in the form of two large flint nodules, was found within the fill; associated finds comprised several large sherds of pottery dated to the middle of the 2nd century AD, contemporary with the phase 3 cremations discovered towards the northern extremity of the site.

Despite the absence of a corresponding feature on the other side of the entrance, the most likely function for this post-hole is as part of a gate structure.

Slot 1043
This feature lay across the entrance and would have been between the postulated internal bank (Figs 21 and

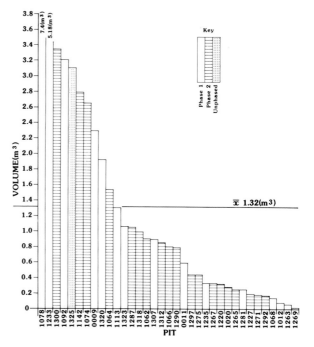

Figure 26   Pit volumes (all pits)

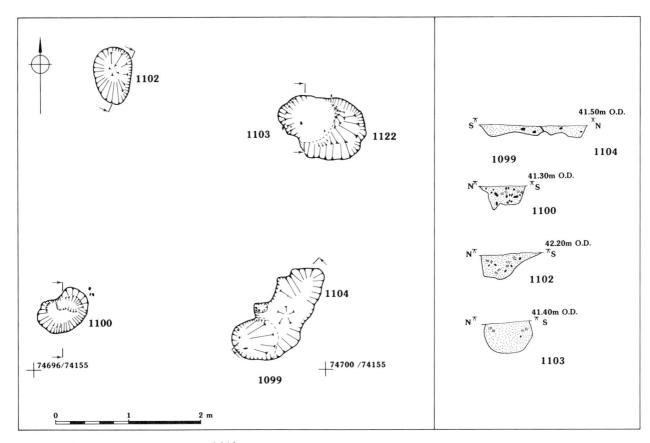

Figure 27   Four-post structure 1410

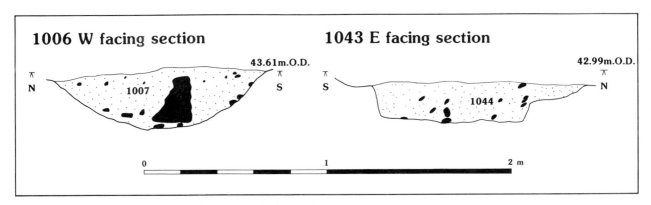

Figure 28   Sections of post-hole 1006 and slot 1043

28). The slot measured 1.2 m long, 0.4 m wide and was 0.25 m deep. It was filled with clay/sand with gravel inclusions but contained no finds. Although not part of any obvious structural pattern its location suggests that it too may have formed part of a gateway, possibly in association with post-hole 1006. It was not possible to assign the slot to a phase.

Linear flint feature 1053
This feature (Fig. 29) consisted of a trench 15 m long, 0.2 m wide, and 0.15 m deep, filled with flint nodules ranging in size from 0.03 m to 0.15 m. It was not associated with any post-holes, building debris or other structural indicators and its relationship with pit 1287

was unclear. Within the fill of 1053, four sherds (24 g) of Romano-British pottery were found, suggesting that it dates to phase 2. The feature could be interpreted as a wall foundation, although its sinuous course, location across the enclosure entrance, and apparent isolation mitigate against this. Alternatively it could have served as a screen foundation, the screen acting as a directional influence to people entering the enclosure, or as a drain.

Features Outside the Enclosure

Archaeological features of known or inferred late prehistoric to Romano-British date were found outside the enclosure in trenches 47, 48H, and 49.

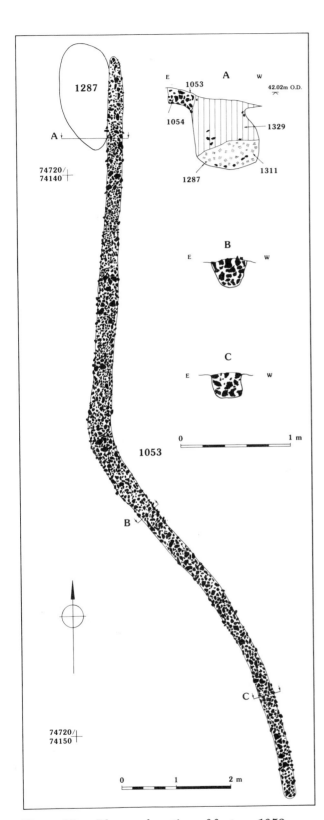

Figure 29   Plan and section of feature 1053

Ditches

Ditch 643

A 26 m length of ditch (Fig. 30) ran diagonally across the contours at the south-west corner of trench 47. The ditch had an average width of 1.3 m and an average depth of 0.5 m. It was cut into loose gravel, had a 'U'-shaped profile, and was filled with silty clay loam with charcoal inclusions. Interpreted as a field boundary, the ditch is tentatively dated to phase 1, Middle–Late Iron Age, by small amounts of pottery recovered from its fills.

Ditch 5087 and recut 5079

A 22.5 m length of ditch 5087 (Fig. 31) running south-west/north-east along the 40 m contour was also investigated in trench 49 (IX). The ditch, 'V'-shaped in profile with a series of sandy loam fills with flint inclusions, had an average width of 1.5 m and an average depth of 0.63 m. Pottery from the fill consisted of a single undiagnostic sherd in a fabric associated with Middle to Late Iron Age (phase 1) forms elsewhere on site.

The southern 1.4 m of the excavated segment of 5087 had been recut by 5079 to the full depth of the earlier ditch and to a maximum width of 1.78 m. The recut contained two sandy loam fills with gravel and flint inclusions. Pottery from the fills dates the recut to the 1st century AD (phase 1).

Ditch 1154

A total length of 95 m of ditch 1154 was uncovered, the feature running across the contours in trench 48H, terminating at the eastern edge of the trench and becoming indiscernible at the bottom of the slope to the west. The ditch was largely traced and excavated by machine (Fig. 32) but incorporated two hand-excavated segments numbered 1158 and 1162. The ditch was on average 1.1 m wide and up to 0.5 m deep, with a stepped profile and an extremely sticky, sandy clay fill which was difficult to distinguish from the surrounding Reading Bed clay. It was unusual in that it contained large amounts of artefacts, including late Romano-British (3rd–4th centuries AD) pottery and two 'fossilised' boot soles (SF 4598 and SF 4599). These consisted of groups of iron hobnails which had corroded together to retain the shape of the original sole. The lower ditch fills contained pottery of mostly 1st–2nd century AD date (phase 2), while the upper fills contained 3rd–4th century AD (phase 4) material and were characterised by a high charcoal content. This suggests that the adjacent feature associated with burning (1152) did not come into operation until the 3rd or 4th century when the ditch was already partially infilled.

Ditch 1166

This ditch 1166 ran north at 90° to 1154, ie along the contours in trench 48H (Fig. 32). Less substantial than 1154, being only 8 m long, 0.3 m wide and 0.15 m deep, the ditch contained a single sandy clay fill almost identical to the natural Reading Beds clay which it cut. It included moderate amounts of fragmentary pottery probably contemporary with that found in the phase 4 upper fills of ditch 1154.

Pit 646

Pit 646 (Fig. 30) was first excavated during the evaluation, trench 47 subsequently being located to investigate its immediate vicinity. The pit was round in plan with a 'U'-shaped profile, 1.16 m in diameter and 0.9 m deep. It had a single fill of sandy silt with much grit and occasional charcoal flecking. Pottery dating to the early Romano-British period (phase 2) was recovered from the fill.

In addition to that found in the two features, a total of 30 sherds of Romano-British pottery was found in the topsoil and subsoil of trench 47.

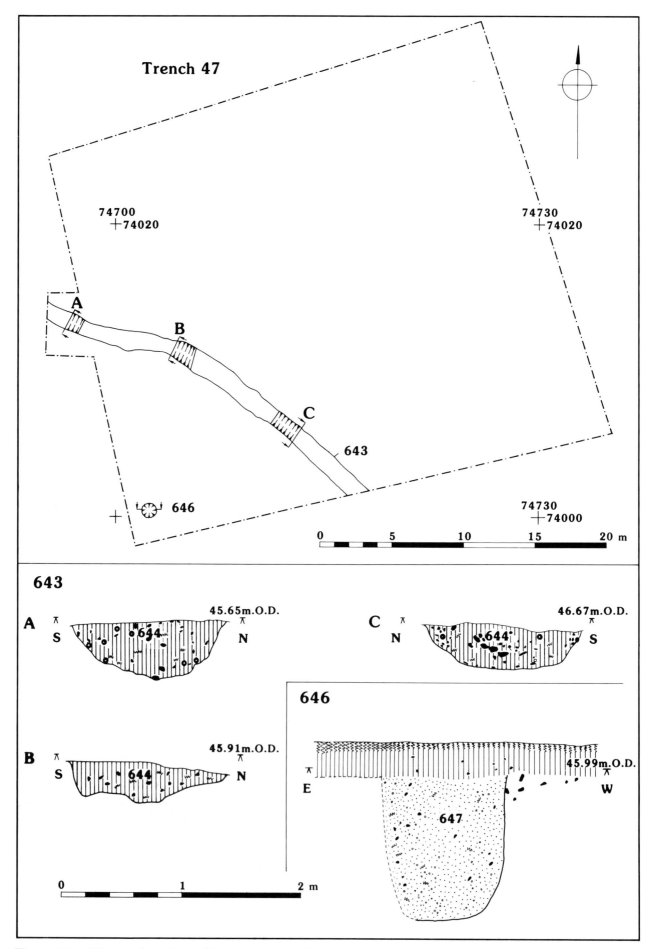

Figure 30   Plan and sections of features in trench 47

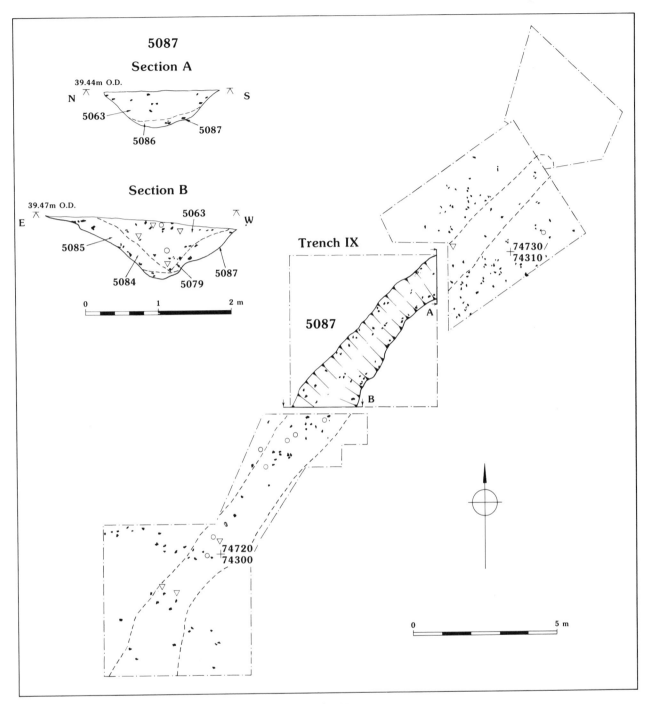

Figure 31   Plan and section of ditch 5087 in trench IX

Cremation burials

Two cremation burial groups (1004 and 1150, Fig. 32) were recovered from trench 48H. One further *in situ* cremation (1409) situated immediately to the west of trench 48H was noted during the second stage of evaluation but was not excavated. Cremated bone was also recovered from the topsoil (1001) in trench 48.

Cremation burial group 1004

This consisted of a 1.5 x 0.5 m spread of pottery and 461.1 g of cremated human bone observed immediately after the removal of the topsoil. There was no cut for the feature, situated on the Reading Beds clay, and it is probable that the cremation burial

was not *in situ*. At least four vessels all dated to the late 2nd century AD (phase 3) were present in the spread, together with two iron nails. The pottery appears to post-date the abandonment of the enclosure and represents the only phase 3 activity recorded outside it.

Cremation burial group 1150

The cremation burial group was contained in a cut in the clay measuring 0.64 x 0.43 m and 0.26 m deep. The sandy loam fill contained 507.3 g of cremated human bone and sherds of pottery from at least two vessels. One vessel was nearly complete, and both dated to the 1st century AD (phase 2). Two iron nails were also found in the cremation.

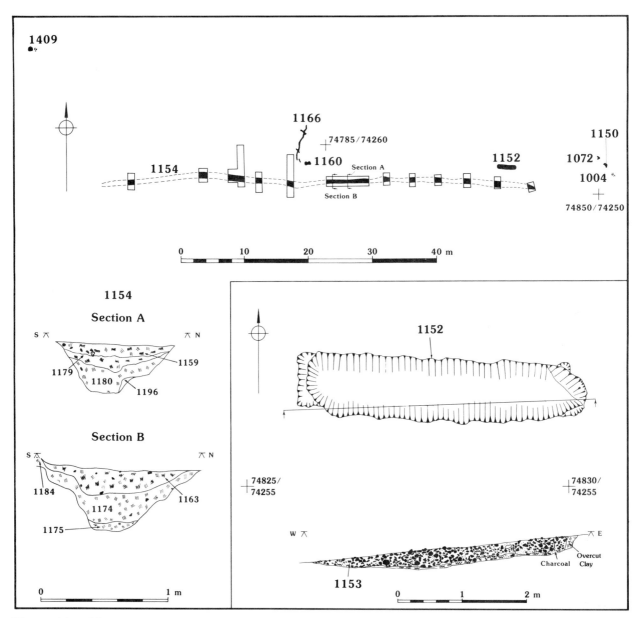

Figure 32   Plan and sections of features in trench 48H

Cremation burial 1409
This cremation burial group was found at the base of the slope directly to the of trench 48H during the earlier evaluation. It comprised two almost complete pottery vessels of Romano-British manufacture which contained and were surrounded by cremated bone, charcoal and burnt flint. It was not excavated but was left *in situ*.

Other features

Feature 1072
This consisted of a circular lens of charcoal, 0.3 m in diameter and 0.13 m deep, sitting in an irregularly shaped patch of silty clay measuring 0.35 x 0.2 m and 0.13 m deep (Fig. 33). No artefacts or bone were found during excavation and only presence of charcoal and the feature's proximity to 1004 and 1150 suggest that it may have been a cremation burial. Not necessarily of ancient date, the feature may be associated with the surrounding Romano-British funerary activity.

Feature 1152
This feature took the form of an elongated pit cut into the hillside approximately 5 m north of the eastern end of ditch 1154 (Fig. 32). It measured 4.4 m east–west, 1 m north–south, was 0.35 m deep, and was almost entirely filled with burnt flint (c. 1800 kg), charcoal, and small amounts of 'sticky' interstitial carbon-rich silt. The clay into which the feature was cut showed marked signs of heat. Whether this indicated the heating of flint *in situ* or the placing of hot flint in the pit was not determined, but the presence of the charcoal suggests that this is where heating or burning took place. The feature is dated to the later Romano-British period (phase 4) by the recovery of small amounts of pottery from fill 1153 and by the presence of large amounts of charcoal, probably derived from the feature, in the phase 4 upper fills of ditch 1154 nearby.

The absence of cremated human (or any other) bone makes it unlikely that this was the site of a funeral pyre; additionally, the two adjacent cremation burials were of earlier date. The form of the feature does not indicate any particular function, including the firing of pottery, but the locally-produced Silchester ware was tempered with burnt flint and it is possible that the feature was a source of this material.

Feature 1160
This circular feature, 0.79 m in diameter, 0.29 m deep, with steep irregular sides and a flat base, was found to the east of ditch 1166 (Fig. 32). It was filled with charcoal-flecked, mottled grey sandy clay loam within which 86 sherds of pottery (773 g) were found. Although the feature had the appearance of a cremation burial and was in close proximity to cremation burials 1004 and 1150, no cremated bone was recovered from the fill. The pottery consisted of a wide variety of material of varying dates but much could be attributed to the 3rd–4th centuries AD (phase 4).

Metalwork

Coin, by I. Barnes
One Roman coin came from the upper fill (1217) of the enclosure ditch. The bronze coin is badly corroded and has not been identified.

Copper alloy objects, by I. Barnes, A.P. Fitzpatrick, and John W. Hawkes
Nine objects of copper alloy were found. Of these, seven are likely to be of Iron Age or Romano-British date on the basis either of context or of identifiable form. Five objects represent jewellery or personal ornaments: one small, and a second possible, brooch fragment, possibly from the same object, a twisted wire bracelet, a second possible bracelet fragment, and a very fragmented length of fine chain, probably a necklace. The remaining two objects are a very small, sheet fragment, from an unidentifiable object, and a ridged tube belt fitting.

The larger of the two possible brooch fragments (Fig. 33: 1) comprises the bow and catch-plate from a decorated brooch. The moulded decoration was probably filled with enamel, and there are traces of what now appears as a yellow substance within the diamond-shaped fields. Decoration of this type appears on the lower part of the bows of Backworth and Polden Hill brooches (Butcher 1982, 107), and while this fragment is too small to be certainly identified, the best parallels are Headstud brooches from Nor'nour, Scilly (Dudley 1968, 40–2, fig. 17, 99–106), Poundbury, Dorset (Green 1987, 95, fig. 66, 5) and *Verulamium* (Frere 1984, 25, fig. 6, 29). These brooches are generally dated to the late 1st or 2nd century AD. A second fragment (Fig. 33: 2), a small piece of curved sheet with a moulded ridge, may be part of the wings which protected the spring or hinge of a brooch, and may derive from the same object; both came from the same phase 4 fill (1163) of ditch 1154 in trench 48H.

The twisted wire bracelet (Fig. 33: 3) consists of two joining fragments, one with part of the expanded and flattened terminal. Bracelets of this type are usually of 3rd or 4th century date (eg Neal 1974, fig. 60, 164; fig. 65, 237–8). A further fragment (Fig. 33: 4), a short length of oval-sectioned rod with an expanded terminal, may be the eye from a bracelet with a hook and eye clasp (Dudley 1968, 22, fig. 9, 33; Frere 1984, 31–3, fig. 10, 68; Stead 1976, 202, fig. 104, 47).

A very fragmented fine chain, made up of small, oval-sectioned links, was found in a pottery vessel, probably of 1st century AD date, together with a glass melon bead (*see* below).

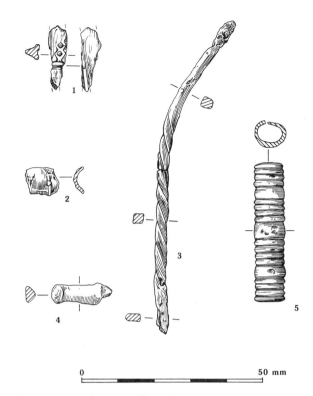

Figure 33   Copper alloy objects

A rolled cylinder of sheet metal decorated with equally spaced sets of four transverse ridges divided by larger mouldings (Fig. 33: 5) has been identified as a late Roman Hawkes and Dunning (1961) type VII tubular-sided attachment-plate from a belt fitting. The edges would have held the belt plate. In terms of size, the closest parallel is an unprovenanced Kentish find which held an elaborate chip-carved buckle (*ibid.*, 68, pl.I, d). Hawkes and Dunning regarded the find, along with other examples from Dorchester-on-Thames, Oxfordshire, and Milton-next-Sittingbourne, Kent, as imports, although this may now be considered less likely.

Discussion
The copper alloy objects were somewhat unevenly distributed across the site. Four came from ditch fills in trench 48H (the twisted wire bracelet, both possible brooch fragments, and the small sheet fragment), contexts all dated by associated pottery to the 3rd or 4th century AD (phase 4); and two objects from within the enclosure (the coin and the chain) were associated with pottery of the 1st century AD (phase 2). The remaining two objects (the smaller bracelet fragment and the belt fitting) were found during topsoil stripping.

The cluster of objects from ditch fill 1163 in trench 48H is worthy of comment: this small collection includes badly worn fragments of a 1st–2nd century AD brooch in addition to a probable 3rd or 4th century bracelet. The age, condition, and concentration of these fragmentary items in a single deposit suggest that they may have been scrap, gathered together for recycling. If this was the case, then scrap or hoarded objects (the fine chain) account for the majority of copper alloy finds from the site.

List of illustrated objects (Fig. 33)

1. Part of the bow and catch-plate of a decorated brooch. SF 11356, context 1163, ditch 1166, trench 48H, phase 4.
2. Small ?brooch fragment, possibly from the same example as No. 5. SF 11358, context 1163, ditch 1166, trench 48H, phase 4.
3. Two joining lengths of a twisted wire bracelet. SF 11354, 11355, context 1163, ditch 1166, trench 48H, phase 4.
4. Short length of oval-sectioned rod, with an expanded terminal; possibly the eye from a bracelet. SF 11353, context 1001, subsoil, trench 48.
5. Decorated copper alloy tube, late Roman type VII tubular-sided attachment-plate from a belt fitting (Hawkes and Dunning 1961). SF 11360, context 5000, topsoil, trench 49.

Iron objects

A total of 439 iron objects was recovered, of which 352 pieces were from well stratified contexts. Of this total, 85 objects were unidentifiable; the remaining 267 objects are discussed here. All items were X-rayed, and from these the pieces were subsequently classified and quantified. Most objects have been identified as nails or hobnails, and rod fragments may represent further nails; other objects comprise three blade fragments, one pin, one ring, and a possible binding fragment. The breakdown of iron objects by type and by context is given in Table 8.

Hobnails

A total of 216 hobnails was found. Of these, 115 were contained within a boot sole and a further 33 in a boot sole fragment (Fig. 34). Both soles were found in the fills of ditch 1154, dated to the 3rd or 4th century AD (phase 4). The hobnails were of standard size and shape, having round domed heads up to 8 mm in diameter with square cross sectioned shafts up to 10 mm long. Of the remaining hobnails, 63 were found within the fills of ditch 1154 and as such are likely to constitute the disturbed remainder of the two soles. Four similar hobnails came from a pit in trench 48H, and a single hobnail was found within the enclosure.

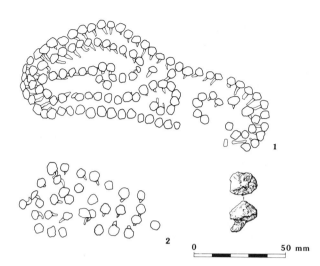

Figure 34   The iron hobnails

Nails

A total of 19 nails was found on the site, although it is possible that many pieces identified as rods could also be so classified. No attempt has been made to classify the nails by type. The majority had square-sectioned shanks, generally around 20 mm in length. Most of the nails came from ditch 1154 in trench 48H.

Rods

A total of 27 pieces of rod were found. All were in a bad state of preservation and in most cases it was not possible to see the shape of the cross-section. They have thus been classified separately from the nails, although many could be nail shanks.

Other objects

The remaining five identifiable objects comprise one blade fragment and a blade/handle fragment, the point from a pin, a ring of uncertain function, and a block with a possible rivet hole, perhaps a binding of some type. The blade/handle fragment, from phase 2 pit 1220 within the enclosure, is very corroded, but the blade appears to be

Table 8 ironwork by context from the terrace area

Feature	Phase	Hobnails	Nails	Rods	Blades	Other	Unidentified
Ditch terminal 1008	2	–	1	1	–	–	–
Post-hole 1090	2	1	–	–	–	–	–
Cremation 1150	2	–	2	2	–	1	2
Pit 1220	2	–	–	–	1	–	2
Pit 1287	2	–	1	–	–	1	–
Cremation 1004	3	–	2	2	–	–	–
Ditch 1154	4	211	13	14	1	1	80
Pit 1160	4	4	–	2	–	–	–
Ditch 1166	4	–	–	5	–	–	1
Post-hole 1055	Unphased	–	–	1	–	–	–
Total		216	19	27	2	3	85

set at a right-angle to the handle, suggesting that this object may be part a pair of shears (cf Manning 1985, 34–5, pl. 14, 4–9). The other blade fragment came from ditch 1154 in trench 48H, and probably derives from a knife. The pin fragment was from cremation burial 1150 and may be from a brooch.

Discussion

Table 8 shows that the majority of the ironwork dates from the later Romano-British period (phase 4) and was found in or around the field boundary ditch 1154 to the north-east in trench 48H, although it should be noted that many of the total represent just two items: the boot soles studded with hobnails. Only nine pieces of iron were found within the enclosure, none definitely from contexts deposited during the initial phases of occupation (phase 1). Eleven iron objects were associated with the cremation burials in trench 48H (1004 and 1150).

List of illustrated objects (Fig. 34)

1. *In situ* hobnails representing a complete boot sole. Context 1159, ditch 1154, trench 48H, phase 4
2. *In situ* hobnails from a partial boot sole. Context 1165, ditch 1154, trench 48H, phase 4.

Metalworking residues

A total of 3629 g of metalworking residues was recovered from the excavation, 391 g of which came from the topsoil and are not discussed. The breakdown of the assemblage by type and context is given in Table 9.

The associated pottery dates most of the metalworking residue (2,823 g) to the early Roman period (phase 2). A further 392 g was found in the fills of recut 5079 of ditch 5087 outside the enclosure, dated to phase 1, whilst 23 g came from insecure contexts in the upper fill of the enclosure ditch (phase 4). Just over half of the assemblage comprises a single piece of limonite (1845 g), a naturally occurring oxide of iron. It was found within the lining of the hearth/oven feature (1127) in northern ditch terminal 1008. Although this is an ore rather than a residue, it has been included here because it may have been brought to the site for smelting but may later have been discarded, and ultimately used in the lining of the hearth. There were no metalworking residues actually within 1127, although seven pieces

were found in stratigraphically earlier contexts and another in a later one. Although evidence may have been obscured by the baulk, there is no compelling reason to conclude that it was a metalworking feature.

Apart from limonite, the bulk of the assemblage falls into the category of smithing slag, as defined by McDonnell (1983, 81–3). There is a small amount of tap slag, but this is too small to be of significance.

Most of the metalworking residues were recovered from northern ditch terminal 1008, and were spread throughout the stratigraphic sequence within phase 2. Only a very small proportion (56 g) came from southern ditch terminal 1359.

The amount of metalworking residue found and, more importantly, the stratigraphic and chronological relationships of the material make it of little significance, but a few general points may be made. Clearly metalworking of some form, probably small-scale, was taking place in the vicinity of the enclosure but not within it, otherwise the quantity of residues found in pit fills would necessarily have been much greater. The concentration of residues within the enclosure ditch contrasts markedly with the distribution of the metal objects found on the site, with very few of the latter being found within the enclosure.

Worked Stone

A total of 38 pieces of worked stone was recovered. This total comprised at least five rotary quernstones, one stone weight and two hones but does not include the flint and hammerstones, which are discussed elsewhere (*see* above). Geological identifications have been provided by Dr. D.F.Williams (University of Southampton). The worked stone is summarised in Table 10.

Rotary quernstones

Thirty-one pieces of stone were identified as parts of rotary quernstones (Fig. 35: 1–3); 30 were from within the Iron Age enclosure and one was from the ditch in trench 48H. In all, five rotary quernstones (two upper and three lower) were represented. No quernstone of any other form was observed.

Table 9 metalworking residues by context and weight (g) from the terrace area

Feature	Phase	Limonite	Haematite	Smithing slag	Smithing/ Smelting slag
Ditch 5079	1	–	–	–	392
Ditch 1008 (lower)	2	–	–	898	–
Hearth/oven lining 1127 within enclosure ditch 1008	2	1845	–	–	–
Pit 1300	2	–	5	–	–
Pit 1312	2	–	–	19	–
Ditch 1359 (lower)	2	–	–	56	–
Ditch 1008 (upper)	4	–	–	23	–
Total		1845	5	996	392

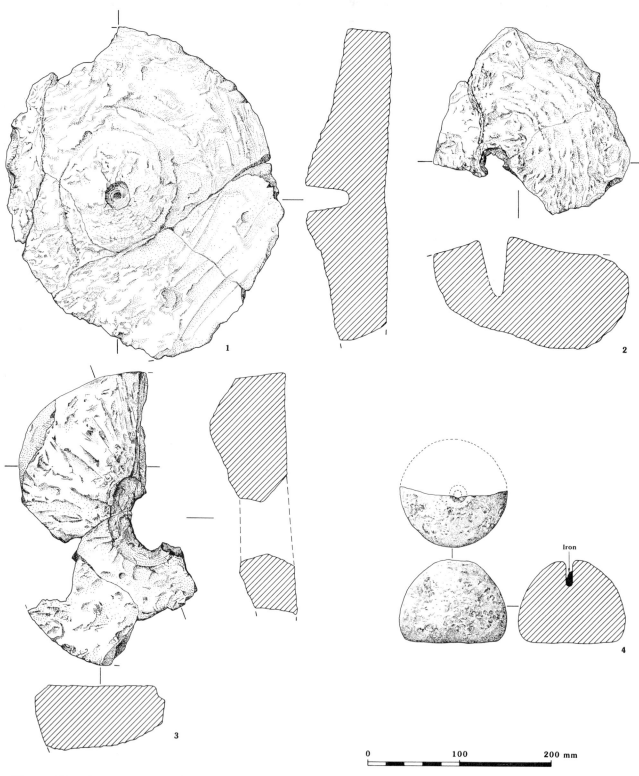

Figure 35   Quernstones and stone weight

Table 10 worked stone by context from the terrace area (number/weight)

Feature	Phase	Lodsworth quern	Quartz conglom. quern	Weight	Hone
Unstratified/ topsoil		–	–	1/894	2/262
Upper fills of pit 1233	2	27/26755	–	–	–
Ditch 1154	4	–	1/290	–	–
Enclosure ditch section 1231	4	–	1/550	–	–
Enclosure ditch section 1257	4	–	2/1090	–	–
Total		27/26755	4/1930	1/894	2/262

Of the total, 27 pieces are of dark grey glauconitic sandstone, characteristic of the Lodsworth quarries in West Sussex (Peacock 1987). These pieces represent at least three individual stones, one upper and two lower, and all were recovered from the pit 1233 within the Iron Age enclosure. Although this is a phase 1 pit, the stones were found in the upper fills which may well represent a phase 2 deposit. One well-worn lower stone was nearly complete (Fig. 35: 1) having a diameter of 0.35 m and a spindle hole which did not penetrate the full thickness of the quern. A localised area of heavy wear on the grinding surface showed that after it had become unsuitable for milling it was used as a hone before being broken and discarded. A second lower stone was less complete (Fig. 35: 2); it had a diameter of 0.3 m. Fill 1250 produced another 14 pieces of glauconitic sandstone, five of which fitted with one or other of the broken lower stones, and the remaining nine pieces of glauconitic sandstone may also derive from the same stones.

Fill 1249 of the same pit (1233) produced 13 more pieces of Lodsworth sandstone, three of which fitted together to form a large portion of a third rotary quernstone (Fig. 35: 3). The stone had a diameter of 0.33 m. It was identifiable as an upper stone by the hollow for the handle and the hopper around the spindle hole. Also from fill 1249 came a small non-fitting fragment of the grinding surface of an upper stone and a further eight pieces of Lodsworth sandstone which could not be assigned to any identified quernstone.

Using the dating criteria proposed by Peacock (1987), ie the thickness of the stones, the presence of a handle slot and hopper, and whether the spindle hole in the lower stone is a complete or partial perforation, these three Lodsworth quernstones can be recognised as belonging to the Late Iron Age.

The remaining quernstone fragments, all dating to the 3rd/4th centuries AD (phase 4), are all of quartz conglomerate rock, probably deriving from the Forest of Dean, Gloucestershire. Two joining fragments were found in the almost sterile fill 1258 of the north eastern spur (1257) of the enclosure ditch. It was not possible to calculate a diameter but the two fragments were part of an upper stone which had a maximum surviving thickness of 55 mm. A third non-fitting piece was found a few metres away in the north-east corner of enclosure ditch 1231. This was part of an upper stone which had a maximum surviving thickness of 35 mm.

The fourth fragment came from field boundary ditch 1154 in trench 48H. This was part of a lower stone which had a maximum surviving thickness of 37 mm.

These four quernstone fragments may represent three stones, but more probably only two. All show the typically Roman characteristics of being thinner than Iron Age examples and of lacking a slot for the handle.

Stone weight

One fragment of bun-shaped stone weight (Fig. 35: 4) in a ferruginous sandstone was recovered from the subsoil (1001) a few metres east of four-post structure 1410, interpreted as a granary, in the north-west corner of the enclosure. It represents approximately half of a complete weight and has a maximum height of 86 mm and a maximum diameter of 115 mm. The weight would have been suspended by an iron hook set into the weight, corroded fragments of which still survived. An original weight of about 1788 g can be calculated from the estimated original volume of about 640 cc and the density of the stone at 2.79 g/cc.

Typologically the weight fits into the Danebury W1 class (Cunliffe 1984a) which belongs to the Middle to Late Iron Age. Other examples have been found at Winklebury Camp (Smith 1977, 108 and 113), Winnall Down (Fasham 1985, 81), and Easton Lane (Fasham et al 1989). These also date from the Middle to Late Iron Age. A possible source for the stone may be found within the Tertiary deposits of the Hampshire basin to the south.

Hones

Four pieces of stone representing two complete hones were recovered from the topsoil in trench 49. One hone was manufactured from grey micaceous sandstone of unknown provenance; the other appears to be an unworked but utilised piece of local valley gravel. Neither is closely datable. As mentioned above, part of one of the broken quernstones had also been used as a hone (Fig. 35: 1).

Discussion

The amount of worked stone found is quite small, quern fragments being the most numerous items. Of the five identifiable querns, three are Lodsworth querns of Late Iron Age type which appear to be redeposited in early

Romano-British contexts (1st century AD). The later use of the quartz conglomerate querns from the Forest of Dean, Gloucestershire may illustrate a change in trade direction at the time of, or sometime after, the abandonment of the enclosure in the late 1st or early 2nd century AD.

Perhaps the most significant find is the Late Iron Age stone weight from within the enclosure. These weights have been used as evidence of increased emphasis on the role of exchange in the southern English Iron Age (Champion in Fasham 1985, 81). The rarity of such weights, and the significance ascribed to them, makes this example of some importance, for it was probably manufactured in the Hampshire basin and it is the most northerly example so far recorded.

List of illustrated objects (Fig. 35)
1. Lower stone from Lodsworth rotary quern. Context 1250, pit 1233, trench 48, phase 2.
2. Lower stone from Lodsworth rotary quern. Context 1250, pit 1233, trench 48, phase 2.
3. Upper stone from Lodsworth rotary quern. Context 1249, pit 1233, trench 48, phase 2.
4. Bun-shaped sandstone weight; corroded fragments of iron inserted in top. Context 1001, subsoil, trench 48.

Glass

With the exception of modern bottle and window glass in the topsoil, only one glass object was found during the excavation: a turquoise glass melon bead, a type dated to the 1st and 2nd centuries AD in Britain (Guido 1978). The bead was found within a pottery vessel of 1st century AD date, together with a very fragmented fine copper alloy chain (*see* above), in a lower fill of the enclosure ditch in section 1259.

Iron Age and Romano-British Pottery, by Lorraine Mepham

Introduction
The complete prehistoric and Romano-British pottery assemblage from Thames Valley Park comprised 11,119 sherds, with a total weight of 99,220 g. The pottery was derived from four main areas: trenches 47, 48, 48H, and 49, and was recovered both from surface collection over unstratified topsoil and subsoil contexts after machine stripping, and also from hand-excavated features and stratified subsoil contexts in the four areas. The problems of interpretation of features whose upper levels have been truncated by machine stripping should be borne in mind when considering the pottery assemblage; there are few securely stratified groups of pottery from features on the site, and some loss of information may have occurred through truncation of later levels within features.

Methods
The pottery was analysed using the standard Wessex Archaeology recording system. Using a hand lens (X8 magnification), the pottery was divided into six fabric groups on the basis of the dominant inclusion type: Group A (fine sandy fabrics), Group B (coarse sandy fabrics), Group C (grog-tempered fabrics), Group D (flint-gritted and flint-tempered fabrics), Group E (shelly fabrics), and organic-tempered fabrics (Group G). These fabric groups were then subdivided into 73 separate fabric types on the basis of the range and size of the macroscopic inclusions; each fabric type has been allocated a unique alpha-numeric code.

Material of Late Neolithic and Bronze Age date has been considered elsewhere in this report. Some sherds were too small to distinguish fabric type with any degree of accuracy; these have been recorded in the archive, but are omitted from further analysis. The assemblage thus examined in detail and discussed in this section consists of 10,753 sherds with a total weight of 97,035 g.

For each context, pottery from each fabric type represented was counted and weighed to the nearest gram. Percentages quoted throughout this report have been calculated by weight, unless otherwise stated. Each rim and base sherd (apart from those too small and/or abraded to be diagnostic), or groups of conjoining rim/base sherds, and any other diagnostic sherds, were allocated unique Featured Sherd Numbers, and these have been used to create a limited vessel type series. Rim and base diameters have been recorded to the nearest centimetre, except where enough of the rim or base survived to make an accurate measurement to the nearest millimetre possible. Details of surface treatment and decorative techniques were also recorded. Full details of all pottery recording are held in the archive. The pottery is discussed by chronological period below.

Early–Middle Iron Age
Thirteen fabric types were identified as Early–Middle Iron Age, largely on the basis of vessel form. These fabrics include coarse sandy fabrics (Group B), flint-gritted or flint-tempered fabrics (Group D), one shelly fabric (Group E), and one organic-tempered fabric (Group G). Fabric totals are given in Table 11. Terms describing the frequency of inclusions in the following fabric descriptions, and throughout this report, are defined as follows: rare (1–3%); sparse (3–10%); moderate (10–20%); common (20–30%); very common (30–40%).

Fabrics
B3 Moderately coarse clay matrix; moderate, poorly-sorted rounded quartz <1 mm; moderate, poorly-sorted grog <2 mm; firing brown–black.

B7 Moderately coarse clay matrix; moderate rounded quartz <1 mm; rare sub-angular flint <2 mm; rare iron oxide; firing orange–red with unoxidised core.

B8 Moderately coarse clay matrix; common to abundant possible glauconite; sparse rounded quartz <1 mm; very rare sub-angular flint; firing grey–brown.

B9 Moderately coarse clay matrix; moderate rounded quartz <0.5 mm; rare subangular/sub-rounded flint <4 mm; rare sub-angular chalk <4 mm; sparse to moderate possible glauconite; firing orange–red with dark grey surfaces.

B10 Moderately silty matrix; sparse rounded quartz <0.5 mm; rare sub-angular flint <1mm; sparse vegetable matter; sparse mica and red iron oxide; firing brown–grey.

B11 Moderately coarse clay matrix; moderate rounded quartz <0.5 mm; sparse mica; firing buff–orange with dark grey core.

D1 Sparsely flint-gritted fabric; moderately silty clay matrix, sparsely micaceous; rare rounded quartz <1 mm; occasional sub-angular flint <1.5 mm; firing dark grey with patchily oxidised exterior.

D4 Moderately coarse sandy flint-tempered fabric; moderately coarse clay matrix; moderate, poorly-sorted sub-angular flint <4 mm; sparse rounded quartz <0.5 mm; unoxidised, with oxidised (orange–red) surface.

D5 Coarse, sandy, flint-tempered fabric; moderately coarse clay matrix; moderate sub-angular flint <1 mm; rare iron oxide; unoxidised, with oxidised (buff/orange) surface.

D7 Coarse, well-finished, flint-tempered fabric; moderately coarse clay matrix; common, fairly well-sorted sub-angular flint <1 mm; unoxidised, firing brown/black.

D11 Moderately coarse flint-gritted fabric; moderately fine, micaceous clay matrix; rare to sparse sub-angular flint <1 mm; unoxidised, firing dark grey/black.

E1 Hard, sandy shelly fabric; moderately coarse clay matrix, sparsely micaceous; moderate, poorly-sorted shell fragments <5 mm.

G1 Soft, silty clay matrix, moderately micaceous, with moderate to common linear voids, indicating vegetable temper; firing buff-brown with dark grey core.

In all cases, where firing conditions allow observation, the clay matrix appears to be relatively iron-rich. The majority of sherds are unoxidised, although some show partial or complete oxidisation of at least the external surface.

With the exception of fabrics B3, E1, and G1, all fabric types can be assigned with some confidence to the Middle Iron Age, with a broad date range of 3rd–1st century BC. Fabrics B3 and E1, each of which is represented by a single vessel only, have been tentatively assigned to the Early Iron Age. Sherds in fabric B3 come from an expanded rim with internal flange, of a type known elsewhere in Early Iron Age contexts, eg at Ashville and Farmoor in Oxfordshire (DeRoche 1978, fig. 31, form A; Lambrick 1979, fig. 21, 1). The shelly fabric E1, represented by two plain body sherds, is of more uncertain date. Shelly fabrics are found throughout central southern England from the Late Bronze Age to the Middle Iron Age, eg in Late Bronze Age contexts at Potterne, Wiltshire (Morris 1991), and in Early–Middle Iron Age contexts in south Oxfordshire (DeRoche 1978; 41, fabric 1; Lambrick 1979, 35, fabric group B).

Fabric G1 is similarly ambiguous. Organic-tempered fabrics are generally considered to be characteristic of the Early–Middle Saxon period in southern England, although similar fabrics are also known in later prehistoric contexts. An organic-tempered fabric was noted at Riseley Farm, Swallowfield, for example, dated to the Middle/Late Iron Age (Lobb and Morris 1994, fabric 26). Fabric G1 again represents a single vessel, a slack-shouldered jar; similar forms are found in the Middle Iron Age fabrics on the site, but the form also occurs in Saxon contexts, and the high proportion of organic material in fabric G1 is certainly more

Table 11 Iron Age pottery: fabric totals

Fabric	No. Sherds	Weight (g)
B3	2	14
B7	254	1870
B8	69	968
B9	22	247
B10	298	2151
B11	141	958
D1	49	330
D4	161	801
D5	108	724
D7	70	957
D11	228	1300
E1	2	17
G1	4	24
C9	268	2232
Total	1676	12593

suggestive of a Saxon date. The vessel was from an unstratified context.

Almost all the fabrics found in the Iron Age assemblage could have been made locally. The site is located on a low terrace on the Thames floodplain, formed from outcrops of Middle and Upper Chalk with overlying loam. Areas of Valley Gravels, Plateau Gravels, and Reading Beds clays all occur elsewhere on the terrace within the development area, and deposits of London Clay are located within 2 km of the site. The similarity of the clay matrix of most of the fabrics might suggest a relatively restricted source area for the bulk of the assemblage, although the presence of possible glauconite in the sandy fabrics B8 and B9 might be indicative of a separate source area, perhaps further afield, for these two fabrics. Glauconite is frequently associated with Greensand formations, which occur approximately 30 km to the south-west in North Hampshire and approximately 30 km to the north-west in Oxfordshire, although glauconitic sand is also found in some locations of the local Reading Beds (White 1907). The possibility that some of the fabrics, notably the well-sorted flint-tempered fabrics D7 and D11, represent a more regionalised mode of production is discussed below.

Forms

Rim sherds and other diagnostic sherds are scarce within the Middle Iron Age assemblage, and those that are present are not always capable of being assigned to particular vessel types. A limited vessel type series has been created using all available diagnostic sherds, including the two complete profiles, rim sherds and decorated body sherds. The correlation of vessel forms to fabric types is presented in Table 12.

1 Saucepan pot; vertical or slightly convex-sided, with plain rim, often with external groove immediately below (Fig. 36, 3, 5).

2   Ovoid or barrel-shaped jar or bowl with inturned, simple rim. Only one example, quite well finished (Fig. 36, 4).

3   Slack-shouldered jar or bowl with vertical or slightly everted rim, simple rounded, or thickened (Fig. 36, 14; Fig. 38, 31).

4   Rounded jar with upright or slightly everted rim, thickened (Fig. 36, 1, 2, 7, 10; Fig. 38, 33, 35, 39, 41).

5   Rounded bowl with upright or slightly everted rim, simple rounded, beaded or thickened (Fig. 36, 6; Fig. 38, 36).

6   Bucket-shaped jar with upright thickened rim emphasised by slight shoulder (Fig. 38, 34). Only one example. This is apparently a very coarse version of the saucepan pot form.

7   Small, bipartite or rounded bowl with upright rim. The only example identified has tooled decoration on the shoulder (Fig. 38, 38)

Surface treatment and decoration
Evidence of either surface treatment or decoration was scarce amongst the Middle Iron Age assemblage. Surface burnishing was recorded for a small proportion of sherds (182 sherds), in both sandy and flint-tempered fabrics. The fabrics which are most frequently burnished are B9 (45.5% of sherds by number), D1 (39.0% of sherds by number), and D11 (43.0% of sherds by number). Other fabrics for which burnishing was recorded were B8 (8.7%), B10 (11.1%), B11 (1 sherd only), and D7 (25.7%). Where vessel form could be identified for burnished sherds, saucepan pots appear to be the most frequently burnished (three examples).

Decoration is restricted to three examples of impressed decoration, the most notable being sherds of a rounded bowl in fabric B10 with impressed curvilinear decoration (Fig. 38, 36). The decoration and vessel form are paralleled at Frilford, Oxfordshire (Cunliffe 1978, A:20, no. 10). Two other sherds in the same fabric have fragments of impressed decoration, and a further sherd, from the rim and shoulder of a rounded or bipartite bowl, has tooled decoration (Fig. 38, 38). All examples of impressed decoration or tooling occur on jar or bowl forms. Some of the saucepan pots are grooved below the rim (Fig. 36, 5), but otherwise this vessel form is undecorated.

Discussion
The Middle Iron Age assemblage from Thames Valley Park appears to be consistent with the general ceramic traditions of the area, as seen at sites such as Alder-

maston Wharf (Cowell *et al* 1978, 24–5); Southcote (Piggott and Seaby 1937); and Riseley Farm (Lobb and Morris 1994). At all these sites, rounded and slack-shouldered plain jar forms, mainly in sandy fabrics, such as those found at Thames Valley Park, are common.

Two other elements, however, may also be discerned, which enable the Thames Valley Iron Age assemblage to be placed within a wider context. The first of these is the presence of a decorated rounded bowl form which appears to have affinities with Cunliffe's 'bowl continuum' covering the south Midlands and north Berkshire (1978, fig. 3:8 and fig. A:20).

The second element is the presence of saucepan pots. These vessels are found widely over central southern England in the Middle Iron Age (Cunliffe 1978, fig. 3:6). The examples from Thames Valley Park fall within the geographical area of the Southcote–Blewburton Hill style as defined by Cunliffe (*ibid.*, fig. A:17), although the lack of decoration on the Thames Valley examples contrasts with the highly decorated vessels from Southcote (Piggott and Seaby 1937) and may find more affinities with, for example, the St Catherine's Hill/Worthy Down style (Cunliffe 1978, fig. A:15). A range of very similar vessels was found, for example, at Brighton Hill South, near Basingstoke (Rees 1995), Hampshire, and a small number at Aldermaston Wharf (Cowell *et al.* 1978, fig. 13). It may be noted that the saucepan pots from both the latter sites, and also from Southcote, occurred almost exclusively in flint-tempered fabrics, and the examples from Brighton Hill South and Aldermaston Wharf are directly comparable with the well-sorted flint-tempered examples from Thames Valley Park. Riseley Farm had no saucepan pots, and this may be explained by the corresponding absence of comparable well-sorted flint-tempered fabrics.

Rees (1995) has noted the difficulties of distinguishing between different modes of pottery production in an area where there are no geologically distinctive fabrics. Pottery manufactured for a regional market rather than a purely local market, might be indicated by standardisation in vessel shape and size, and/or by the frequency of burnishing and decoration. The sample of diagnostic Iron Age pottery from Thames Valley Park is too small for any standardisation to be discerned, but a number of sherds indicate that some care was taken both in the preparation of the clay and in the finishing of the vessel. Though decoration is rare, surface burnishing is fairly common on certain fabrics, and some attempt has been made to sort inclusions such as

Table 12 Middle Iron Age pottery: vessel forms by fabric

	B7	B8	B10	B11	D1	D5	D7	D11	G1	Total
Saucepan pot	–	–	–	–	–	–	1	5	–	6
Small ovoid jar	–	1	–	–	–	–	–	–	–	1
Slack-shouldered jar	1	–	4	–	1	1	–	1	1	9
Rounded jar	–	–	4	2	1	2	1	1	–	11
Rounded bowl	–	1	1	–	–	–	–	–	–	2
Rounded/bipartite bowl	–	–	1	–	–	–	–	–	–	1
Total	1	2	10	2	2	3	2	7	1	30

crushed flint. Fabrics B9 and D11 exhibits the most frequent evidence of surface burnishing amongst the Iron Age assemblage (45.5% and 43.0% respectively). The same may also be true of fabric D7, sherds of which indicate that some care was taken in the sorting of the crushed flint inclusions; it is frequently burnished. Both these flint-tempered fabrics are most commonly found in saucepan pot forms, and are comparable to fabrics at Brighton Hill South for which Rees proposes a regional mode of production (in prep., fabrics 1 and 4). It may also be noted that fabric B9 contained possible glauconite, for which a non-local source has been suggested (*see* Fabrics, above).

The Middle Iron Age assemblage from Thames Valley, therefore, could be seen as comprising largely locally produced wares, with a secondary element of more standardised wares representing a more regionalised mode of production. The sample of diagnostic sherds is small, and it is not possible to discern any chronological development in the use of particular fabrics or vessel forms; the contemporaneity of saucepan pots with slack-shouldered and rounded jars, the most common vessel types represented, is well attested from other sites in the area, such as Aldermaston Wharf and Southcote (Cowell *et al.* 1978; Piggott and Seaby 1937).

Late Iron Age (1st century BC–1st century AD)

One fabric type within the prehistoric assemblage appears on the basis of manufacturing technique and vessel forms present, to be of Late Iron Age date (see Table 11 for fabric totals).

C9　Soft grog-tempered fabric with a soapy feel; moderately fine clay matrix; moderate, fairly well-sorted grog <1 mm; sparse rounded quartz <0.5 mm; sparse iron oxide. Handmade, although a few examples may be wheelthrown. Unoxidised, with patchily oxidised exterior.

This fabric is well-finished, and occurs in beaded rim jar forms (Fig. 38, 30). Some of these vessels may be wheelthrown. Also in this fabric is a single pedestal base, probably from a wheelthrown vessel (Fig. 36, 8). This fabric would appear to fall within the tradition sometimes defined as 'Belgic' grog-tempered ware, found widely over south-eastern England from the 1st century BC until the middle of the 1st century AD (Thompson 1982). A comparable fabric type was identified, for example, at Brighton Hill South (Rees 1995, fabric 7), and handmade bead rims in grog-tempered fabrics were recovered from Site I at Aldermaston (Cowell *et al* 1978, 26).

Romano-British

Romano-British pottery formed the bulk of the Thames Valley Park ceramic assemblage. The Romano-British assemblage has a general date range of 1st–4th century AD, with an emphasis on the early Roman period, particularly middle 1st to early 2nd century AD.

Fabrics and forms
Fabric types identified included both fine (Group A) and coarse sandy wares (Group B), grog-tempered fabrics (Group C), and flint-gritted or flint-tempered fabrics (Group D). All four groups contain fabric types of known type or source. Fabric totals are given in Table 13.

Group A: fine sandy fabrics: Within the fine sandy fabric group, imports are represented by a number of sherds of samian, and single examples of Lyon ware (Greene 1979, 13) and possible Central Gaulish glazed ware (*ibid.*, 90). No attempt has been made to assign the samian to particular sources; only one sherd was decorated, a very abraded and unidentifiable body sherd. Vessel forms present include a Drag. 15/17 platter, Drag. 18, 18/31 and 31 platters (eight examples), an unrouletted example of a Drag. 24/25 cup, a Drag. 38 bowl, and a Drag. 42 platter. The Drag. 15/17 platter and the Drag. 24/25 cup have pre-Flavian or Flavian currency in Britain (middle–late 1st century); the Drag. 18/31 platters have a broad date range of AD 90–150; the Drag. 42 platter is likely to be of early–middle 2nd century date, and the Drag. 31 platter and the Drag. 38 bowl are the latest forms (mid–late 2nd century AD),

The single sherd of Lyon ware is from a roughcast cup or beaker with a red–brown colour coat. The possible Central Gaulish sherd, in a soft, micaceous buff-coloured fabric with traces of a brownish glaze may be from a bowl or flagon. This sherd was identified by D.F. Williams (University of Southampton), whose full report can be found in archive. Both these wares have a Claudian–Neronian currency (*c.* AD 40–70) in Britain.

Other recognised fine wares include colour-coated and plain oxidised wares and white wares from the Oxfordshire region (Young 1977), and colour-coated and plain white wares from the New Forest (Fulford 1975a). The distinction between products of the two centres is not always possible for plain, undiagnostic sherds. No vessel forms could be identified within the New Forest group, but a broad date range of *c.* AD 260–400 may be suggested for these wares (*ibid.*, 39–42). The Oxfordshire colour-coated wares occur in forms copying samian platters and bowls (Young 1977, type C46, imitating Drag. 18/31 platter; type C48, imitating Drag. 36 bowl; Fig. 38, 54); there are also two mortaria in an oxidised fabric with white colour coat (*ibid.*, types WC4, WC7). These Oxfordshire products, like the New Forest wares, are of late Roman type; the vessel forms present are dated no earlier than the middle of the 3rd century AD.

Fine sandy fabrics of unknown source are listed below.

A2　Terra Rubra imitations: fine, soft, silty clay matrix, moderately micaceous, with rare rounded quartz <0.5 mm, firing orange–red.

A3　Fine, soft, silty clay matrix, sparsely micaceous, with rare iron oxides, firing buff–orange to orange–red, with unoxidised surfaces.

A4　Fine, soft, moderately fine clay matrix with moderate, well-sorted rounded quartz <0.25 mm; rare iron oxides; firing salmon–pink.

A5　Very fine, soft, micaceous silty clay matrix without visible inclusions; unoxidised, firing pale grey.

A9　Hard, moderately fine clay matrix with sparse rounded quartz <0.5 mm; sparse iron oxide; firing yellow–cream.

A10　Very soft, fine, slightly micaceous clay matrix with sparse black iron oxide <0.5 mm; firing pale buff–grey.

A11 Fine, silty clay matrix, moderately micaceous, with very rare rounded quartz <0.25 mm; sparse black iron oxide; firing blue–grey.

A12 Fine, silty clay matrix with common rounded quartz <0.25 mm; rare red iron oxide; firing pale pink–buff.

A14 Hard, fine sandy fabric; rare rounded quartz <0.5 mm; sparse black iron oxide; firing orange–buff.

A15 Hard, fine, silty clay matrix, sparsely micaceous, with rare quartz grains <0.5 mm; sparse red iron oxide; firing buff–orange with unoxidised core.

A16 Possible Gaulish import; hard, fine, silty clay matrix without visible inclusions; firing cream–white with brown–red colour coat.

A18 Very soft, fine, silty clay matrix, sparsely micaceous, without visible inclusions; firing pink–buff.

A19 Soft, moderately fine clay matrix with rare black and red iron oxide; firing white–grey.

A20 Possible imitation Terra Nigra; hard, fine, silty clay matrix, moderately micaceous, without visible inclusions; unoxidised, firing brown/black.

With the possible exception of fabric A16, all these fabric types are likely to be of British source, although several can be seen to imitate vessel forms of Continental origin, particularly Gallo-Belgic forms which were current in Britain in the middle–late 1st century AD.

Fabrics A2 and A20 occur in platter forms which imitate Gallo-Belgic originals (Hawkes and Hull 1947, form Cam. 17; Fig. 38, 49). Other examples of this form were identified in fabric A11, which may be a product of the Alice Holt kilns (Lyne and Jefferies 1979, fabric A; fig. 18). Gallo-Belgic wares were imported into Britain before the conquest, but imitations continued to be produced throughout the 1st century AD.

Beakers, imitating the Gallo-Belgic butt and girth beakers, occur in fabrics A3, A5, and A15 (Fig. 37, 26), and sherds of fabric A5 also derive from at least two rounded beakers, one with barbotine dot decoration. A 1st century, or possible early 2nd century AD date can be suggested for these beakers. One rim sherd from a reeded rim bowl (Fig. 37, 27) in fabric A5 is likely to be of similar date, as is a flagon in fabric A9 with a double-beaded rim (Fig. 37, 21).

Only two vessel forms were identified which might be later in date than 1st century AD: a platter base with an illiterate stamp in fabric A14 (Fig. 38, 46), probably an early 2nd century AD imitation of a samian Drag. 18/31 form (V. Rigby pers. comm.); and the base of a possible flagon in fabric A16 (Fig. 38, 47). The latter vessel has an internal brown–red colour coat, and has been tentatively identified as an imported Gaulish flagon (V. Rigby pers. comm.); associated pottery suggests a late 2nd century AD date.

Group B: coarse sandy fabrics: Amongst the coarse sandy group, imported wares comprise two amphora fabrics: sherds from Dressel 20 amphorae, commonly found in Britain from the Late Iron Age at least as late as the 3rd century AD (Williams and Peacock 1983); and a single sherd from either a Dressel 1 or a Dressel 2–4 amphora. Both the latter amphora types shared common fabrics, although the context of this sherd (pit 1233, *see* below), suggests that this is a Dressel 1 amphora, produced from the late 2nd century BC to the end of the 1st century AD (*ibid.*). The amphorae have been

identified by D.F. Williams (University of Southampton), whose full report can be found in archive.

British coarsewares of known source include sherds of Black Burnished ware of Poole Harbour type (BB1; Seager Smith and Davies 1993, 249, fabric 1), and Alice Holt greywares (Lyne and Jefferies 1979, fabrics B and C). Both wares are found in both early and late Roman vessel forms, bead rim jars and hemispherical, flat-rimmed bowls of 1st century type, everted rim jars of 1st/2nd century type, and dropped flange bowls and everted rim jars of 3rd/4th century type. A small group of sherds in a coarse sandy fabric, firing a dirty yellow colour, may represent another Alice Holt product; a similar fabric was identified at Portchester in 4th century contexts (Fulford 1975b). Imitations of Black Burnished ware (eg fabrics B6, B24) are discussed below.

There are a small number of sherds from mortaria of the *Verulamium* region. One vessel, possibly from the Brockley Hill kilns, is stamped RICAII (Fig. 37, 20). These kilns were producing mortaria from the late 1st to early 2nd century AD (Corder 1941; Castle 1976, figs. 5–6).

Coarse sandy fabrics of unknown source are listed below. The correlation of fabrics and vessel forms is given in Table 14.

B1 A 'catch-all' group for moderately coarse unoxidised sandy wares, with moderate/abundant rounded quartz <0.5 mm; rare black iron oxide; probably includes products of more than one source.

B2 A 'catch-all' group for moderately coarse oxidised wares, with moderate/abundant rounded quartz <0.5 mm; probably includes wares from more than one source.

B4 A 'catch-all' group for coarse unoxidised sandy wares (coarser than B1), with moderate, poorly-sorted rounded quartz <1mm; very rare sub-angular flint <2mm; rare black iron oxide.

B6 Moderately fine sandy fabric; moderate to common rounded quartz <0.5 mm, moderately micaceous; unoxidised, firing black.

B17 Hard, coarse sandy fabric; common rounded quartz <0.5 mm; 'catch-all' group for coarse oxidised sandy fabrics (as unoxidised group B4).

B20 Hard, coarse sandy fabric; thick-walled vessels; common, poorly-sorted quartz <1 mm; rare iron oxide; oxidised.

B21 Soft, sandy fabric; moderately fine clay matrix with moderate, poorly sorted rounded quartz <0.5 mm; sparse to moderate grog <1 mm; rare charcoal flecks; 'speckled' appearance.

B22 Soft sandy fabric; moderately coarse, micaceous clay matrix with moderate rounded quartz <0.25 mm; rare grog <1 mm; sparse to moderate charcoal; unoxidised.

B24 Moderately fine sandy fabric; common, well-sorted rounded quartz <0.25 mm; firing orange–red. Black Burnished ware imitations; unoxidised.

In contrast to the fine sandy fabrics, these coarse-wares are found almost exclusively in utilitarian vessel forms such as everted rim jars and bowls of various forms. Much of this group comprises non-distinctive grey sandy wares which have been grouped together as fabrics B1 and B4. These fabrics undoubtedly include the products of more than one source, and the vessel

Table 13   Romano-British pottery: fabric totals (No. and weight (g)) from the terrace area

Fabric	No. sherds	Weight	Fabric	No. sherds	Weight
Samian	204	1128	Grog-tempered fabrics contd.		
Lyon ware	1	1	C16	18	189
Central Gaulish glazed ware	1	10	Total grog-tempered fabrics	4025	49464
Oxfordshire wares	119	670			
New Forest colour-coats	3	6	Silchester ware	206	1703
Oxford/New Forest whitewares	1	4	D6	103	1063
A2	101	435	D8	25	412
A3	30	66	D16	9	53
A4	3	28	D17	19	148
A5	72	373	D18	2	36
A9	12	126	Total flint-tempered fabrics	364	3415
A10	17	127			
A11	47	226	Total Romano-British	9077	84442
A12	28	211			
A13	9	47			
A14	1	122			
A15	4	14			
A16	13	112			
A18	2	15			
A19	6	16			
A20	1	20			
Total fine sandy fabrics	675	3757			
Dr 1/2–4 amphora	1	256			
Dr 20 amphorae	7	1161			
Verulamium region mortaria	34	2150			
Alice Holt greywares	508	3757			
Black Burnished ware (BB1)	138	383			
Portchester fabric D	13	84			
B1	1365	6845			
B2	216	943			
B4	992	7091			
B5	2	26			
B6	180	1796			
B17	347	1236			
B20	9	256			
B21	114	1195			
B22	59	351			
B24	28	276			
Total coarse sandy fabrics	4013	27806			
Wessex grog-tempered ware	11	181			
C1	53	511			
C2	2515	30446			
C4	585	7838			
C7	50	727			
C10	250	2761			
C13	442	5292			
C15	101	1519			

forms present indicate a date range throughout the Roman period, with an emphasis on the early Roman period (1st/2nd century AD). Some of these greywares may be unrecognised Alice Holt products; another possible source is the Hamstead Marshall kilns near Newbury, Berkshire, which were in operation from the middle of the 2nd century to the 4th century AD, producing a range of plain jars and bowls (Rashbrook 1983). Vessel forms present at Thames Valley include beaded rim and cordoned jars of 1st/early 2nd century type, hemispherical, flat-rimmed bowls of similar date, everted rim jars of both early and late Roman type, and flanged and dropped-flange bowls of late Roman type.

Other fabrics are used for a similar, though more restricted range of vessels. Fabrics B6 and B24 include imitations of Black Burnished ware forms: beaded rim and everted rim jars, and flanged bowls.

Group C: grog-tempered fabrics: One grog-tempered fabric was tentatively identified as Wessex grog-tempered ware, identified at Portchester in late 3rd–late 4th century contexts (Fulford 1975b, fabric A). This ware probably represents the products of more than one centre, with a distribution concentrated in south Hampshire. All eight remaining grog-tempered fabrics are of unknown, though probably fairly local origin. The correlation of fabrics and vessel forms is given in Table 14.

C1   Soft, soapy, grog-tempered fabric; moderately coarse clay matrix with moderate to common grog <1 mm; sparse charcoal flecks; unoxidised with patchily oxidised surfaces.

C2   Moderately coarse grog-tempered fabric; moderate to common grog <2 mm; sparse rounded quartz <2 mm; very rare sub-angular flint <1 mm; rare black iron oxide. Firing as C1; C2 may be a finer version of C1.

C4   Soft, soapy grog-tempered fabric; moderately fine clay matrix; moderate to common grog <2 mm; rare rounded quartz <2 mm; oxidised, firing orange–red.

Table 14 Romano-British pottery: vessel forms from the terrace area

	1	2	3	4	5	6	7	8	9	10	11	12	13	14	15	16	Total
Bead rim jar	1	–	1	–	1	–	–	–	9	–	–	–	9	1	–	–	22
Globular jar	–	–	–	–	–	–	–	–	–	–	–	–	–	–	–	1	1
Cordoned jar	–	–	3	2	1	–	–	–	9	10	–	–	–	–	–	–	25
Jar C1/2	–	8	14	15	–	4	3	–	49	–	–	–	–	–	–	–	93
Jar C3/4	3	4	2	2	–	–	1	2	–	–	2	–	–	–	–	–	16
Storage jar	–	–	–	–	–	–	–	–	14	–	2	1	3	–	1	–	21
Beaker	–	1	1	–	1	–	–	–	–	9	–	–	–	–	–	–	12
Platter	–	–	–	–	–	–	–	–	–	16	–	–	–	–	–	–	16
Flat-rim bowl	–	2	7	2	–	–	–	–	–	–	–	–	–	–	–	–	11
Plain dish	–	–	–	–	–	–	–	–	2	–	–	1	–	–	–	–	3
Flanged bowl	–	–	1	–	1	–	–	–	–	–	–	–	–	–	–	–	2
Dropped-flange bowl	–	1	3	1	–	–	–	–	–	–	–	–	–	–	–	–	5
Lid	–	–	–	–	–	–	–	–	1	–	–	–	–	–	–	–	1
Total	4	16	32	22	4	4	4	2	84	35	4	2	12	1	1	1	228

1 = Black Burnished ware; 2 = Alice Holt; 3 = B1/B2; 4 = B4/B17; 5 = B6; 6 = B21; 7 = B24; 8 = Wessex grog-tempered ware; 9 = C2/C4; 10 = C10; 11 = C13; 12 = C15; 13 = Silchester ware; 14 = D6; 15 = D8; 16 = D18

C7 Coarse grog-tempered fabric; moderate grog <1.5 mm; sparse sub-angular flint <2 mm; sparse rounded quartz <0.5 mm; unoxidised.

C10 Soft, grog-tempered fabric; moderately fine clay matrix; moderate, fairly well-sorted grog <1 mm; sparse sub-angular flint <0.5 mm; sparse charcoal flecks; sparse iron oxides; a 'speckled' appearance; oxidised orange–red with unoxidised core. Probably manufactured on site.

C13 Moderately coarse sandy grog-tempered fabric; very coarse clay matrix; moderate to common, poorly-sorted grog <2 mm; moderate rounded quartz <0.5 mm; rare sub-angular flint <1 mm; sparse charcoal flecks; sparse iron oxides; firing as C1.

C15 Hard, sandy grog-tempered fabric; moderately coarse clay matrix; moderate, poorly-sorted grog <2 mm; rare sub-angular flint <1 mm; rare iron oxide.

C16 Soft, sandy grog-tempered fabric; moderately fine clay matrix; sparse, poorly-sorted grog <2 mm; very rare sub-angular flint <1 mm; sparse iron oxide; oxidised with unoxidised core.

The grog-tempered fabrics make up the largest group within the assemblage (58.6% by weight). As coarse sandy wares, these fabrics are dominated by plain, utilitarian vessel forms, predominantly beaded rim jars, everted rim jars and large storage jars of 1st/2nd century type (Fig. 36, 15, 17, 18); there are also simple dishes (Fig. 36, 19) and a lid (Fig. 38, 37). Most, if not all of these fabric types are likely to be of at least fairly local origin; in fact, evidence suggests that one fabric type (C10) might have been manufactured on the site itself (*see* below), in the middle of the 1st century AD. This fabric is represented by a number of vessels in three fairly standardised forms: platters, high-shouldered, cordoned jars, and small jars or beakers (Fig. 36, 11–13).

Few of the grog-tempered fabrics occur in vessel forms of late Roman (3rd/4th century) type, and most vessel forms could be accommodated within a date range of middle 1st to early 2nd century AD. These exceptions are the possible Wessex grog-tempered ware, and fabric C13, used for everted rim jars of 3rd/4th century type (Fig. 38, 50, 51).

Group D: flint-tempered fabrics: One very coarse flint-tempered fabric, found in handmade beaded rim (Fig. 38, 32) and everted rim jar forms, is comparable to a fabric identified as Silchester ware. This ware was produced near Silchester from the latest pre-conquest period to the end of the 1st century AD (Charles 1979), and in its choice of tempering agent and vessel forms represents the continuation of a native Late Iron Age potting tradition. Four other flint-tempered or flint-gritted fabrics were defined.

D6 Hard, coarse, flint-tempered fabric; moderately fine clay matrix, sparsely micaceous, with moderate to common sub-angular flint <2 mm; sparse iron oxide; unoxidised, with patchily oxidised surfaces.

D8 Hard, sandy fabric, sparsely flint-tempered; moderately coarse clay matrix; sparse to moderate sub-angular flint <2 mm; sparse grog <2 mm; sparse to moderate charcoal flecks <3 mm; sparse iron oxides; unoxidised, sometimes with oxidised surfaces.

D16 Soft, moderately flint-gritted fabric; moderately coarse clay matrix; sparse calcined, sub-angular flint <1 mm; moderate iron oxides. Oxidised with unoxidised core.

D17 Soft, soapy, sparsely flint-gritted fabric; moderately fine clay matrix; sparse, calcined, sub-angular flint <1 mm; sparse grog/clay pellet <1.5 mm. Oxidised with unoxidised core.

D18 Hard, sparsely flint-tempered fabric; moderately fine clay matrix; moderate, poorly-sorted sub-angular calcined flint <2 mm; rare iron oxide; unoxidised, with oxidised surfaces.

These four fabrics can also be seen within the context of native ceramic traditions, and are likely to have a similar date range to the Silchester ware. Vessel forms identified include a bead rim jar in fabric D8, a small, barrel-shaped vessel with an inturned rim in fabric D18 (Fig. 38, 40), and an everted rim storage jar in fabric D8.

Discussion

Despite the introduction of imported wares from the middle 1st century, the Romano-British assemblage displays a bias towards wares which could have been locally produced, particularly the grog-tempered fabrics which dominate the assemblage, both in the 1st/early 2nd centuries and later in the Roman period. Indeed, the production of grog-tempered pottery in one particular fabric on the site itself is suggested in the middle 1st century AD. The existence of a large proportion of grog-tempered fabrics within the early Roman period assemblage indicates a fairly conservative potting tradition in the area; such fabrics are well attested in the Late Iron Age in the area, and many of the vessel forms represented are clearly influenced by native forms, eg the high-shouldered cordoned jars. A substantial proportion of the imported fine wares that do occur on the site appear to have had a function other than domestic, as accessory vessels in cremation burials. Their presence in the enclosure is restricted to a few odd sherds, probably of later (3rd/4th century) date, and a somewhat anomalous deposit in a post-hole in the enclosure entrance. Even the usually ubiquitous samian is largely absent from the enclosure; apart from a few odd sherds, the only recognisable vessel is a Drag. 18 bowl associated with the large deposit in the ditch terminal 1008, which does not in any case appear to be a normal domestic deposit.

Enclosure ditch (trench 48): Fifteen sections were dug across the enclosure ditch. These produced 2,666 Iron Age and Romano-British sherds with a total weight of 39,808 g (41% of the total Iron Age/Romano-British assemblage), plus two residual sherds of Middle–Late Bronze Age date. The breakdown of pottery by ditch section is given in Table 15.

The assemblage from the ditch sections ranged in date from Middle Iron Age to late Roman (3rd–4th century AD). A total of 214 sherds (2327 g) were of coarse sandy and flint-tempered fabrics datable to the Middle Iron Age on the basis of vessel forms. These sherds tended to be concentrated in the lower ditch fills (*see* Table 15). Section 28 produced only coarse sandy Iron Age sherds of undiagnostic form from the primary fills (99, 100); the primary fill of section 1139 (1218) produced one sherd of Middle Iron Age material; and fragments of a largely complete saucepan pot in a coarse, flint-tempered fabric (Fig. 36, 3) were found right at the base of ditch terminal 1359 (1339). The relatively complete and unabraded nature of the sherds in the latter deposit argues against redeposition, and the presence of this vessel at the very bottom of the ditch must therefore indicate a Middle Iron Age date for the original construction of the enclosure ditch.

A large proportion of the assemblage from the ditch (65.9%) consisted of coarse grog-tempered fabrics dated to the mid 1st to early 2nd century AD on the basis of vessel form, and this total was dominated by substantial deposits in the two excavated ditch terminals, 1008 and 1359, neither of which could be regarded as ordinary domestic deposits. Ditch terminal 1008 produced 839

sherds (18,169 g), of which 563 sherds (14,434 g) fell into this category. Almost all of these occurred as what appeared to be a deliberate dump above possible hearth feature 1127. Joining sherds from within feature 1127 and from overlying contexts 1085 and 1095, indicate that the pottery is contemporary with the feature, and was dumped during, or immediately after, its period of use. The group was fairly homogeneous, consisting of two shallow dishes, one with incised decoration (Fig. 36, 19), and a series of partially complete everted rim jars of various forms (Fig. 36, 15, 17, 18), some wheelthrown and some handmade, and all in two grog-tempered fabrics (C2, C4). This group was associated with a virtually complete carinated jar in a form and fabric paralleled at the Farnham kilns (Fig. 36, 16; Millett and Graham 1986, fig. 59, 65), a samian dish (Drag. 18), and a sherds of a very abraded Brockley Hill mortarium. The most closely datable form is the samian dish, which is found in both pre-Flavian and Flavian contexts in Britain; and a date in the middle to late 1st century AD can be suggested for this deposit.

Another large group of pottery was recovered from the opposite ditch terminal 1359, associated with a deposit of burnt clay (1098). This group (206 sherds: 2774g) consisted largely of sherds of a fine grog-tempered fabric (C10), comprising several well-made, wheelthrown vessels, mostly burnished, in three basic forms: platters, cordoned jars and beakers (Fig. 36, 11–13). Several factors indicate that this was probably not a normal deposit of domestic refuse, but the products of a small pottery kiln on the site. Several vessels of different forms but in the same fabric were found together, with more than one vessel of each form, though rim diameters indicate some standardisation. The presence of wasters was suggested by the generally underfired nature of the sherds, and many sherds which showed signs of spalling, which involves the splitting of the vessel wall when the vessel is heated too quickly (Rye 1981, 114 and fig. 115). The shallow feature in which the pottery was found was apparently clay-lined, and also contained a rectangular fired clay 'brick' (*see Fired Clay*, below). This may represent the remains of a 'slab-type' pedestal kiln of 1st century AD date, with portable kiln furniture (Swan 1984, 59). Kilns of very similar construction and with comparable products have been excavated in Northampton (Shaw 1979), dated to the middle 1st century AD. The small number of vessels in the group, and the temporary nature of the possible kiln furniture, would suggest that this represents perhaps only a single firing episode. Very few sherds in this fabric were recovered from elsewhere on the site. All three vessel forms would be consistent with a date in the middle 1st century AD.

The evidence from ditch terminal 1008 seems more ambiguous. Although the group of grog-tempered pottery from feature 1127 was fairly homogeneous, it was also mixed with pottery of other fabrics, some from known sources elsewhere. The feature itself showed little evidence of burning, apart from some burnt soil on the floor of the feature, and there was no evidence that it had ever been lined with clay or any similar substance. Sherds of the same fabric as the group in the opposite terminal were found within the feature, suggesting that the two deposits are contemporary; if this was another

Table 15 pottery by no. and weight (g) from the enclosure ditch sections

Ditch section	Contexts	MIA	LIA (C9)	C1/2 Gp A	C1/2 Gp B	C1/2 Gp C	C1/2 Gp D	RB gen Gp B	C3/4 Gp A	C3/4 Gp C	Total
15	upper fill	–	–	–	–	6/36	–	–	–	–	6/36
	lower fills	1/8	–	1/2	–	–	–	–	–	–	2/10
19	upper fills	1/28	–	1/5	–	3/32	–	1/32	–	1/67	7/164
	lower fills	6/19	–	8/27	–	43/885	–	71/512	–	–	128/1443
28	upper fill	1/3	–	31/190	–	31/505	9/86	5/47	–	–	77/831
	lower fills	15/80	–	2/17	–	23/213	11/69	9/28	–	–	60/407
	primary fills	21/124	–	–	–	–	–	–	–	–	21/124
112	upper fill	–	–	6/59	–	28/415	–	21/146	–	–	55/620
	lower fills	15/214	–	5/29	–	45/471	34/476	35/256	–	–	134/1446
1005	upper fill	13/108	–	13/65	–	142/1478	12/129	37/196	–	–	217/1976
	lower fills	10/154	–	2/17	–	17/150	2/23	7/47	–	–	38/391
1008	upper fill	8/54	–	1/12	5/41	9/107	9/72	29/273	1/2	2/91	64/652
	1085/1095/1127	5/71	–	11/226	19/763	538/13795	9/139	101/956	1/3	–	684/15953
	lower fills	27/453	15/157	3/6	8/179	16/532	4/67	15/155	3/15	–	91/1564
1036	upper fill	5/39	7/74	1/1	6/19	25/222	1/1	15/126	2/32	1/6	63/520
	lower fills	11/109	1/7	7/27	7/99	37/483	–	37/376	1/2	–	101/1103
1139	upper fill	2/21	–	1/1	–	7/91	–	46/680	2/12	–	58/805
	lower fills	1/11	–	–	–	–	–	–	–	–	1/11
	primary fill	1/4	–	–	–	–	–	–	–	–	1/4
1216	upper fill	8/50	25/141	13/79	8/42	55/867	12/104	33/140	3/4	–	157/1427
	lower fill	–	7/67	–	1/5	56/724	8/92	–	–	–	72/888
1231	upper fill	5/55	–	15/147	20/1312	69/989	1/40	20/275	–	3/74	133/2892
1257	(one fill)	2/7	–	–	–	–	–	8/29	–	–	10/36
1259	upper fill	4/29	–	2/4	–	16/185	3/75	13/131	–	–	38/424
	lower fills	–	–	–	–	20/1038	–	–	–	–	20/1038
1306	upper fill	3/25	14/160	1/10	1/5	4/38	5/120	45/382	–	–	73/740
1356	upper fill	–	–	–	–	–	–	1/45	–	–	1/45
1359	upper fill	8/82	1/1	25/193	1/5	53/516	5/118	23/120	–	–	116/1035
	'oven' 1098	9/130	3/44	1/6	–	180/2467	13/127	–	–	–	206/2774
	lower fills	32/449	–	–	–	–	–	–	–	–	32/449
Total		214/2327	73/651	150/1123	76/2470	1423/26239	138/1738	572/4952	13/70	7/238	2666/39808

Table 16 pottery totals by no. and weight (g) from pits within the enclosure

Pit	Contexts	MIA	LIA (C9)	C1/2 GpA	C1/2 Gp B	C1/2 GpC	C1/2 GpD	RB gen Gp B	C3/4 GpA	C3/4 Gp C	Total
9	upper fills	77/1399	–	–	–	1/3	2/63	1/2	–	–	81/1467
	primary fill	1/19	–	–	–	–	–	–	–	–	1/19
11	upper fills	12/85	–	2/3	–	–	–	1/6	–	–	15/94
	primary fills	3/8	–	–	–	–	–	–	–	–	3/8
1012	all fills	1/1	–	–	–	–	–	–	–	–	1/1
1020	all finds	3/10	–	–	–	–	1/8	–	–	–	4/18
1062	one fill	18/140	1/6	–	3/33	72/955	6/28	7/29	–	–	107/1201
1064	upper fill	7/39	–	–	–	–	1/1	1/1	–	–	9/41
	primary fill	1/6	–	–	2/7	–	–	–	–	–	3/13
1066	all fills	32/81	–	–	–	2/4	1/3	–	–	–	35/88
1068	upper fills	5/30	–	–	–	11/12	–	1/1	–	–	17/43
	primary fill	13/71	–	–	–	–	–	–	–	–	13/71
1074	all fills	4/15	–	–	–	1/5	3/11	–	–	–	8/31
1078	upper fills	6/13	–	–	–	–	1/1	–	–	–	7/14
	primary fill	2/5	–	–	–	–	–	–	–	–	2/5
1092	upper fills	4/22	–	5/8	–	–	2/13	23/365	1/1	–	35/409
	primary fill	2/5	–	–	–	–	–	–	–	–	2/5
1113	all fills	14/44	–	–	–	–	–	–	–	–	14/44
1142	one fill	–	–	1/1	3/17	6/66	1/4	–	–	–	11/88
1220	one fill	37/306	19/100	–	1/9	3/49	1/2	–	–	–	61/466
1227	one fill	27/125	–	–	–	1/5	1/4	–	–	–	29/134
	primary fill	3/21	–	–	–	–	–	–	–	–	3/21
1235	one fill	6/9	–	–	–	–	–	–	–	–	6/9
1263	one fill	3/21	–	–	–	–	–	–	–	–	3/21
1265	one fill	7/21	1/1	–	1/1	–	–	–	–	–	9/23
1267	all fills	35/244	1/1	–	1/4	–	2/61	2/8	–	–	41/318
1269	one fill	–	–	–	–	1/5	–	–	–	–	1/5
1271	all fills	8/47	–	–	–	–	4/17	23/602	–	–	35/666
1275	all fills	2/10	–	–	–	–	–	2/5	–	–	4/15
1287	all fills	3/15	2/4	3/10	1/64	12/121	1/16	8/36	–	2/20	32/286

Table 16 continued

Pit	Contexts	MIA	LIA (C9)	C1/2 GpA	C1/2 Gp B	C1/2 GpC	C1/2 GpD	RB gen Gp B	C3/4 GpA	C3/4 Gp C	Total
1290	upper fill	3/23	–	–	–	–	–	–	–	–	3/23
	primary fill	6/96	–	–	1/4	–	–	–	–	–	7/100
1292	all fills	3/12	–	4/26	–	8/37	2/14	5/28	–	–	22/117
1297	one fill	6/26	8/49	–	–	272/3935	13/290	1/7	–	–	300/4307
1300	all fills	16/72	–	–	–	–	1/1	–	–	–	17/73
1307	upper fill	2/8	–	–	–	30/141	1/41	17/77	–	–	50/267
	primary fill	1/2	–	–	–	–	–	–	–	–	1/2
1312	one fill	27/162	–	–	–	–	1/6	–	–	–	28/168
1318	all fills	21/47	–	1/3	–	–	1/1	–	–	–	23/51
1320	upper fills	6/27	–	–	1/7	–	2/14	–	–	–	9/48
	primary fill	12/36	–	–	–	–	–	–	–	–	12/36
1323	one fill	8/66	–	–	–	–	–	–	–	–	8/66
Total		496/4742	32/171	16/51	14/146	421/5340	50/630	93/1168	1/1	2/20	1125/12269

Pit fills have been divided into upper and primary fills where a potential difference in pottery dating can be distinguished

kiln, it might have been expected to be of the same form as the other. One piece of possible kiln furniture, part of a wedge-shaped bar in a grog-tempered fabric, was recovered from an upper context within this ditch terminal, but this cannot definitely be associated with the underlying feature. A similarly ambiguous group was excavated with the kilns at Northampton, and it was suggested that this might have been some kind of oven (Shaw 1979, 21).

Pottery of forms and fabrics similar to that from ditch terminal 1008, ie 1st or early 2nd century everted rim jars in coarse sandy and grog-tempered fabrics, was recovered from all other excavated ditch sections. A large part of a Brockley Hill mortarium, with stamped rim (Fig. 37, 20) came from the upper fill of section 1231. Pottery of possible 3rd or 4th century date was confined exclusively to upper ditch fills or unstratified contexts within the ditch. This consisted almost entirely (11 sherds) of Oxfordshire and New Forest fine wares, though two late rim forms were also recovered: a storage jar rim in Wessex grog-tempered ware (Fig. 37, 28), and part of a middle 3rd/4th century jar with a band of burnished lattice decoration, in a wheelthrown fabric imitating Black Burnished ware (Fig. 37, 29).

Pits in trench 48: Of the excavated pits in trench 48, 35 contained pottery; 33 of these can be dated to the Iron Age or Romano-British period (pits 1243 and 1245 have already been discussed). All but one were located within the enclosure; pit 1012 was situated immediately outside the ditch to the east. The breakdown of pottery recovered from the pits is presented in Table 16.

A large number of pits contained Iron Age material; this accounted for nearly one-third of the total from the pits. Five pits (1012, 1113, 1235, 1263, 1323) contained exclusively Middle Iron Age material, and a further eight (9, 11, 1068, 1078, 1092, 1233, 1307, 1320) produced only Middle Iron Age material from primary fills. Vessel forms represented in the Middle Iron Age assemblage from the pits include rounded bowls, and slack-shouldered and rounded jars (Fig. 38, 30, 33) in coarse sandy fabrics; saucepan pots in flint-tempered fabrics; and a very coarse bucket-shaped jar (Fig. 38, 34) in a coarse sandy fabric. The number of diagnostic sherds is very small: a minimum of six saucepan pots and four rounded or slack-shouldered jars are represented. None of the pits contained both saucepan pot and jar/bowl forms, though several have sherds in both sandy and flint-tempered fabrics.

Along with the only example of a bucket-shaped jar from the site, pit 1233 also contained, within the upper fills, a sherd of amphora of either Dressel 1 or Dressel 2–4 form. The associated pottery suggests Dressel 1, a form which was produced from the late 2nd century BC until the end of the 1st century BC (Peacock and Williams 1986). A nearby pit 1320 produced the only two sherds of shell-tempered pottery from the site (fabric E1), associated with a non-distinctive jar/bowl rim.

The remaining pit fills can be dated to the 1st century AD or later. All but two produced wheelthrown Romano-British wares; pits 1074 and 1300 contained only handmade wares but included sherds of Silchester ware, which would date them to the middle–late 1st century AD. Again, a large proportion of the total assem-

blage from the pits comprised sherds in coarse grog-tempered fabrics similar to those found in ditch terminal 1008, though these were unevenly distributed, being concentrated in just two pits: 1062 and 1297. Pit 1062 produced 107 sherds (1201 g), of which 72 sherds (955 g) were in these grog-tempered fabrics; and pit 1297 contained an even larger amount of pottery (300 sherds: 4307 g), of which 272 sherds (3935 g) were in grog-tempered fabrics. The latter group was of a different character from other pit deposits, and resembled more the large deposit from ditch terminal 1008. The group included several partially complete vessels: a shallow dish (Fig. 38, 43), a cordoned jar, a coarse handmade globular jar (Fig. 38, 40), a coarse storage jar and a lid. All except the globular jar were in wheelthrown, grog-tempered fabrics, and all the grog-tempered forms are paralleled in the ditch terminal deposits, suggesting a date for this feature in the middle–late 1st century AD.

Only one sherd of possible 3rd–4th century material was recovered from any of the pits: a small sherd of Oxfordshire oxidised ware in pit 1092.

In general, the pits contained the same range of fabrics as the enclosure ditch, though with a greater proportion of Iron Age material (Iron Age pottery made up only 7.4% of the total from the ditch). Only six pits contained fine wares (11, 1092, 1142, 1287, 1292, and 1318), and these produced only a very small amount (16 sherds: 51 g).

Post-holes in trench 48: Twenty-seven post-holes were excavated in trench 48, all within the enclosure; 14 contained pottery. A breakdown of pottery by post-hole is given in Table 17.

As was noted for the pits in trench 48, there was a fairly high proportion of Iron Age material from the post-holes, though in nearly every case, Iron Age material occurred in association with later material. Only two post-holes, 1088 and 1102, contained exclusively Middle Iron Age material; post-hole 1279 produced only sherds in the Late Iron Age fabric type C9. Sherds of a decorated rounded bowl (Fig. 38, 36) came from post-hole 1221, and the same feature produced the largest assemblage of any post-hole, all but one sherd of Middle Iron Age date. Only one other feature contained any diagnostic Middle Iron Age material: a jar rim from post-hole 1088. As was noted for the pits, the jars and bowls are found in features away from the centre of the enclosure. No diagnostic sherds of saucepan pot forms were recovered from post-holes.

The Romano-British material from the post-holes covered the same range as that from the pits, though very few diagnostic sherds were recovered. One exception was post-hole 1006, which was somewhat anomalous both in its position, right in the enclosure entrance, and contents. These included an non-distinctive sherd of samian and a platter base in a fine sandy oxidised fabric (A14) with an illiterate stamp (Fig. 38, 46), probably an imitation Drag. 18/31 of early 2nd century date; as well as the partial profile of an Alice Holt grey ware everted rim jar (Fig. 38, 45), of a form dating no earlier than about AD 120 (Millett 1979, fig. 3, type 21: c. AD 120–375). This was the only feature associated with the enclosure which had a probable date in the 2nd century AD. Only six sherds of fine wares

Table 17 pottery: fabric totals by no. and weight (g) from post-hole fills within the enclosure

Post-hole	MIA	LIA (C9)	C1/2 GpA	C1/2 GpB	C1/2 GpC	C1/2 GpD	RB gen. GpB	C3/4 GpB/C	Total
1006	–	–	3/163	6/123	–	–	14/272	–	23/558
1018	17/50	–	–	1/2	–	6/29	1/2	–	25/83
1047	–	–	–	–	1/1	–	–	–	1/1
1049	–	–	–	–	1/1	–	–	–	1/1
1051	1/2	–	1/1	–	2/3	–	1/3	–	5/9
1055	1/1	1/2	–	–	1/8	–	2/5	1/2	6/18
1088	1/10	–	–	–	–	–	–	–	1/10
1090	9/90	–	2/15	1/5	1/11	7/98	6/11	–	26/230
1099	10/41	–	–	–	–	1/2	–	–	11/43
1100	–	–	–	–	1/4	–	–	–	1/4
1102	2/10	–	–	–	–	–	–	–	2/10
1221	67/344	–	–	–	–	1/2	–	–	68/346
1277	7/6	–	–	–	60/542	–	4/4	–	71/552
1279	–	1/36	–	–	–	–	–	–	1/36
Total	115/554	2/38	6/179	8/130	67/570	15/131	28/297	1/2	242/1901

were recovered from the post-holes, three of which derived from post-hole 1006. Only one sherd of diagnostically 3rd/4th century material was recovered.

Ditch 1154 (trench 48H): Several sections were excavated across ditch 1154 in trench 48H, which produced 1553 sherds with a total weight of 11,151 g, from two main fills (1157, 1155). All the pottery from the ditch, bar seven sherds (18 g) of Middle–Late Iron Age date, was of Romano-British origin, and included both early and late vessel forms. The earliest distinctive sherds were two Silchester ware bead rims (Fig. 38, 52) from the lower fill (1155). Other early material included everted rim jars (eg Fig. 38, 53, 54), of 1st or 2nd century date. Sherds of the same grog-tempered fabrics as were recovered from the enclosure ditch (C2, C4) occurred in ditch 1154, though proportionally the amount (22.4%) was not so great as in the enclosure ditch.

Later Romano-British material from ditch 1154 included several everted rim jars (Fig. 38, 55, 56) in both sandy and coarse grog-tempered fabrics, two dropped-flange bowl rims (Fig. 38, 58), and fragments of an almost complete Oxfordshire colour-coated bowl, an imitation of a samian Drag. 36 form (Fig. 38, 54).

There did seem to be some chronological sequence within the ditch, with 3rd/4th century material being concentrated in the upper fill, and only occasionally found in the lower fill (see Table 18). Although there was only one definite late rim form, an everted rim jar from the lower fill, there were also several sherds of a coarse grog-tempered fabric (C13) which occurs largely in later vessel forms in the upper fill, and one rim sherd in Wessex grog-tempered ware. The grog-tempered fabrics similar to those from the enclosure ditch (C2, C4) were concentrated in the lower fill; they appear to be replaced by the coarser fabric C13, which is largely confined to the upper fill.

This mixing of material of different dates may be largely the result of the difficulty of distinguishing between the different fills during excavation; joining sherds are recorded from the two fills.

Cremation burials: Two cremation burials were excavated in trench 48H (1004, and 1150). Although the two features were situated in the same general area, they do not appear to be contemporary with each other. A third cremation burial was observed, but not excavated, 150 m west of these during the evaluation.

Cremation 1150 was contained in a coarse, wheel-thrown cordoned jar in the sandy fabric B4 (Fig. 38, 48). It was accompanied by an imitation Gallo-Belgic platter (Fig. 38, 49) in imitation Terra Rubra (fabric A2). The two vessels would be consistent with a date in the latter half of the 1st century AD.

Cremation 1004 was contained in a coarse ware jar (fabric B17), of which only the bottom half survived. Associated with this vessel were a samian Drag. 38 bowl and a Drag. 42 platter, and the bottom half of a fine ware vessel, in a fine creamy sandy fabric (A16) with a purple–red slip on the interior, possibly an imported flagon (Fig. 38, 47). There were also a few coarse-ware sherds in various fabrics, none diagnostic, and a rim sherd of a Drag. 31 samian platter. The samian vessels within the group all have a probable date in the 2nd century AD, although Drag. 42 forms were current in the first half of the 2nd century, whilst Drag. 31 and 38 forms were more common in the second half of the 2nd century. The possible imported flagon would be consistent with a date for the feature in the latter half of the 2nd century, since by this period flagon production in this country was declining.

The cremated bone in unexcavated context 1409 had been deposited with two vessels, both of which were comparatively intact. A photograph allowed the identifi-

Table 18 pottery totals by no. and weight (g) from features on the terrace area outside the enclosure

Feature	Context	MIA	LIA (C9)	C1/2 GpA	C1/2 GpB	C1/2 Gp C	C1/2 Gp D	RB gen. Gp B	C3/4 Gp A	C3/4 GpB/C	Total
Ditch 1154	upper fill	–	1/7	7/32	49/374	105/1507	–	821/4326	45/224	252/2717	1280/9187
	lower fill	5/8	1/3	6/41	108/306	68/988	17/163	54/392	6/7	8/56	273/1964
Cremation burial 1004		–	–	124/647	302/742	32/120	–	–	–	–	458/1509
Cremation burial 1150		–	–	68/223	279/1900	–	–	–	–	–	347/2123
Pit 1160		1/1	–	6/4	14/235	21/237	1/3	42/266	1/27	–	86/773
Ditch 1166		1/1	–	4/9	7/145	2/12	–	55/483	3/11	5/47	77/708
Ditch 5079		14/184	7/48	–	1/1	12/89	20/98	–	–	–	54/420
Total		21/194	9/58	215/956	760/3703	240/2953	38/264	972/5467	55/269	265/2820	2575/16684

cation of one as an everted rim vessel, probably of Romano-British manufacture. The second was similar.

Pit 1160 in trench 48H: One other feature was excavated to the west of the two cremation burials in trench 48H (1160). However, despite its proximity to the latter features, the group of pottery which it contained was completely different in character. The feature produced a mixed assemblage, including both samian and Oxfordshire ware sherds, and a flanged bowl rim. There were no complete or even partial vessels, and no evidence of cremated bone.

Trench 49: A small amount of pottery was recovered from trench 49 (548 sherds: 2461 g), of which 368 sherds (2093 g) are of Iron Age or Romano-British date. This was derived almost entirely from topsoil and subsoil contexts; only one excavated feature could be dated to the Iron Age or Romano-British period. Ditch 5079 produced 54 sherds (420 g) of Iron Age or Romano-British material. Five rims were recovered: two grog-tempered beaded rims, two rims of rounded jars (Fig. 36, 1, 2) in flint-tempered fabrics and one everted rim jar in a grog-tempered fabric. All would be consistent with a date sometime in the 1st century AD, probably pre-Flavian. This ditch was a recut of an earlier ditch 5087, which produced one undiagnostic sherd (41 g) in a coarse sandy fabric, found elsewhere on the site in Middle Iron Age vessel forms.

General comments

The Iron Age and Romano-British assemblage from Thames Valley Park does show some spatial patterning within the site. Iron Age material is found in trench 48, with greater proportions in the features within the enclosure than in the enclosure ditch itself. The material that does occur in the ditch fills appears to be largely mixed with later material, with one or two exceptions, whereas some of the features within the enclosure can be definitely dated to the Iron Age. The differential distribution of various vessel forms within the enclosure has been mentioned above.

Though the amount of diagnostic material present in the enclosure is relatively small, it appears to support the idea of continuity from the Iron Age into the Romano-British period. There does not appear to be any marked change in distribution of Romano-British features from the earlier features, and a large proportion of the features produced a mixture of Iron Age and later pottery.

The terminals were used for some form of industrial activity, possibly involving pottery manufacture, in the middle–late 1st century, and by this time the ditch was two-thirds silted up; there appears to have been no attempt at any stage to recut the ditch after the 1st century. There are no sherds within the ditch which can definitely be dated to the 2nd century AD, though some of the of the less closely datable everted rim jar forms may cover this period. Some 3rd/4th century sherds are present, though in small quantities, from the upper ditch fills. It might then be suggested that the enclosure was largely abandoned by the beginning of the 2nd century AD, though some activity in the later 2nd

century is attested by a single cremation burial in trench 48H and a post-hole in the enclosure entrance.

The presence of 3rd/4th century material in the upper ditch fills of the enclosure may be connected with later use of ditch 1154 in trench 48H, which produced the greatest concentration of later material, though the earlier use of this feature appears to have been contemporary with the 1st century activity in the enclosure.

Iron Age material was almost entirely absent from trench 48H, though a ditch north of this area, in trench 49, could be dated to the Late Iron Age/1st century AD.

List of illustrated sherds

Fig. 36

1 Rounded jar, Fabric D5. FSN 11746, Context 5063, ditch 5079, trench 49.
2 Rounded jar; Fabric D11. FSN 11744, Context 5063, ditch 5079, trench 49.
3 Saucepan pot; Fabric D7. FSN 4699, Context 1339, ditch terminal 1359, trench 48.
4 Small ovoid jar or bowl; Fabric B8. FSN 4667, context 1141, ditch terminal 1008, trench 48.
5 Saucepan pot; Fabric D11. FSN 4663, context 1141, ditch terminal 1008, trench 48.
6 Rounded bowl; Fabric B8. FSN 11200, context 1041, ditch section 1005, trench 48.
7 Rounded jar; Fabric B10. FSN 4697, context 1124, ditch terminal 1359, trench 48.
8 Base from pedestal jar, burnished exterior, ?wheelthrown; Fabric C9. FSN 4698, context 1124, ditch terminal 1359, trench 48.
9 Everted rim jar, wheelthrown, burnished decoration on rim; Fabric B24. FSN 11224, context 1040, ditch section 1036, trench 48.
10 Rounded jar; Fabric B11. FSN 4655, context 1135, ditch terminal 1008, trench 48.
11 Platter, wheelthrown; Fabric C10. FSN 4670, context 1098, ditch terminal 1359, trench 48.
12 Cordoned jar, wheelthrown, burnished exterior; Fabric C10. FSN 4669, context 1098, ditch terminal 1359, trench 48.
13 Beaker, wheelthrown, burnished exterior; Fabric C10. FSN 4657, context 1133, ditch terminal 1008, trench 48.
14 Slack-shouldered jar; Fabric B7. FSN 4651, context 1098, ditch terminal 1359, trench 48.
15 Large, high-shouldered, everted rim jar, wheelthrown; Fabric C2. FSN 4611, context 1085/1095, ditch terminal 1008, trench 48.
16 Carinated, everted rim jar, wheelthrown; Alice Holt greyware. FSN 4654, context 1085, ditch terminal 1008, trench 48.
17 Small, pulled beaded rim jar, handmade; Fabric C2. FSN 4614, context 1085, ditch terminal 1008, trench 48.
18 Large, ovoid, everted rim jar, wheelthrown; Fabric C2. FSN 4626, context 1085, ditch terminal 1008, trench 48.
19 Shallow dish, wheelthrown, incised design on underside of base; Fabric C2. FSN 4630, context 1085, ditch terminal 1008, trench 48.

Fig. 37

20 Mortarium, wheelthrown, stamped RICAII on rim; *Verulamium* region, probably Brockley Hill. FSN 11280, context 1230, ditch 1231, trench 48.
21 Flagon with double-beaded rim, wheelthrown; Fabric A9. FSN 11268, context 1232, ditch 1231, trench 48.

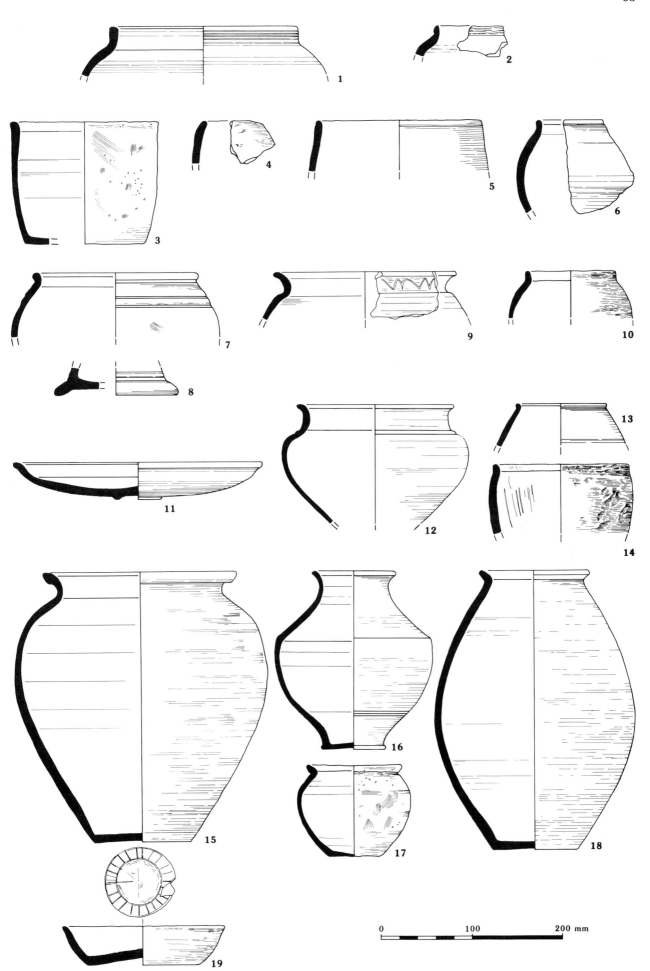

Figure 36   Iron Age and Romano-British pottery

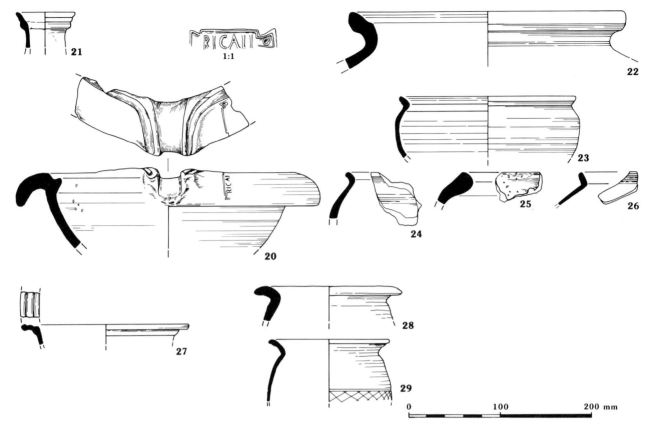

Figure 37   Iron Age and Romano-British pottery

22   Large storage jar, wheelthrown; Fabric C15. FSN 4619, context 1085, ditch terminal 1008, trench 48.

23   Wide, hemispherical bowl with everted rim, handmade; Fabric C2. FSN 4635, context 1095, ditch terminal 1008, trench 48.

24   Rounded jar, handmade; Fabric D1. FSN 4621, Context 1085, ditch terminal 1008, trench 48.

25   Beaded rim jar, handmade; Silchester ware. FSN 11274, context 1232, upper fill of ditch 1231, trench 48.

26   Beaker or small jar, wheelthrown; Fabric A15. FSN 4637, context 1095, ditch terminal 1008, trench 48.

27   Reeded rim bowl, wheelthrown; Fabric A5. FSN 240, context 116, ditch 112, trench 48.

28   Large, everted rim jar, ?wheelthrown; Wessex grog-tempered ware. FSN 3, context 18, upper fill of ditch section 11, trench E.

29   Everted rim jar, wheelthrown; Fabric B24. FSN 228, context 109, upper fill of ditch section 1036, trench 48.

Fig. 38

30   Beaded rim jar, post-firing hole below rim; handmade; Fabric C9. FSN 11315, context 1219, pit 1220, trench 48.

31   Slack-shouldered jar, handmade; Fabric B10. FSN 11318, context 1219, pit 1220, trench 48.

32   Beaded rim jar, handmade; Silchester ware. FSN 11327, context 1299, pit 1267, trench 48.

33   Rounded jar, handmade; Fabric B10. FSN 11321, context 1222, post-hole 1221, trench 48.

34   Bucket-shaped jar, handmade; Fabric B7. FSN 11322, context 1249/1250, upper fills of pit 1233, trench 48.

35   Rounded jar, handmade; Fabric B10. FSN 11348, context 1313, pit 1312, trench 48.

36   Rounded bowl, impressed decoration, handmade; Fabric B10. FSN 11312/11313, context 1222, post-hole 1221, trench 48.

37   Lid, wheelthrown; Fabric C2. FSN 11342, unstratified within pit 1307.

38   Rounded or bipartite bowl, diagonal tooled decoration on shoulder, handmade; Fabric B10. FSN 95, context 23, pit 9, trench 48.

39   Rounded jar, impressed decoration, handmade; Fabric B10. FSN 57, context 23, pit 9, trench 48.

40   Small ovoid jar, handmade; Fabric D18. FSN 11335, context 1298, pit 1297, trench 48.

41   Everted rim jar, wheelthrown; Fabric C2. FSN 11341, context 1298, pit 1297, trench 48.

42   Base of jar, wheelthrown; Fabric C2. FSN 11333, context 1298, pit 1297, trench 48.

43   Shallow dish, wheelthrown; Fabric C15. FSN 11332, context 1298, pit 1297, trench 48.

44   Flanged bowl, wheelthrown; Fabric B1. FSN 11374, context 1206, pit 1205, trench 48.

45   Everted rim jar, wheelthrown; Alice Holt greyware. FSN 11372, context 1007, post-hole 1006, trench 48.

46   Platter, wheelthrown; illiterate stamp on base; Fabric A14. FSN 11750, context 1007, post-hole 1006, trench 48.

47   Base of possible flagon, colour-coated interior, wheelthrown; Fabric A16. FSN 4500, context 1003, cremation burial 1004, trench 48H.

48   Cordoned jar, wheelthrown; Fabric B4. FSN 11376, Context 1151, cremation burial 1150, trench 48H.

49   Imitation Gallo-Belgic platter, wheelthrown; Fabric A2. FSN 11378, context 1151, cremation burial 1150, trench 48H.

50   Everted rim jar, wheelthrown; Fabric C13. FSN 11724, context 1159, ditch 1154, trench 48H.

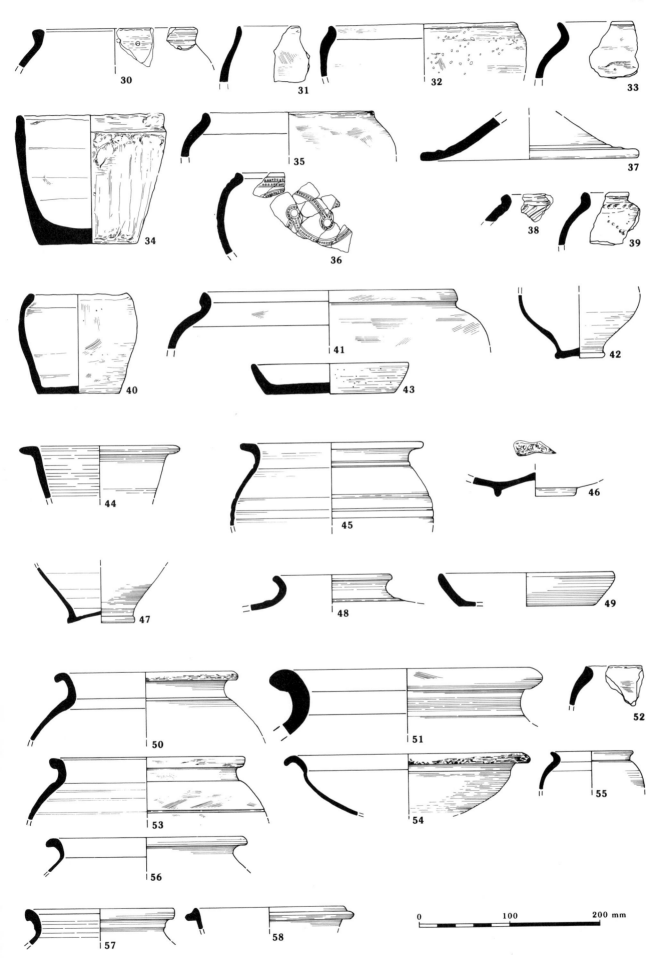

Figure 38   Iron Age and Romano-British pottery

Table 19   ceramic building material: fabric totals by type from the terrace area (no./weight (g))

Fabric	Tegula	Brick	Tile unspecified	Unclassified	Total
1	11/2302	3/418	27/1582	30/355	71/4657
2	–	1/1075	7/1160	–	8/2235
3	–	14/645	90/4701	208/1218	312/6564
Total	11/2302	18/2138	124/7443	238/1573	391/13456

51 Large storage jar, handmade? Fabric C13. FSN 11729, context 1159, ditch 1154, trench 48H.

52 Beaded rim jar, handmade, Silchester ware. FSN 11733, context 1155, ditch 1154, trench 48H.

53 Everted rim jar, wheelthrown; Fabric B21. FSN 11396, context 1163, ditch 1154, trench 48H.

54 Imitation Drag. 36 bowl, wheelthrown; Oxfordshire colour-coated ware; abraded and all slip gone. FSN 11720, context 1159, ditch 1154, trench 48H.

55 Small everted rim jar, wheelthrown; Fabric B1. FSN 11392, context 1161, ditch 1154, trench 48H.

56 Everted rim jar, wheelthrown; Fabric B4. FSN 11379, context 1155, ditch 1154, trench 48H.

57 Everted rim jar, wheelthrown; Fabric B1. FSN 11386, context 1165, ditch 1154, trench 48H.

58 Dropped flange bowl, wheelthrown; Fabric B1. FSN 11389, context 1165, ditch 1154, trench 48H.

Ceramic Building Material

A total of 1,025 pieces of ceramic building material (46,603 g) was recovered from the excavation, of which 634 pieces (33,147 g) from the topsoil, or modern features, represent post-medieval and modern brick and roof tile and are not considered here. The remaining 391 pieces (13,456 g) derived from 23 separate contexts, both within and outside the enclosure.

Within the assemblage from stratified contexts, three distinct fabrics were identified when the material was examined at x10 magnification:

1. Iron rich clay matrix with clay pellet (<5%), quartz (<1%) and iron oxide (<1%) inclusions.
2. Iron rich clay matrix with quartz (<5%), iron oxide (<1%), clay pellet (<2%) and grog (<10%) inclusions.
3. Iron rich clay matrix with quartz (<10%) and iron oxide (<1%) inclusions.

Table 20   ceramic building material: no. and weight (g) by context from the terrace area

Context	Phase	Tegula	Tile Unspec.	Brick Unspec.	Unclassified	Total
Unstrat/topsoil		–	29/630	1/108	15/161	45/899
Subsoil 1001		7/1075	69/3239	9/930	184/1221	269/6465
Post-hole 1088	1	–	–	–	2/6	2/6
Ditch 1005	2	–	2/28	–	4/36	6/64
Ditch 1036	2	1/428	–	1/1075	5/18	7/1521
Linear 1053	2	–	–	–	1/2	1/2
Pit 1062	2	–	3/482	–	1/1	4/483
Pit 1064	2	–	–	–	1/1	1/1
Post-hole 1090	2	–	–	–	1/1	1/1
Feature 1127 in ditch 1008	2	–	2/636	–	–	2/636
Ditch 1306	2	–	2/178	–	–	2/178
Ditch 1354	2	–	1/136	–	–	1/136
Post-hole 1006	3	–	–	–	2/1	2/1
Ditch 1005	4	–	1/144	–	4/13	5/157
Ditch 1008	4	–	–	–	4/25	4/25
Ditch 1139	4	1/164	–	–	1/19	2/183
Pit 1152	4	–	–	7/25	5/15	12/40
Ditch 1154	4	–	8/532	–	–	8/532
Pit 1160	4	–	1/72	–	1/2	2/74
Ditch 1216	4	–	1/122	–	–	1/122
Ditch 1231	4	2/635	5/1244	–	7/51	14/1930
Total		11/2302	124/7443	18/2138	238/1573	391/13456

The fabric types are tabulated by form in Table 19. There were no complete bricks or tiles, though several diagnostic pieces were present, allowing a division into *tegulae*, undiagnostic tile, and undiagnostic brick, although it should be noted that the bulk of the assemblage consisted of unclassifiable fragments. All *tegulae* fragments were of fabric 1, which suggests that the other 60 pieces of fabric 1 might represent further *tegulae*. One piece of *tegula* still retained the upper cut-away where the adjacent tile would have overlapped. The majority of the undiagnostic tile was in small pieces and was featureless apart from four pieces which bore signs of keying to aid the adhesion of plaster; these fragments are likely to represent hypocaust flue tiles.

A breakdown of the ceramic building material by context is presented in Table 20. It can be seen that the material from dated contexts is divided almost equally between phases 2 and 4. The majority of the *tegulae* fragments from stratified contexts were found in the upper fills of the enclosure ditch, or from the subsoil. Within the enclosure virtually all the material is later than the first phase of occupation, although two fragments came from post-hole 1088, which is dated to the Middle Iron Age (phase 1); either these fragments are intrusive, or the pottery is residual.

The excavation failed to produce any significant structural evidence, but the moderate amount of brick and tile found on the site implies the presence of a substantial structure in the vicinity of the enclosure. An alternative location for the structure, perhaps associated with the cropmarks on the hill-crest to the east, must therefore be suggested. The date of associated material indicates that demolition of any such structure probably occurred during the later Romano-British period, ie after the abandonment of the enclosure.

Fired Clay

A total of 25,026 g of fired clay was recovered, of which 22,376 g came from stratified deposits of Romano-British date. The remainder (2,650 g) was from the topsoil, modern features, or was unstratified. Only the stratified material is discussed here. Of the stratified material, 10,921 g came from a single feature (1098).

Fabrics

Six distinct fabrics were identified when the material was examined at X8 magnification.
1. Iron rich clay matrix; vegetable tempering (<25%), flint (<0.1%) and quartz (<0.1%) inclusions.
2. Iron rich clay matrix; quartz (<10%), and flint (<1%).
3. Iron rich clay matrix; quartz (10%) inclusions.
4. Iron rich clay matrix; vegetable tempering (<10%) and quartz (<1%) inclusions.
5. Iron rich clay matrix; rare flint (<0.1%) and quartz (<0.1%) inclusions. These seem to be restricted to the exterior of the artefact.
6. Iron rich clay matrix; common grog (<10%), rare quartz (<0.5%) and sparse iron oxide (<0.1%) inclusions.

Fabric 3 predominates, of which fabrics 2 and 4 are variant forms. Fabrics 1, 5, and 6 appear to have had specific uses. Fabric 1 was used in the construction of possible kiln 1098, discussed below. Fabric 5 was found only once, as a brick in the possible oven 1127 in the

Table 21 fired clay: no. and weight (g) by functional type from the terrace area

Fabric	Loom-Weight	Kiln (1098)	Undiag.	Total
F1	–	10,021	86	10,107
F2	1620	–	2338	3958
F3	1070	–	6019	7089
F4	234	–	322	556
F5	–	–	568	568
F6	–	–	98	98
Total	2924	10,021	9431	22,376

northern ditch terminal, 1008. Fabric 6 is grog-tempered, usually only found in pottery fabric, but the piece is too massive to have been part of any known vessel form.

Forms

The fired clay can be subdivided into three categories: material associated with the possible kiln in feature 1098; fragments of loomweights; and featureless, undiagnostic fragments. The correlation of fabrics to these categories is presented in Table 21, and the fired clay is discussed by category below.

Fired clay kiln

Feature 1098 comprised a block or 'brick' of fired clay of fabric 1 c. 0.3 x 0.12 x 0.24 m, sitting in a 'basin' of the same material, the latter being only 7 mm thick (Figs 21 and 23). 1359, in the southernmost ditch terminal, had been constructed when the ditch was at least two-thirds silted up. The fired clay 'basin' was intact when excavated, and, because of the fragile nature of the fabric and the thinness of the walls, it is likely that it was fired *in situ*. The block itself must also have been fragile and cannot have been moved far.

The block and clay 'basin' were associated with at least two lenses of burnt material which included small pieces of poorly fired clay or daub and sherds of middle 1st century AD pottery. Some sherds were identified as wasters (*see* Pottery, above) and suggest that 1098 may have been a kiln. The block is probably an example of a portable rectangular clay pedestal as used inside a 'slab-type' pedestal kiln (Swan 1984, 59) during firing. This type of kiln is attributed to the La Tène III or immediately post-conquest period, a date which is consistent with that for the pottery.

Loomweights

Eleven of the pieces of fired clay (2,924 g) were identified as fragments of loomweights (Fig. 40). All bar one of these, which came from an unphased feature, were found in deposits dated to the early Romano-British period (phase 2). Where the shape can be discerned all are triangular with perforations through the corners, a form occurring widely throughout lowland areas of southern England from the 5th century BC into the Romano-British period (Champion 1975, fig. 2). Three of the loomweights are in fabric 2, and all were found in

Table 22 fired clay: total weight (g) by context from the terrace area

Context	Phase	F1	F2	F3	F4	F5	F6	Total
Subsoil 1001		–	–	2242	–	–	–	2242
Post-hole 1033	unphased	–	–	782 332*	–	–	–	782 332*
Pit 1113	1	–	12	3	–	–	–	15
Pit 1263	1	–	26	–	–	–	–	26
Pit 1320	1	–	95	20	–	–	–	115
Recut 5079	1	–	–	341	–	–	–	341
Enclosure ditch (lower fills)	2	86	35	44	–	–	–	165
Ditch terminals (lower fills)	2	–	937	921 422*	194*	–	–	1858 616*
Pit 1020	2	–	84	5	–	–	–	89
Linear 1053	2	–	–	6	–	–	–	6
Pit 1062	2	–	–	11	–	–	–	11
Pit 1064	2	–	–	1	–	–	–	1
Pit 1066	2	–	–	5	–	–	–	5
Pit 1074	2	–	–	5	–	–	–	5
Post-hole 1090	2	–	–	26	176 40*	–	–	202 40*
Pit 1092 (upper fills)	2	–	–	3 294*	–	–	–	3 294*
Kiln 1098	2	3962 6059**	900	–	–	–	–	4862 6059**
Hearth/oven 1127	2	–	–	–	–	568	–	568
Pit 1227	2	–	–	5	–	–	–	5
Pit 1233 (upper fills)	2	–	13 1620*	12	–	–	–	25 1620*
Pit 1267	2	–	–	22 22*	–	–	–	22 22*
Pit 1275	2	–	–	34	–	–	–	34
Post-hole 1277	2	–	–	112	–	–	–	112
Post-hole 1279	2	–	–	180	–	–	–	180
Pit 1287	2	–	–	32	–	–	–	32
Post-hole 1006	3	–	236	586	–	–	–	822
Enclosure ditch (upper fills)	4	–	–	489	146	–	98	733
Ditch 1154	4	–	–	100	–	–	–	100
Ditch 1166	4	–	–	32	–	–	–	32
Total		10107	3958	7089	556	568	98	22376

* = loomweight(s) ** = kiln furniture

pit 1233; of the others, six are in fabric 3 and two in fabric 4, most of these coming from northern ditch terminal 1008. None was found in a position which could reasonably be interpreted as being *in situ*.

Featureless fragments
The remaining 9431 g of fired clay consisted of featureless fragments. None of the pieces showed wattle impressions nor were any structural fragments recognisable. The remainder of the fired clay is likely to represent debris from ovens and hearths.

Discussion
Table 22 presents the breakdown of fired clay by context. The chronological distribution shows fabrics 1, 2 and 5 to be predominantly used during phases 1 and 2, whilst fabric 6 appears in later contexts. Fabrics 3 and 4 appear as a 'universal' fabric. It is of note that all datable identified pieces, ie the loomweights and possible kiln fragments, date to the early Romano-British (phase 2) use of the enclosure.

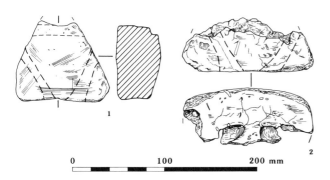

Figure 39   Loomweights

List of illustrated objects (Fig. 40)
1. Triangular loomweight, three perforations, fabric 2. Context 1250, upper fill of pit 1233, phase 2.
2. Part of triangular loomweight, two perforations surviving, fabric 3. Context 1034, post-hole 1033, unphased.

Human Bone, by Jacqueline I. McKinley (submitted 1988)

In all, ten collections of bone were examined, all except one cremated. Age was assessed on the degree of bone fusion; sex was assessed from sexually dimorphic traits where sufficient evidence remained.

Cremation burial group 1004 (late 2nd century AD)

In total, six collections of cremated bone were made in the immediate area of this phase 3 cremation burial group, consisting of 2 pots/urns containing bone and at least two other accessory vessels. The group had been substantially disturbed by ploughing which was doubtless responsible for the spread of bone, no doubt originally all deposited in the two urns. Taken as a whole the collection consisted of 461.1 g of well cremated bone (ie all organic content oxidised), 20.3% of which was identifiable, (max. frag. 33.5 mm). There was no indication that the collection represented other than a single individual, no duplication of bones was noted and the collection was compatible in terms of condition and age. It was not unusual in the Romano-British period to deposit the remains of one individual in two adjacent urns with other accessory vessels in groups such as this (several such collections were noted by the author when examining the Romano-British cremation burials from Baldock (McKinley 1984).

- Adult; mature/older ?male.
- No pathology was noted.

Cremation burial group 1150 (1st century AD)

A cremation burial group consisting of urn and accessory vessel, situated several metres north-west of 1004 but dated to the earlier phase 2 of Iron Age/Romano-British activity. A total of 507.3 g of well cremated bone, 19.7% of which was identifiable (max. frag. 42 mm).

- Adult; mature/older sex?
- No pathology was noted.

Context (1001)

Cremated bone recovered from the ploughsoil in trench 48H in the vicinity of the other cremation burials. A total of 98.1 g of well cremated bone, 21.1% of which was identifiable (max. frag. 32 mm).

The bone was well cremated and both its condition and identification would make it compatible with either 1004 or 1150.

Context 1159 (3rd/4th centuries AD)

A total of 0.9 g of very fragmentary burnt bone was recovered from ditch 1154. Probably animal.

Context 1352 (Middle–Late Iron Age)

Bone was recovered from the lowest fill of phase 1 pit 1320 within the sub-rectangular enclosure. The collection represented most of the skeleton of a foetus/neonate (7–8 months in utero). These were found in conjunction with a the skull and feet of a 1.5–2 year old lamb and a mature, butchered cow skull (*see* Animal Bone below).

Discussion

Both cremation burials were fairly small, representing by weight *c.* 20% of the total weight of a cremated adult (McKinley 1993). The bone was well fragmented, most being between 5–10 mm in size. Both the small quantity of bone and the level of fragmentation may partly be the result of disturbance, spreading the bone and crushing that which remained. Fragmentation may result from the methods of tending the pyre, and on the method of collection after cremation (McKinley 1994).

Animal Bone, by M. Maltby

Introduction

The animal bones were examined by the author at the Faunal Remains Unit, Department of Archaeology, University of Southampton, where a copy of the archive is stored. Only one context produced a substantial number of bones (1352) and these will be considered separately from the others.

Context 1352

This was the lowest fill of a phase 1 Middle–Late Iron Age pit 1320. A total of 144 animal bones was recorded from this fill (Table 23). These formed the following groups:

Cattle skull, mandibles, and hyoid

The skull was intact and belonged to an adult animal. The tooth eruption sequence was complete; most sutures were fused and the horn cores were compact. The horn cores were flattened, short in proportion to their basal circumference and curved slightly downwards. All these characteristics are typical of bulls (Armitage and Clutton-Brock 1976). The cores were very small, possessing an outer curvature length of only *c.* 82 mm and a greatest diameter at the base of 38.9 mm (min. diameter of base 22.3 mm). The skull as a whole measured 401 mm along its profile length.

The mandibles were also complete and all permanent teeth were in wear. The teeth were not, how-

Table 23 animal bone: from phase 1 context 1352, pit 1320, within the enclosure

	Foetal Cattle	Other Cattle	Sheep	Toad	Sheep-Sized Mammal
Skull fragments	1	1	1	1	–
Mandible	2	3	2	1	–
Hyoid	–	1	–	–	–
Loose teeth	–	1	–	–	–
Scapula	2	–	–	1	–
Humerus	1	–	–	1	–
Radius and ulna	–	–	–	2	–
Ulna	2	–	–	–	–
Os coxae	2	–	–	2	–
Femur	2	–	–	2	1
Tibia	–	–	–	2	–
Carpals	–	1	–	–	–
Centroquartal	–	2	–	–	–
Other tarsals	–	2	–	2	–
Metacarpus	1	1	1	–	–
Metatarsus	–	2	1	–	–
Metapodial	–	–	1	3	–
1st phalanx	–	6	2	–	–
2nd phalanx	–	4	–	–	–
3rd phalanx	–	4	–	–	–
Phalanges	–	–	–	6	–
Sesamoids	–	14	–	–	–
Ribs	17	–	–	–	1
Vertebrae	37	–	–	2	–
Total	67	42	8	25	2

ever, in very heavy wear. Taking this evidence in conjunction with the evidence for suture closure on the skull, it is likely that the animal was between five and eight years of age.

The third molars of the mandible possessed only vestigial posterior cusps. The posterior cusps of the upper third molars had suffered some compensatory abnormal wear. Mandible and maxillae displaying this condition, which is probably genetic in origin (Andrews and Noddle 1975), are commonly found in small numbers in Iron Age and Romano-British assemblages.

The skull was recovered in an inverted position a few centimetres above the base of the pit. The mandibles appear still to have been in articulation with it. However, marks on the skull indicate that the animal may have been skinned. These consisted of knife cuts running along the right frontal bone. The other frontal bone had been depressed, probably reflecting the damage inflicted during pole-axing. A possible knife cut was also found on the right occipital condyle, although modern damage had almost obliterated it. Such a cut could have been made when the skull was detached from the vertebral column.

Bones from cattle feet
These consisted of a pair of metatarsi, a left metacarpus and associated carpals, tarsals, phalanges and sesamoids (36 bones in all, see Table 23). It is possible that all these bones belonged to the feet of the same animal.

Metrical analysis of the metapodia revealed that the metacarpus had a greatest length of 172.8 mm and the metatarsi one of 197.3 mm. Converting these measurements into withers heights using the factors recommended by Foch (1966), the metacarpus gave an estimated height of 105.8 cm and the metatarsi one of 107.5 cm; such a variation in the estimates is well within the range encountered for a single animal. Comparisons of width and length measurements suggested that both bones fell into the female range because of their slenderness. Therefore, although they may have belonged to the same animal, they probably did not belong to the same skeleton as the skull and mandibles, which probably belonged to a bull. The size of the metapodia is typical of the small cattle encountered in contemporary deposits in Hampshire (eg Owslebury: Maltby nd). All bones in this group were fused and belonged to an animal(s) probably over three years of age (Grigson 1982, 22). Knife cuts were found on several bones in this group. Both centroquartals had cuts on the anterior surface made during the disarticulation of the feet from the upper hindlimb. The metacarpus bore several cuts on the anterior, lateral and medial surfaces of the lower part of the shaft running in a medio-lateral direction. These were probably the marks left during the initial stages of skinning (Binford 1981, 107). A similar cut was encountered on the shaft of one of the metatarsi. One of the hind first phalanges had a knife cut on its outer surface, which could also have occurred during skinning.

Table 24 animal bone: from terrace area contexts other than 1352

Feature	Type	Phase	Bones	Total
Ploughsoil		unphased	Cattle femur; large mammal fragment; unidentified mammal fragment	3
Subsoil		unphased	Cattle tooth fragment; sheep-sized longbone fragment	2
1005 (lower fills)	ditch	1	Sheep-sized mammal fragment	1
1092 (lower fills)	pit	1	Sheep scapula; pig deciduous lower 4th premolar; 2 unidentified mammal fragments	4
1113	pit	1	Cattle axis and skull fragment; sheep/goat metacarpus; 2 large mammal fragments	5
5079	ditch	1	Unidentified mammal fragment	1
1018	post-hole	2	Unidentified mammal fragment	1
1036 (upper fills)	ditch	2	2 cattle tooth fragments	2
1062	pit	2	Sheep-sizes mammal fragment	1
1078 (upper fills)	pit	2	Cattle tooth fragment	1
1092 (upper fills)	pit	2	Large mammal fragment	1
1127	hearth/oven	2	Cattle upper molar	1
1290	post-hole	2	Unidentified mammal fragment	1
1300	pit	2	49 water vole bones; skull and mandibles of short-tailed vole; 4 unidentified rodent bones	56
1318	pit	2	Dog metapodial	1
1320 (upper fills)	pit	2	Sheep/goat radius and tibia; 2 sheep-sized longbone fragment; cattle radius; cattle mandible; sheep/goat mandible and frontal/horn core; sheep-sized rib fragment	9
1160	pit	4	Unidentified bird fragment	1
Total				91

Bones of a cattle foetus

Sixty-seven bones were recovered, most of which consisted of ribs and vertebrae fragments; bones from the head and all four limbs were also represented (Table 23). The porosity and size of the bones indicated that they belonged to a foetus rather than a neonatal mortality.

Sheep skull and mandibles

The skull was incomplete but one of the maxillae survived to show that it articulated with the pair of mandibles. Tooth eruption data revealed that only the deciduous premolars and the first molar had erupted. The first molar was in an early stage of wear (Grant 1982 — Stage b). Such an animal was probably between six months and a year old.

Bones from sheep feet

An immature sheep was also represented by a metacarpus, a metatarsus, an associated metapodial distal epiphysis and two first phalanges. The distal epiphysis of the metapodia and the proximal epiphyses of the phalanges were unfused and therefore the bones may have belonged to the same skeleton as the skull and mandibles.

Bones of a toad

Nineteen bones from large toad were recovered. They probably belonged to a common toad (*Bufo bufo*). The animal probably fell into the bottom of the pit and was unable to escape.

The context also produced a few other fragments of animal bone. The only ones identifiable to species were a cattle incisor and mandible fragment, which were probably associated. A femur of a probably foetal sheep-sized mammal was also recorded.

The layer, therefore, was associated with the primary disposal of carcass waste not required for food. All the groups of the major domestic mammal bones had relatively little meat value, consisting either of foetuses or of head and limb extremities. The separation of skull or limb extremities from the more valuable meat-bearing parts of the skeleton has been noted on several Iron Age sites.

Animal bones from other contexts

Only 91 fragments from 25 bone-producing contexts were recorded. The species and anatomies involved are listed in Table 24. In general, the bones were poorly preserved, particularly close to the ground surface. Of the contexts sampled for pH readings, none of those with values of 7 produced animal bones, whereas four contexts with values of 8–10 did contain animal bones. Further analysis of this sort would be a worthwhile exercise. Even so, the good preservation of bones in context (1352) demonstrated that bones could survive on the site in good condition and their paucity may also reflect a low rate of deposition.

Four further contexts in the phase 2 upper fills of pit 1320 produced small numbers of animal bones. Small amounts of bone were recovered from the upper fill of the pit, including a sheep/goat tibia which had been partially destroyed by canid gnawing. Animal bones from lower layers included another cattle mandible fragment, bringing the minimum number of cattle represented in this pit to four (including the foetal skeleton), though these may have been deposited over a considerable length of time. A sheep/goat mandible from the upper layers belonged to an older animal than the one represented in 1352. This specimen had all its permanent teeth erupted with the third molar in an early stage of wear (Grant 1982 – Stage d). It probably belonged to an animal aged between two and four years old.

Phase 1 pit 1092 produced five fragments including the only identification of pig and a scapula of a young sheep. Five fragments were also recovered from phase 1 pit 1113, including a canid gnawed sheep/goat metacarpus and a cattle axis bearing a chop mark probably made during dismemberment. The only bones recovered from phase 2 pit 1300 belonged to rodents, 49 of these were from a skeleton of a water vole (*Arvicola terrestris*); the remainder could all have belonged to the same short-tailed vole (*Microtus agrestis*) skeleton. Both animals were probably pit fall victims.

Three other pits, all phase 2 deposits, (1062, 1078, and 1318), each produced one bone fragment. A metapodial of an immature, short, stocky type of dog was found in pit 1318. Other features produced very little faunal data (Table 24), most of which was poorly preserved.

Carbonised Plant Remains, by W.J. Carruthers (submitted 1989)

Introduction

An environmental sampling programme was set up during the early stages of the excavations. Environmental samples were taken from a range of contexts across the site. The majority were from contexts associated with the Iron Age/Romano-British enclosure, but in addition large quantities of soil were processed from a number of 5 x 5 m squares where there was evidence of human activity elsewhere on the site; the results from these latter contexts have been outlined previously (*see* above). Samples associated with Food vessels have also already been considered.

The soil samples ranged in size depending on the type of deposit, but wherever possible they were taken in multiples of 10 litres. The total volumes of soil processed for each phase are given at the bottom of the species list (Table 25). A modified Siraf tank was used for the flotation. Hydrogen peroxide solution was added to the sample prior to flotation where particularly cohesive soils were encountered in order to help disaggregate the soil. The flots were dried, bagged and sent to the author unsorted.

Results

A total of 43 samples produced results. A summarised list of the taxa recovered is given in Table 25. The full list of data is presented in the archive.

Notes on identification

Both emmer (*Triticum dicoccum* Schubl.) and spelt wheat (*T. spelta* L.) were identified using the patterns of venation on the glume bases and measurements of glume base widths. The caryopses of emmer/spelt were generally too poorly preserved to indicate which species was present, although a few well-preserved grains were tentatively identified as emmer wheat.

The caryopses of bread/club wheat (*T. aestivo-compactum* sl.) were distinctive in their much broader, more rounded profile and absence of hump on the dorsal side. The single bread/club wheat rachis section was incomplete and so could not be identified to species, but the nature of the fragmentation indicated that it was from a free threshing wheat.

Where the preservation allowed the distinction to be made, all of the barley appeared to be hulled. Six-row barley (*Hordeum vulgare* L. emend.) was only identified where twisted grains were present, otherwise the identification was given as *Hordeum* sp. The rachis fragments were not in a sufficiently good state of preservation to be identified to species level.

It was not possible to say whether the oat (*Avena* sp.) caryopses were from cultivated or wild oats, since no floret bases were present. The large numbers of oat awn fragments could have come from just a few highly fragmented awns.

Discussion

Middle–Late Iron Age to early 2nd century AD (phases 1 and 2)
Considering the quantities of soil processed, surprisingly few carbonised plant remains were recovered from the Iron Age and Romano-British samples. This is despite the fact that many of the pits within the enclosure were of the size and form usually considered characteristic of grain storage pits. In some cases the tops of the pits appeared to be plugged with clay or chalk in the fashion described by Reynolds (1974), a practice necessary to ensure that grain within the pit is maintained in the correct storage conditions. However, samples from eleven possible storage pits produced very few carbonised plant remains, the average being 8 fragments per 10 litre soil sample.

The primary fills of grain storage pits are frequently found to be rich in carbonised remains. These assemblages can be composed of either charred grain representing the burnt remains of the stored crop such as was found by Jones (1984) at Danebury, Hampshire, or chaff fragments and weed seeds, deposits that may represent some sort of lining (Monk and Fasham 1980, Carruthers 1989). No such assemblages were present in any of the primary fills of the pits at Thames Valley Park. The pits also contained few pottery sherds or fragments of bone. Thus, there is little evidence of secondary usage of the pits for the deposition of domestic waste, as appears to be common with abandoned storage pits on other sites.

Most of the examples of Iron Age sites containing large numbers of grain storage pits have been found on the chalklands of south-east England (eg Danebury, Jones 1984), Winnall Down (Monk in Fasham 1985), Brighton Hill South (Carruthers 1995). The local sand

Table 25 carbonised plant remains from the terrace area

Taxa	Habitat	Mesolithic	Early Bronze Age	Phase 1/2 Enclosure Ditch	Phase 1/2 Features in Enclosure	Phase 1/2 Features Outside	Phase 3/4 Features
T. spelta (spelt glume bases)	–	–	–	32	13	6	1
T. dicoccum Schubl (emmer glume bases)	–	–	–	16	1	–	–
T. dicoccum (emmer spikelet forks)	–	–	–	9	–	–	–
T. cf. dicoccum (cf. emmer caryopses)	–	–	–	6	–	–	–
Triticum dioccum/spelta (emmer/spelt caryopses)	–	4	–	30	36	3	2
Triticum dioccum/spelta (emmer glume bases)	–	–	–	78	29	4	1
Triticum dioccum/spelta (emmer spikelet forks)	–	–	–	15	7	3	–
Triticum aestivocompactum. s.l. (bread/club wheat caryopses)	–	–	–	3	–	20	–
Triticum aestivocompactum. s.l. (bread/club wheat rachis fragment)	–	–	–	–	1	–	–
Hordeum vulgare L. emend (6-row hulled barley)	–	–	–	2	1	–	–
Hordeum sp. (hulled barley caryopses)	–	2	–	58	4	1	–
Hordeum sp. (barley rachis fragments)	–	–	–	13	–	3	–
Avena sp. (oat caryopses)	–	–	1	13	1	–	1
Avena sp. (oat awn fragments)	–	–	–	127	5	–	–
Indeterminate cereals	–	6	1	298	82	20	9
CARYOPHYLLACEAE							
Silena cf. alba (Mill.) E.H.L. Krause (cf. white campion)	CDH	–	–	–	2	–	–
S. cf. dioica (L.) Clairv. (cf. red campion)	HW	–	–	6	1	–	–
Stellaria media (L) Vill. (chickweed)	CD	–	–	1	1	–	–
CHENOPODIACEAE							
Atriplex hastata/patula (orache)	CD	–	–	2	1	–	–
Chenopodium album L. (fat hen)	CD	–	–	10	4	–	–
C. polyspermum L. (all-seed)	CD	–	–	–	1	–	–
Chenopodium sp.	–	–	–	–	–	–	1
Indeterminate (without seed coat)	–	–	–	12	–	–	–

Table 25 continued

Taxa	Habitat	Mesolithic	Early Bronze Age	Phase 1/2 Enclosure Ditch	Phase 1/2 Features in Enclosure	Phase 1/2 Features Outside	Phase 3/4 Features
COMPOSITAE							
Anthemis cotula L. (stinking mayweed)	ADh	–	4	–	–	1	1
Tripleurospermum maritimum ssp. inodorum (scentless mayweed)	AD	–	–	3	–	–	–
CORYLACEAE							
Corylus avellana L. (hazlenut shell fragments)	HSW	317	–	1	2	–	–
CYPERACEAE							
Eleocharis subg. Palustres (spike-rush)	MR	–	–	1	–	–	1
GRAMINEAE							
Bromus sect. Bromus (chess)	ADG	–	–	54	15	5	1
Indeterminate (grasses)	DG	–	–	21	14	2	–
LEGUMINOSEAE							
Trifolium sp. (clover)	DG	–	–	1	–		
Vicia sp./Lathyrus sp. (vetch, tare)	–	1	–	17	15	5	1
Indeterminate	–	–	–	1	1	–	–
PLANTAGINACEAE							
Plantago major L. (great plantain)	CDo	–	1	–	–	–	–
POLYGONACEAE							
Bilderdykia convolvulus (L.) Dumort, (black bindweed)	AD	–	–	2	4	–	–
Polygonum aviculare agg. (knotgrass)	AD	–	–	–	1	–	–
Polygonum lapathifolium L. (pale persicaria)	CD	–	–	12	–	–	–
P. persicaria L. (red shank)	CD	–	–	3	–	–	–
Rumex acetosella agg. (sheep's sorrel)	CEGa	–	–	2	4	1	–
Rumex sp. (dock)	–	–	–	27	8	2	1
PRIMULACEAE							
Anagallis arvensis L. (scarlet pimpernel)	C	–	1	–	2	–	–
RANUNCULACEAE							
Ranunculus acris/bulbosus/repens (buttercup- no seed coat)	DG	–	–	–	–	1	–

Table 25 continued

Taxa	Habitat	Mesolithic	Early Bronze Age	Phase 1/2 Enclosure Ditch	Phase 1/2 Features in Enclosure	Phase 1/2 Features Outside	Phase 3/4 Features
ROSACEAE							
Crataegus monogyna L. Jacq. (hawthorn)	HSW	–	–	–	–	1	–
Rosa sp. (rose)	HSW	2	–	–	–	–	–
RUBIACEAE							
Galium aparine L. (cleavers)	DH	–	–	1	1	–	–
Galium sp.	–	1	–	–	1	–	–
Sherardia arvensis L. (field madder)	AD	–	–	1	–	–	–
SCROPHULARIACEAE							
Euphrasia sp./*Odontites verna* (eyebright/red bartsia)	CD	–	–	2	4	9	–
TOTAL		333	8	880	262	87	19
Total volume of soil processed (litres)		1180	131	127	311	334	139
Number of contexts sampled		5	2	10	23	6	4

Habitats: A = arable; C = cultivated land: D = disturbed ground; E = heath; G = grassland; H = hedgerows; M = marsh; R = riverside; S = scrub; W = woodland; a = acid soils; h= heavy soils; o = open habitats

and clay soils at Thames Valley Park would appear to be less suitable for pit storage, being more retentive of moisture than chalk. However, pit storage experiments carried out by Reynolds (1974) using a variety of subsoil types including clay, clay-with-flints, and sand and gravel demonstrated that almost all of the pits produced edible grain and the majority retained the grain in a condition fit for use as seed corn. But it was noted that where a pit became flooded temporarily, the grain within it soon rotted. This could be a reason for pit abandonment at Thames Valley Park. In addition, if the pits had only been used for a short period they may not have been sterilised by burning. Thus, any crop remnants or lining present would not have been preserved by carbonisation but would have rotted away *in situ* leaving no archaeological trace. The presence of, as Reynolds puts it, 'a mass of rotting stinking grain' could be one reason for rapidly backfilling the pits with relatively clean material. However, without the supporting evidence the suggestions given are mere speculation.

The analysis of the assemblage from the pit fills showed a roughly equal proportion of grain, chaff, and weed, though the fragment numbers were low, 34 fragments of seed and chaff being the maximum recovered from any one pit.

The enclosure ditch samples produced approximately eight times as much carbonised material per litre of soil as the samples from the features. However, this is mainly due to the presence of a few rich deposits within the ditch. The actual percentage compositions of the assemblages, ie percentage grain, chaff and weed seeds, were similar in the ditch deposits to the samples from the features, indicating that the same type of waste was being deposited in both cases. The species composition for the cereals and weed seeds was also not notably different.

One of the rich deposits was recovered from the remains of a probable kiln (1098) dated to the 1st century AD (phase 2) found in one of the enclosure ditch terminals. This was the most productive sample processed and the cereal caryopses present were recovered in by far the best state of preservation. Most of the grain recovered from the rest of the site was vacuolated, indicating carbonisation at high temperatures. The good state of preservation of grain from the kiln indicates that the burning was of a much more controlled nature.

Fired clay/pottery from the kiln contained plant impressions, some of which were identifiable. These included the following :

- *Triticum spelta/dicoccum* glume bases 2
- *Triticum* spikelet forks 2
- *Bromus* sect. *Bromus* (chess) 1

Comparing the results from the kiln with those from another rich deposit, a possible hearth/oven (1127) contemporary with the kiln but situated in the opposite ditch terminal, it can be seen that a much higher occurrence of chaff was found in the kiln. One explanation for these differences could be that the chaff and weed seeds in the kiln were a waste product of crop processing that had been used as a tinder. The grain in the hearth might be the result of parching small amounts of grain over the fire, and other domestic

activities involved in the preparation of food. However, the differences in carbonisation temperatures between a kiln and a domestic fire could also account for these results. As the grain in the kiln was clearly in a better state of preservation, it is possible that some of the more delicate chaff fragments had been burnt away in the fiercer, less controlled heat of the hearth. Carbonisation experiments carried out by Wilson (1984) have shown that the preservation of remains depends to a great extent on factors such as temperature and duration of heat.

The few features sampled outside the enclosure contained comparable percentages of grain, chaff, and weed seeds to those from the enclosure. The species composition was also similar.

For phases 1 and 2 as a whole, the range of cereals recovered was typical of many Iron Age sites examined to date. Spelt wheat appears to have been the predominant crop (many of the remains could not be identified further than spelt/emmer), although emmer was more in evidence in these samples than on some other Late Iron Age sites in Wessex, such as Lains Farm, near Andover (Carruthers 1991), Brighton Hill South (Carruthers 1995) and Danebury (Jones 1984). The small amount of bread/club wheat present was mostly found in the enclosure ditch terminal and feature 1152. Hulled barley was of lesser importance than wheat, as is usual on sites of this date, and a few oat caryopses were present, probably as a crop weed.

The few weed seeds recovered were also typical of the period, in particular chess (*Bromus* sect. *Bromus*), field madder (*Sherardia arvensis* L.), stinking mayweed (*Anthemis cotula* L.) and spike-rush (*Eleocharis* subg. *Palustres*). The latter two taxa indicate the cultivation of damp ground, such as might be found on the alluvial soils of the floodplain. However, very few seeds of these damp soil taxa were recovered when compared to some Iron Age sites. Kay (1971) notes that stinking mayweed may be replaced by scentless mayweed (*Tripleurospermum maritimum* ssp. *inodorum*) on lighter soils, and this species was slightly more common on the Thames Valley Park site.

There is also the possibility that some hay was represented amongst the weed assemblage, since quite a few grass (unidentified Gramineae), vetch/tare (*Vicia* sp./*Lathyrus* sp.), sheep's sorrel (*Rumex acetosella* agg.) and clover (*Trifolium* sp.) seeds were present. However, these taxa may grow in a range of habitats including areas of waste ground and as arable weeds on newly cultivated soils.

An analysis, on the lines of that given by Jones (1985), comparing the percentages of grain, chaff and weed seeds present in carbonised assemblages from Iron Age and Romano-British sites was undertaken. Jones suggests that differences between producer and consumer sites can be observed. Much higher percentages of grain are likely to occur around a site of production due to spillages during crop processing than on a consumer site where the imported grain would have been a highly valued commodity which must not be wasted.

The Thames Valley Park samples appear to fall into the Jones (1985) producer category, being primarily grain rather than chaff or weed seeds. However, only a few samples produced enough material to be included so representivity may be a problem. In addition, differential preservation under high temperatures, as suggested earlier, and the possibility of grain being burnt deliberately for ritual purposes or because of disease may have affected the results to some extent. Nevertheless, the surrounding loams and gravel soils on the river terraces would have provided a suitable growing medium for cereals, particularly for the wheats.

Late 2nd–4th century AD (phase 3 and 4)
Only six samples were taken from four contexts of this phase, both in the enclosure and from features outside. Therefore, it is not possible to compare the few remains recovered with those from the earlier phase, except by noting that no new taxa were found. Emmer/spelt caryopses, spelt glume bases, oat, chess and a few other weed species were present.

A greater occurrence of free threshing wheat (*Triticum aestivo-compactum*) was recorded in one sample taken outside the enclosure. This was from rectangular cut 1152 (phase 4).

4. Floodplain Excavations and Observations (W244),1988

by C.A. Butterworth and John W. Hawkes

Introduction

Following the 1986 evaluation and the terrace area excavations of 1987, further archaeological work was carried out at Thames Valley Park between April and October 1988. The original archaeological strategy based on the planning application submitted in 1985, had envisaged that only a limited response would be necessary at this stage in the development, largely confined to observation of road construction within the development area with little disturbance to the floodplain zone.

However, during the course of 1987 the scale of the operation was changed. An appraisal of the practicalities of transporting the pulverised fuel ash (PFA) off-site had identified a major, unwelcome effect on the local residential area, and an alternative strategy was developed. This involved burying the PFA in sealed holes within the floodplain following the stripping of the alluvium and extraction of the underlying gravel.

In view of the comparatively small areas then threatened, only limited examination of the southern part of the floodplain had been carried out during the 1986 evaluation. This had not indicated any great density of archaeological activity and it was initially thought that a watching brief would be the most appropriate means of recording the archaeology of the area; features exposed during the contractors' excavations might be isolated and examined as the earth-moving work continued. In practice it very quickly became clear that the scale and speed of excavation were too great to guarantee the discovery of anything but the largest features; the damage caused by earth-moving machinery to the often wet alluvium surface was very considerable, and the watching brief team was stretched to (and sometimes beyond) its capacity to deal effectively and promptly with archaeological recording over a wide area.

Following consultations with the resident engineer, it was agreed to modify the archaeological approach. A limited number of trenches were dug in areas of perceived potential ahead of the contractors' operations, thus allowing features to be identified, excavated, and recorded more carefully away from the immediate threat of the earth-moving. Wherever the presence of significant archaeological deposits was established, it proved possible to negotiate an agreed timetable for further investigation which involved the minimum of disruption to the development programme. Where predicted delays to the contract were likely to be prohibitively expensive, the less costly option of a temporary increase in the size of the archaeological team to speed the work was followed. A watching brief was still maintained on all operational areas.

The Floodplain

Over 20 ha of floodplain lay within the development site, although not all of that area was to be affected; a broad strip across the site was reserved for a future Thames road crossing, and the routes of two existing gas pipelines were also excluded. At least another 11 ha of floodplain at the eastern side of the site were buried beneath PFA dumped during the lifetime of the power station, but surface stripping before the ash had been deposited appeared likely to have destroyed most, if not all, archaeological deposits in that area. Archaeological trial trenches and areas extracted for the dumping of fuel ash totalled some 7 ha (Fig. 40).

Although low lying, at around 35–36 m OD, and generally level, some minor undulations, probably the result of changes in the course of the river, were noted across the floodplain. A ridge running parallel with the present course of the Thames at the northern side of Area X was one of the most well-defined and prominent of these areas of higher ground, but others occurred to the south and east (Fig. 40). Trenches dug on the northern ridge disclosed that it was formed of both alluvium and gravel, the latter intermittently occurring directly below topsoil. Alluvium, as might be expected, extended across the greater part of the floodplain, the only other deposits encountered being of peat or very organic silt in some sections of former river channels.

The natural ground water level on the site was high until lowered by pumps installed before the start of the development and run continuously throughout the earth-moving operations thereafter. Conditions for the preservation of organic artefacts and environmental evidence were thus initially good and, influenced by the proximity of the Thames and the nature of the alluvium capping the gravel, remained so for some considerable time in those areas not being worked.

Archaeological Strategy

The contractors' excavations were to start at the northern end of the floodplain, in Area Y, before expanding southwards and westwards into Areas X and Z. Once started, the scale of their operation effectively sterilised much of Area Y, so that when the main archaeological response was diverted from the watching brief to machine trenching ahead of the contractors' excavations, only the southern part of that area was still accessible. Eleven trenches were opened as the first phase of archaeological prospection; one, trench D, in Area Y, seven, trenches A, C, E–H, and L, north-west of the gas pipeline which formed the northern boundary of

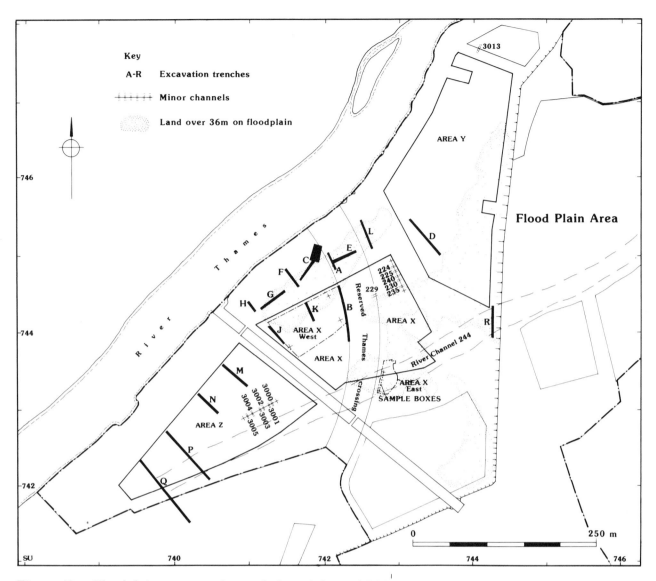

Figure 40   Floodplain area trenches and plan of channel 244

Area X, and three, trenches B, J, and K, in Area X West. Trenches A and E and part of trench B lay within the area reserved for the future Thames crossing. All trenches except D and H were placed across or along the ridge described above (Fig. 40). The trenches, excavated with the ditching bucket of a mechanical excavator, were between 2.1 m and 4 m wide and between 23 m and 94 m long; topsoil, seldom more than 0.3 m deep, and in some areas some of the subsoil, were removed mechanically.

Occasional, unstratified worked and burnt flints were recovered from all trenches except E and L, but features were only recognised in trench C. Despite the apparent scarcity of features, however, it was considered worthwhile to extend the area of investigation to cover as much of the northern part of Area X West, the southern half of the ridge, as possible. Discussion with the resident engineer and contractors resulted in a change in their work schedule sufficient to allow the complete excavation of the northern half of Area X West.

Later in the development, four more trenches, M, N, P, and Q, were opened in Area Z, and a fifth, R, south of Area Y. No features were seen in any of the trenches,

nor were any finds recovered from them and no further advance work was done in these areas. Trench R confirmed the eastward course of river channel (244) which was also confirmed by other observations. The watching brief, although on a reduced scale, was maintained on all operational areas and resulted in the recording of a number of former stream channels (Fig. 40). It also led to the excavation of part of a much larger river channel in Area X East and the subsequent preservation of much of its course across the site. Work on the floodplain was carried out under a new site code, W244. A unique numbering system was used, with blocks of numbers given to different parts of the site. The difficulties encountered in dating many of the features precludes description by phase, and the site is considered by area.

Artefact and Environmental Sampling and Processing, by Sarah F. Wyles

The sampling strategy was developed during the course of the excavation to investigate the range of environmental and artefactual evidence. Bulk samples were

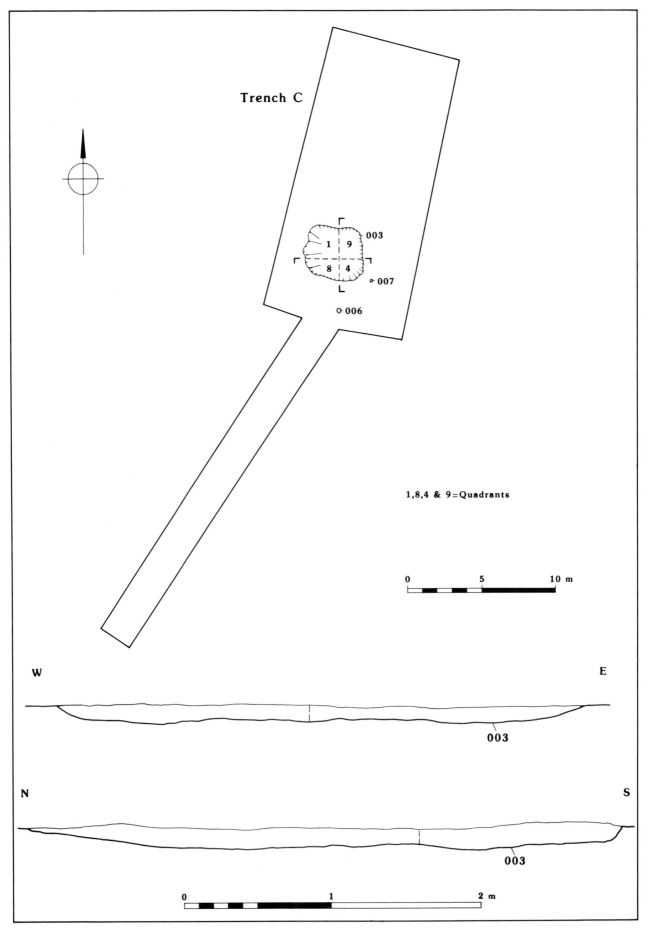

Figure 41   Trench C: Mesolithic hollow, plan and section, and other features

processed by standard flotation methods (flots retained on a 0.5 mm mesh sieve and residues fractionated to 5.6 mm, 2 mm and 1 mm) or wet sieved on a 1 mm mesh. Artefacts were sorted from the 5.6 mm and 2 mm fractions of floated samples. Waterlogged samples (1 litre) were processed by laboratory flotation with residues and flots retained on 300 μ mesh.

Area X west
A series of 19 samples of between 10 and 18 litres were taken and processed from Romano-British features for flotation and all residues were sorted for artefacts.

Area X east
Channel 244 was extensively sampled with over 120 bulk samples of between 2 and 22 litres being taken from the peat channel. This was augmented by a series of six 1 litre samples as a sequence through the peat channel and processed for the waterlogged plant remains. These samples are reported upon by Carruthers.

Standard bulk flotation was not a successful method of processing larger bulk samples from the peat channel and were wet sieved. All residues were fully sorted before discarding.

Twenty one samples of between 3 and 33 litres were taken from other channels and 17 (between 3 and 42 litres) were taken from other features and processed by flotation. Samples from other channels were sorted for both environmental material and artefacts, but from other non-channel features artefacts were only sorted from the 5.6 mm residue.

Area Y
Two 4 litre samples were taken and processed by flotation and the residues sorted for both environmental material and artefacts.

Trench C

A concentration of worked flint noted in subsoil exposed during the machining of trench C, suggested the possible presence of archaeological deposits. The trench was extended and careful cleaning revealed two post-holes, 6 and 7, and a larger feature, 3, possibly a working hollow, possibly of Mesolithic date (but see below; Fig. 41). Immediately to the south of trench C, the subsequent stripping of Area X West (Fig. 40) revealed a more extensive spread of potentially contemporaneous

worked and burnt flint. This material extended across the gravel ridge but was present in lesser quantities in the topsoil and on the alluvium surface to the south. Available time and resources precluded the total collection of the unstratified finds, although items of intrinsic interest were retained. The quantities of flint recorded from excavated features and hollows in Area X West give an indication of the extent of the distribution.

Feature 3: the Hollow
The hollow was c. 3.3 x 4 m in area and a maximum of 0.14 m deep (Fig. 41). Its edge was poorly defined, with a darker central fill becoming lighter and merging with the surrounding dark yellowish–brown sandy silt. No discrete layers were recognised. Excavation was carried out in quadrants, the first two (north-west and south-east) each excavated as a single context. The remaining two quadrants were sub-divided into 0.2 x 0.2 m squares (of which 149 were excavated), the spoil from each square being reserved for sieving for artefacts. All 149 samples were 100% sieved through a 1 mm mesh after pre-soaking with hydrogen peroxide, and the residues sorted. Many flint chips were recovered during this exercise, up to 1,021 (42 g) from a single 0.2 m² square. Much of this material is probably of natural origin (*see* below) but some may represent debitage.

Flint, by P.A. Harding
The flint was sorted, and the quantities from trench C are shown in Table 26, the totals for the other trenches on the floodplain are given in Table 31. The majority of the material was recovered either from the hollow itself (contexts 1, 8, and 9 or from the immediate area. The chips from the sieved residues in contexts 8 and 9 have been counted and are listed in archive but are not included in Table 26. Most of these chips were probably produced by natural action during the course of gravel deposition, although diagnostic debitage chips are also present. Table 26 shows that 45% of the stratified assemblage comprises blades and bladelets (hereafter referred to as blade/lets) of which 70% are broken. The condition, colour, and raw material, together with refitting pieces, suggest that this assemblage was *in situ*. The stratified material has therefore been analysed in some detail to characterise the assemblage, but the unstratified collection has been examined more superficially.

Table 26 quantification of worked flint from trench C

Location	1		2	3	4	5			6			7	8
	A	B				A	B	C	A	B	C		
Unstratified	4	8	9	16	16	157	34	11	177	18	20	40	10
Fill 1 of hollow 3	3	1	–	–	2	21	19	10	33	39	20	20	2
Fills 8/9 from hollow 3	–	–	–	3	–	10	1	5	28	9	15	14	6
Total from hollow 3	3	1	–	3	2	31	20	15	61	48	35	34	8

1 = cores; 2 = core fragments; 3 = debitage; 4 = chips; 5 = unbroken; 6 = broken; 7 = burnt; 8 = retouched tools
A = blade; B = flake; C = bladelets

Distribution
The totals from each context, for the whole assemblage within the hollow, indicated that most of the flint was concentrated in the north-west quadrant. This area also contained refitting pieces; however, neither detailed analysis nor the reconstruction of possible knapping clusters was possible given the absence of three-dimensional coordinates.

Condition and raw material
The flint from the hollow is mottled light grey in colour with small areas of light blue patination. It is in mint condition, although the material from the unstratified collection is more mixed, including deeply patinated pieces and others with a light brown stain. Some patinated pieces have edges which show post-depositional damage. Gravel nodules, including 'bullhead' flint derived from Reading Beds deposits, were readily available at the site but were used less frequently than chalk flint. This latter source, outcropping locally on the terrace edge only some 250 m south of the hollow, provided larger nodules of better quality flint. Some pieces with incipient thermal fractures could be broken into smaller angular pieces which were suitable for blade core preparation. This flint is naturally dark grey or black in colour with cherty inclusions. The cortex ranges from a thickness of 5 mm to a thin, weathered rind.

Mode
The examination of material from the hollow showed that where mode could be determined, 41% of flakes and blade/lets were characterised by vague points of percussion, diffuse bulbs, and lipped butts. These features are characteristic of soft hammers (Ohnuma and Bergman 1984, 169), which were probably used for direct percussion. It could not be determined whether the hammer was of an organic material or soft stone.

Cores
Table 26 shows that three cores from the hollow were prepared for the removal of blade/lets. The one core classified as a flake core may also have been a blade/let core rejected during core preparation. The ratio of cores to flakes and blade/lets is 1:52, which is comparable to the *in situ* knapping cluster from the terrace site (*see* above) where it was 1:47. This appears to confirm that the assemblage is complete. The cores are similar to those from the terrace excavations. They were probably prepared initially with a single striking platform which was used as the main source of blade/let production. Blade/lets were sometimes removed from an opposed platform, although these were used more often for core rejuvenation. Cresting was employed to shape or modify the front of the core and to narrow the base, while sides and back were trimmed if this was necessary. Striking platforms were abraded to strengthen the edge, remove overhang, and isolate the point of aim before the blank was removed. Striking platforms were rejuvenated by removing rejuvenation tablets or were modified by faceting.

The three blade/let cores from the hollow were all rejected after they had produced usable blade/lets. The causes of rejection are similar to those for the cores from

Table 27 analysis of unbroken flint flakes/blade/lets from trench C

Sample Size		61
		%
Hammer:	hard	8
	soft	41
	indet.	51
Butts:	plain	48
	punctiform	10
	linear	21
	others	21
Butts:	0–1	47
	2–3	33
	4–5	10
	6–7	2
	8–9	6
	10+	2
Cortext:	0	59
	25	30
	50	3
	75	6
	100	2
Length:	0–9	–
	10–19	7
	20–29	36
	30–39	26
	40–49	18
	50–59	6
	60–69	5
	70+	2
Breadth:	0–9	8
	10–19	36
	20–29	26
	30–39	23
	40–49	3
	50–59	2
	60–60	2
	70+	–
Breadth:length:	1.5:5	11
	2.5:5	28
	3.5:5	18
	4.5:5	11
	5.5:5	18
	6.5:5	7
	6.6+:5	7
Thickness:	0–3	23
	4–6	44
	7–9	13
	10–12	10
	13–15	8
	16–18	–
	19+	2

the terrace site excavations. The edges of the striking platforms were maintained carefully; only occasionally did the flaking angles increase to a position beyond which further flaking was not possible. Hinge fractures were present on each of the cores, in one case being responsible for its rejection.

Flakes and blade/lets
The total number of flakes and blade/lets from the hollow is listed in Table 26. This shows that broken flakes and blade/lets account for 68% of the collection. A collection of 61 unbroken flakes (those with proximal ends intact) and blade/lets were analysed and the results confirm observations made from the cores. Table 27 shows that the flakes and blade/lets can be summarised as elongated in plan with narrow plain or linear butts, some of which were strengthened by platform abrasion. The butt width was usually insufficient to permit measurement of the flaking angle. Flakes with a squat or broad plan correspond to core rejuvenation tablets or partially cortical trimming flakes. Approximately 70% of the sample measures less than 40 mm in length and 30 mm in breadth, which corresponds to the final blade/let lengths on the cores. Residual scars on the dorsal surfaces of analysed artefacts confirm that both single platform and opposed platform cores were used for blade/let production. Truncated scars orientated at right-angles to the axis of percussion have been interpreted as indicators of cresting, and some of the flakes have been regarded as the products of this process. The large proportion of broken blade/lets and the absence of complete refitting sequences suggests that unbroken blade/lets were taken away for use as tools. Areas of residual cortex are rare, which implies that core preparation may not have taken place at site.

Retouched material
Three obliquely blunted points, two retouched blade/lets, and two microburins were found in the hollow. Five of these items were recovered from sieved samples. The obliquely blunted points include one example which was supported on an anvil and flaked at the proximal end using abrupt retouch. The remaining examples, which include one with a transverse truncated base, are both broken and are pointed at the distal end. This may have been due to impact fracture. The microburins comprise one of the proximal end and one of the distal end.

Unstratified material
The unstratified collection includes blade/lets which are clearly contemporary with those from the hollow. Attributes here include refitting pieces, soft hammer mode, blade/let cores, and platform abrasion. However, Table 26 shows that blade/lets and broken blade/lets account for only 16% of the collection. The majority consists of flakes which include some heavily patinated examples and others with post-depositional edge damage. The visual scan has shown that the flakes are both larger and more robust than the stratified examples.

The retouched pieces show a similar variation in condition and patination. Most pieces are unpatinated and are in mint condition. They include an obliquely truncated blade, a notched bladelet, and an end scraper made on the proximal end of a flake using direct, irregular retouch. However, an end scraper made on a large flake is heavily patinated, and much of the retouch has been removed by subsequent edge damage.

Other finds
The presence of other materials, such as burnt clay, and copper alloy fragments (details in archive), does not necessarily preclude a Mesolithic date for the feature; there is a strong likelihood that intrusive material had become incorporated in the upper fill of the hollow via the topsoil. For this reason it was decided not to amalgamate the charcoal recovered from sieving in an attempt to obtain a radiocarbon date.

Other Features

Two post-holes, 6 and 7, were recorded in trench C immediately south of, but not apparently associated with, the hollow (Fig. 41). The post-holes were both 0.21 m in diameter and 0.12 m (6) and 0.25 m (7) deep. Both were filled with dark brown silty sand, and post-hole 6 also contained fragments of charcoal, fired clay, and burnt flint. It is possible that they were connected with the complex of features recorded to the south in Area X West.

Area X West

The excavation trench in Area X West (Fig. 42) comprised approximately 3,900 m², extending from trench J eastwards to trench B and encompassing trench K.

Topsoil was removed by machine to expose gravel over the northern part of the trench, that is toward the apex of the ridge, but to the south the gravel dipped beneath deepening deposits of pale yellow sandy silt. All features were planned (Fig. 42), most were half-sectioned. Features occurred mainly in the northern and eastern part of the trench and fell into four categories:

i.   One Late Neolithic pit.
ii.   Two later prehistoric, probably Late Iron Age, features.
iii. A group of Late Iron Age/ Romano-British pits and possibly related post-holes.
iv.   A group of soil-filled hollows in the gravel, some, but not all, containing knapped or burnt flint. These features otherwise showed no clear evidence of having been deliberately dug.

Few of the features were very closely datable; all of those for which dates have been suggested lay in the eastern part of the trench. Details of all excavated features in Area X West are summarised in Table 28.

Late Neolithic pit 1518

The single Late Neolithic pit, 1518, lay at the northern edge of Area X West (Figs 42 and 43). The feature was filled with dark brown silty soil, in which sherds of three vessels were found during excavation (*see* below); a few additional sherds were recovered during general cleaning of the surrounding area. Other finds associated with the pit included burnt flint and knapped flints.

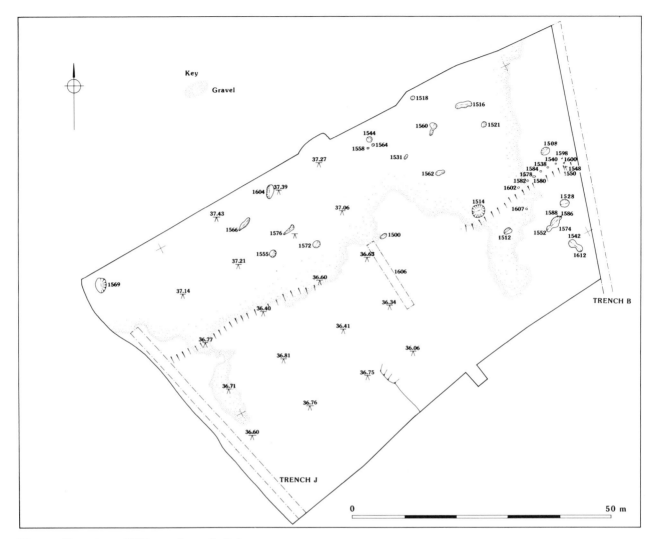

Figure 42   Area X West: plan of all features

Later Prehistoric Pits 1508 and 1516

Two 'later prehistoric' features, pits 1508 and 1516, were identified (Figs 42 and 43). Both are possibly of Late Iron Age date. They lay to the north of a cluster of features with which they may have been associated and which, where datable, proved to be of Late Iron Age/Romano-British date.

Few finds were found in pit 1508 but amongst those which were were three iron objects, one a knife blade (*see* below). Although the base of the pit had silted up naturally, the upper levels, from which the iron objects came and which also contained much charcoal and animal bone, had been deliberately backfilled. The pit was cut into the sandy silt above gravel and may have had four stake-holes cut into its northern edge; the pit was only half-sectioned, however, and the presence of stake-holes around the whole circumference was not established.

Pit 1516 had very poorly defined edges. It was probably cut into a natural silty loam-filled depression in the gravel and was filled with very similar material. This feature may perhaps have belonged to the fourth group of 'natural' features listed above; it has been included

here by virtue of the number and type of finds recovered from it.

Late Iron Age/Romano-British Features

Features of the third group were confined to the south-eastern corner of Area X West (Fig. 44).

Few of the excavated features have been very precisely dated, a broad date range of Late Iron Age/Romano-British has been suggested for pits 1514, 1528 and 1574, and for pit complex 1542/1612 (Figs 44 and 45). The other features within the group have been assigned to it on the basis of their relative proximity.

Pit 1514 and pit group 1542/1612, the deepest features of this group, both contained preserved worked wood, *in situ* in the latter but not certainly so in the former.

Pit 1514 was cut into the gravel to a depth of depth of 2.15 m, the lowest 0.5 m of which remained wet throughout excavation despite the site pumping operation, which had by then been in progress for some months. The pit was predominantly filled with homogeneous silty clay, the wood, all oak (identification by R.

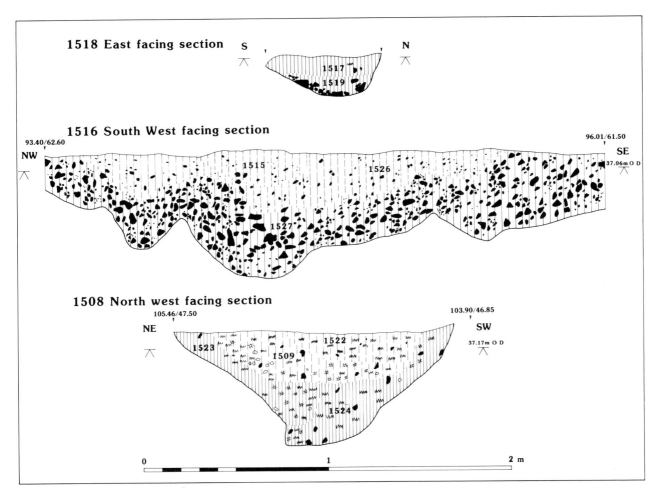

Figure 43   Area X West: section of features 1508, 1516, and 1518

Gale), being found just above the base. Two thin, plank-like timbers were butted against each other to form a right-angle with approximately northern and eastern sides. A larger tapering timber (Fig. 45: 1627) lay across the centre of the pit just below the two planks, parallel with the eastern one and not extending beyond the northern one, and may have been held in position by a vertical stake at its northern side. An iron plough-share tip was also found near the base of the pit and may originally have been attached to the wood, the whole possibly having been thrown into the pit as rubbish.

Pit complex 1542/1612 was composed of a deep conical southern section (1612) connected with, or perhaps cut by, a broader shallower feature (1542) to the north. Most of the wood was found in 1612; three vertical stakes, two rounded (one hazel, one unidentifiable) and one squared (oak), held in position an oak plank set on edge lengthways, above which lay a second horizontal timber, a roughly squared beam of poplar/willow. Immediately north of the upper timber, at the same level as its top surface and approximately parallel with it, were four smaller cut stakes (three of hazel, one of alder/oak) lying horizontally. None of the vertical timbers appeared to have been eroded or truncated; they, the top of the plank and the smaller horizontal pieces all lay only a little below the base of pit 1542. Set into the base of 1542 were two upright stakes of unidentified species (Fig. 44:

1615 and 1616) aligned approximately on the centre of the higher horizontal timber in 1612 and approximately 0.55 m and 0.9 m away from it respectively. The upper levels of both 1542 and 1612 were filled with heavily charcoal-flecked clay loam, beneath which were lighter coloured sandy silts. Fired clay, fragments of ceramic building material, pottery, and a worked bone needle were recovered from 1542. 1542 was only half-sectioned, but almost the whole of 1612 was excavated to allow the wood to be removed.

The only other features from which datable finds were recovered were pits 1528 and 1574 (Figs 44 and 45), both of which contained pieces of slag, fired clay, and ceramic building material in addition to sherds of Romano-British (pit 1528) and Iron Age (pit 1574) pottery; also found in 1574 were part of a pair of copper alloy tongs and a single iron nail. Two post-holes, 1586 and 1588, approximately 0.25 m apart, lay within 0.4 m of the north-eastern edge of 1574 and may have been associated with it. Pit 1512 contained no pottery, but fired clay and slag were recovered from it.

Twelve post-holes were excavated within the area of the pits described above (Fig. 45). Two of the 12 superseded earlier versions: 1548 replaced 1550 and 1578 replaced 1580. Eleven of the post-holes may have formed the northern (longer) and eastern sides of a rectangular building, at least 10.5 x 2.5 m in area. A single isolated

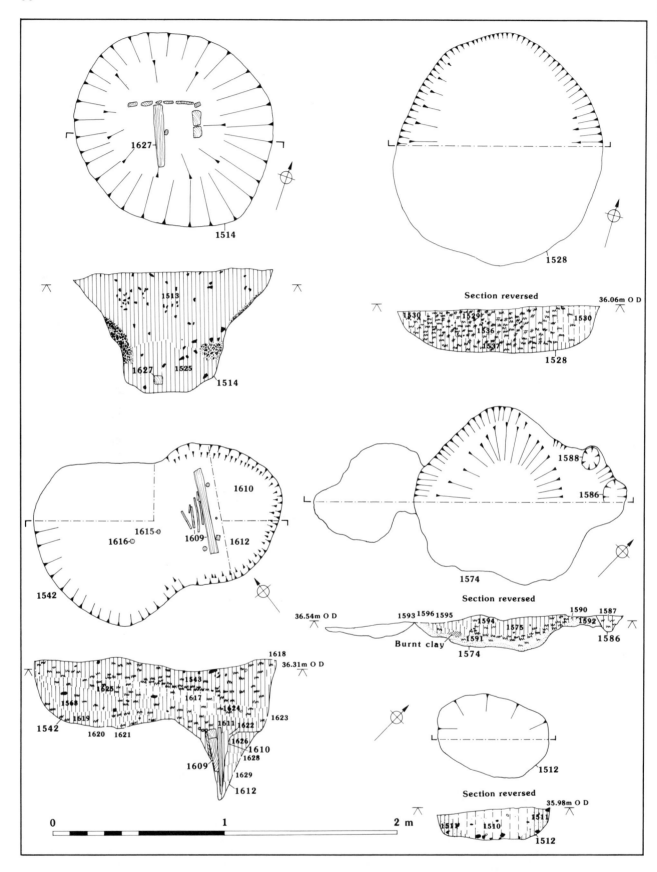

Figure 44   Area X West: plans and sections of Late Iron Age / Romano-British features

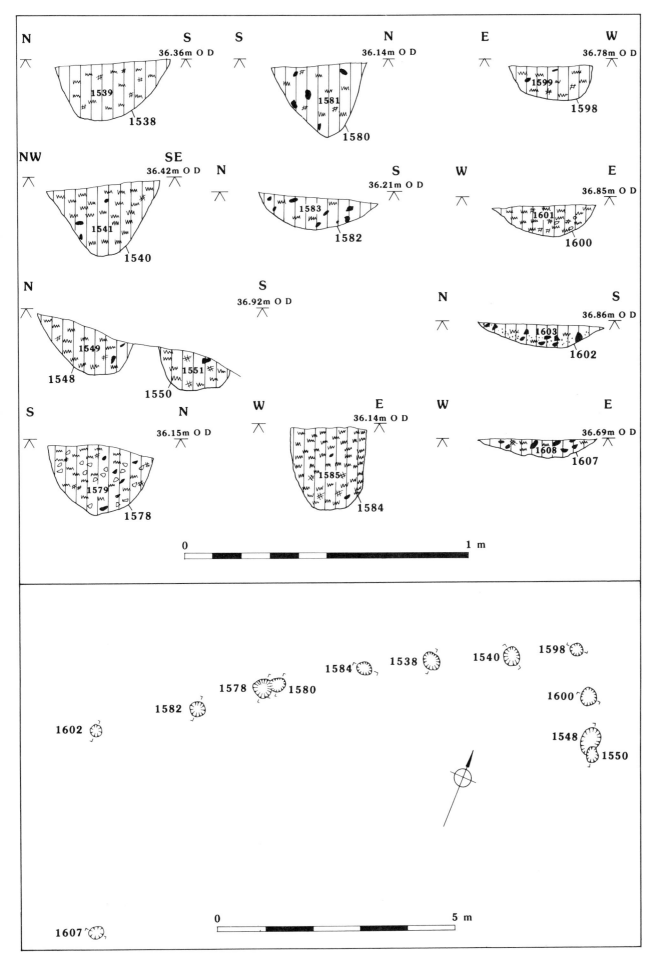

Figure 45   Area X West: plan and sections of post-holes forming a possible structure

Table 28 Area X West: summary of excavated features

Feature	Date	Type	Shape	Profile	Length (m)	Width (m)	Diameter (m)	Depth (m)
1518	Neolithic	pit	ovoid	'U'-shaped	0.63	0.58	–	0.15
1508	LIA	pit	sub-circular	irregular	–	–	1.50	0.67
1516	LIA	pit	irregular	irregular	3.10	1.00	–	0.69
1514	L IA/RB	pit	sub-circular	conical	2.15	2.07	–	1.33
1528	LAI/RB	pit	circular	'U'-shaped	–	–	2.00	0.55
1542	LIA/RB	pit	ovoid	'U'-shaped	2.80	2.0	–	0.80
1574	LIA/RB	pit	irregular	irregular	2.32	1.97	–	0.38
1612	LIA/RB	pit	circular	'V'-shaped	–	–	1.30	1.80
1500	undated	hollow	ovoid	shallow 'U'	2.10	0.70	–	0.20
1512	undated	pit	ovoid	'U'-shaped	1.40	1.00	–	0.30
1521	undated	hollow	ovoid	shallow 'U'	1.10	0.65	–	0.10
1531	undated	hollow	ovoid	shallow 'V'	1.10	0.60	–	0.20
1538	undated	post-hole	circular	'U'-shaped	–	–	0.40	0.19
1540	undated	post-hole	circular	'U'-shaped	–	–	0.40	0.25
1544	undated	hollow	ovoid	shallow 'U'	1.28	1.00	–	0.14
1548	undated	post-hole	circular	'U'-shaped	–	–	0.30	0.17
1550	undated	post-hole	circular	'U'-shaped	–	–	0.15	0.12
1552	undated	hollow	ovoid	shallow 'U'	1.32	0.98	–	0.13
1555	undated	hollow	sub-rect.	shallow 'U'	1.50	1.40	–	0.46
1558	undated	post-hole	ovoid	'U'-shaped	0.29	0.20	–	0.17
1560	undated	hollow	irregular	shallow 'V'	1.50	0.85	–	0.42
1562	undated	post-hole	circular	'U'-shaped	–	–	0.42	0.11
1564	undated	post-hole	ovoid	shallow 'U'	0.56	0.52	–	0.07
1566	undated	hollow	irregular	irregular	2.80	1.00	–	0.25
1569	undated	pit	ovoid	'U'-shaped	3.00	2.25	–	0.73
1572	undated	hollow	circular	shallow 'U'	–	–	1.20	0.14
1576	undated	hollow	irregular	irregular	1.60	0.80	–	0.23
1578	undated	post-hole	circular	'U'-shaped	–	–	0.36	0.22
1580	undated	post-hole	circular	'U'-shaped	–	–	0.28	0.26
1582	undated	post-hole	circular	shallow 'U'	–	–	0.36	0.10
1584	undated	post-hole	circular	'U' -shaped	–	–	0.22	0.28
1586	undated	post-hole	circular	'U'-shaped	–	–	0.26	0.15
1588	undated	post-hole	circular	'U'-shaped	–	–	0.28	0.18
1598	undated	post-hole	circular	'U'-shaped	–	–	0.30	0.14
1600	undated	post-hole	circular	'U'-shaped	–	–	0.33	0.12
1602	undated	post-hole	circular	'U'-shaped	–	–	0.38	0.08
1604	undated	hollow	ovoid	'V'-shaped	2.80	1.40	–	0.44
1607	undated	post-hole	circular	shallow 'U'	–	–	0.35	0.03

LIA = Late Iron Age; RB = Romano-British

post-hole, 1607, lay approximately 4 m south of the main group (Fig. 45). The post-holes were between 0.15 m and 0.4 m in diameter and 0.03 m and 0.28 m deep, all were filled with slightly darker sandy silt than that through which they were cut. None contained any useful dating evidence but may possibly be considered to be contemporary with the Late Iron Age/Romano-British pit group.

Soil-filled hollows

The eleven features of the fourth category, those of uncertain origin, were all in the higher, gravelly part of the trench. They were often quite regular in plan and profile, usually filled with dark yellowish–brown silty clay, but contained no finds other than a few knapped or burnt flints. These features may well be of natural origin.

Metalwork, by Rachael Seager Smith

Copper alloy objects

Only one identifiable copper alloy object was found: one 'arm' of a pair of tongs (Fig. 46: 1), with a slightly inturned, leaf-shaped blade from the upper layer (1575) of pit 1574 in Area X West. The date of this object remains unknown, as no published parallels have been found, although sherds from a round-bodied jar of Middle–Late Iron Age date were also found in this context. Numerous tiny fragments, thought to be of copper alloy, were also recovered during the wet sieving of the fills of feature 3 in trench C, but these were thought to be intrusive in disturbed upper deposits.

Illustrated object (Fig. 46: 1)
1.   Fragment of copper alloy tongs. SF117, context 1575, pit 1574.

Iron objects

Five iron objects were recovered, all from Area X West. All the items were subjected to X-ray examination but no conservation has been undertaken. None of the items appear to be closely datable. Three objects, an unidentifiable fragment, a rod and a knife, were recovered from pit 1508. The knife (Fig. 46: 2), tanged with a leaf-shaped blade, is comparable to Manning's type 5 knives (1985, fig. 28, 5), dated to the 2nd century AD, but his example has a well-preserved, decorated bone handle and may therefore be of later date. A single nail was found in pit 1574, while a plough-share tip (Fig. 46: 3) was recovered from pit 1514. Although likely to be of Late Iron Age or Romano-British date, the precise date range of this object is uncertain for, although broadly similar examples occur in an Iron Age context at Hunsbury, Northampton (Rees 1981, fig. 9, b) and in a Ceramic Phase 7 (c. 300–100 BC) and an unphased post-hole at Danebury (Sellwood 1984, fig. 7, no. 14; Poole and Cunliffe 1991, illus. 2.207, 351), the floodplain example is considerably larger and heavier than might normally be expected for the Iron Age (Rees 1981, 12). Heavier, broad spade-shaped share tips with wide curving ends are, however, known from Romano-British contexts, such as the 1st–2nd century AD. example from Blackburn Mill (Rees 1981, 12, fig. 11, c), although these items are not common finds. Unfortunately, the only other datable material recovered from this feature, the pottery, could be of either Iron Age or Saxon date.

Illustrated objects (Fig. 46)
2.   Iron knife with leaf-shaped blade. SF202, context 1509, pit 1508.
3.   Tip of iron plough share. SF200, context 1525, pit 1514.

Pottery, by Rachael Seager Smith and Rosamund M.J. Cleal

A small ceramic assemblage comprising 196 sherds (721 g) was recovered from the floodplain excavations, and a further 58 g was recovered during the sieving of samples. This material ranges in date from the later Neolithic Peterborough Ware to a sherd of post-medieval glazed coarseware.

The pottery has been recorded using the same system as for the larger assemblage recovered from the terrace excavations (*see* above), and where possible, fabric types have been matched with the latter assemblage. Seven broad fabric groups were identified. Groups A–E correspond to the fabric groups present in the terrace assemblage, while sherds of limestone (Group F) and organic-tempered fabrics (Group G) were also recorded. All fabrics were examined using a binocular microscope (x20 magnification).

Earlier prehistoric pottery

A small assemblage of prehistoric pottery, comprising 123 sherds (weighing 310 g) was recovered from the excavation of feature 1518 in Area X West, and a further 58 g of pottery was later extracted from the sieving of sample 168 from this feature. All this pottery is likely to be of later Neolithic date, and to belong to the Peterborough tradition. Pottery fabric totals are given in Table 29.

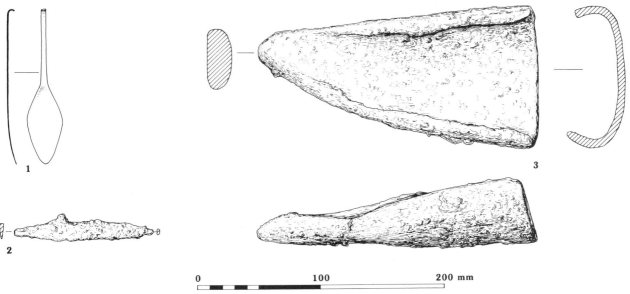

0   100   200 mm

Figure 46   Area X West: metalwork

Fabrics

Three fabrics were identified, and are described below. Terms used to describe the frequency of inclusions are defined as follows: rare (1–3%); sparse (3–10%); moderate (10–20%); common (20–30%).

D19 Soft fabric with a smooth feel and a hackly fracture. Contains: flint; moderate to common, ill-sorted (<8 mm, most <6 mm), sub-angular, unevenly distributed; quartz sand — moderate, well-sorted (<0.5 mm), rounded, evenly distributed; mica: sparse, well-sorted (<0.25 mm), plate-like, evenly distributed; iron oxides: sparse, well-sorted (<1 mm), rounded, unevenly distributed. Exterior surfaces generally oxidised (orange), core and interior surfaces unoxidised (black).
Diagnostic material: no decorated sherds, but one sherd angle from a flattened base.

D20 Hard fabric (not easily scratched with the fingernail) with a soapy feel and a laminated fracture. Contains: flint: rare, well-sorted (<2 mm), angular; quartz sand: rare, well-sorted (<0.5 mm), rounded, unevenly distributed. Exterior surfaces abraded, core and interior unoxidised (dark grey).
Diagnostic material: two sherds with traces of incised lattice.

C19 Soft fabric with a smooth feel and a hackly fracture. Contains: grog: sparse to moderate, ill-sorted (<7 mm, most <4 mm), sub-rounded to sub-angular, unevenly distributed; flint: rare to sparse, well-sorted (<3 mm), sub-angular, unevenly distributed; iron oxides: rare, well-sorted (<1 mm); mica: rare, fine (unmeasurable, less than 0.25 mm); quartz sand: sparse, well-sorted (c. 0.25 mm–0.5 mm), rounded, evenly distributed. Exterior surfaces oxidised (orange to orange–red), core and interior surfaces oxidised, partially oxidised, or unoxidised (orange, pale brown, grey).
Diagnostic material: sherds with twisted cord decoration.

Form and decoration

None of the featured sherds are illustrated, as the decorated and carinated sherds were too small for this to be practical, and the flattened base angle sherd shows only a very little of the profile. Although Peterborough Ware bowls of the Mortlake and Ebbsfleet sub-styles are generally round-bottomed, it is not uncommon for the base to be slightly flattened; this is almost certainly a result of the pot having been rested upright while drying, if not also during manufacture, so that the considerable weight of the vessel causes some flattening of the base. The presence of two small carinated sherds demonstrates that the usual form of hemispherical bowl with carinated shoulder is present in the assemblage.

The only sherd with clear decoration is a small worn body sherd in fabric C19 which has a single length of 'S'-twisted cord impression (ie made with an 'Z'-twisted cord); one other sherd may also have twisted cord impressions (*see* Catalogue, below). Two small sherds of fabric D20 show traces of very abraded incised lattice decoration.

Discussion

Three vessels appear to be represented in the assemblage, although only by a very small proportion of each. Two are certainly Peterborough Ware, one each in

Table 29 earlier prehistoric pottery from pit 1518 in Area X West

Context	Fabric F1	F2	G1
1517	18/130	–	33/16
1519	–	2/4	61/36
1534 (cleaning over 1518)	6/121	–	3/3
Total	24/251	2/4	97/55
Sieved sample*	58 g	–	–

Quantities are given by number/weight in grams
* pottery from sieved sample not counted as it comprises extremely small sherds and fragments

fabrics D19 and C19. That in fabric D19 must, on the basis of the flattened (ie rather than flat) base belong to the Mortlake or Ebbsfleet sub-styles. The coarseness of fabric D19 also suggests that the former is slightly more likely to be correct than the latter (Smith 1965, 74). The profile of the lower body of this vessel is likely to be similar to that of P15 and P22 at West Kennet, both of which are Mortlake Ware (Piggott 1962, 33, fig. 12). The single sherd with certain twisted cord impression, and the sherd with possible twisted cord decoration, are in the grog-tempered fabric C19. This vessel also belongs to either the Mortlake or Ebbsfleet sub-styles. The two sherds with traces of incised lattice decoration are in a fabric not typical of the later Neolithic, although the firing and decoration could easily be accommodated in the Peterborough tradition. Lattice is a common motif on Beakers, but the fabric would be as unusual in that tradition as in Peterborough Ware. Such decoration does occur on Peterborough Ware, especially in the Ebbsfleet sub-style (eg at Green Howe, Yorkshire, Wood 1971, fig. 4: 1–2). On balance, an attribution to the Peterborough tradition seems reasonable, even for these two sherds, as the decoration is acceptable, although the fabric is unusual. There is no evidence from the feature of later intrusion. Peterborough Ware, although well represented in the lower and upper Thames Valley, appears scarce in the middle reaches, in spite of the extensive gravel working which has brought finds of other periods to light. However, although there are no large concentrations of material, the number of find-spots is slowly increasing, and it is becoming clear that there was a presence of users of Peterborough Ware, although not on the scale of, for instance, the area around Oxford, or the Staines/Runnymede area. Finds near Reading include part of a single Mortlake Ware vessel from Field Farm, Burghfield (Mepham 1992) and sherds of several Peterborough Ware vessels (of Mortlake Ware and possibly Ebbsfleet Ware) from Englefield (Cleal 1991–3).

Catalogue

The sherds may be assigned to the following vessels. It should be noted that this is an estimate of minimum number of vessels, and more may be represented.

Table 30 later prehistoric and Romano-British pottery from the floodplain

Trench	Feature	Fabric	No. sherds	Weight (g)	Date
B	unstratified	B26	2	12	? Late Bronze Age/Iron Age
		B27	1	3	Post-medieval glazed coarseware
C	hollow (3)	D7	1	1	Late Iron Age/Romano-British?
		E2	2	2	Late Bronze Age
	unstratified	A6	3	3	240–400+ AD
		B5/B6	11	59	Romano-British
		B6	2	3	Romano-British
		C17	4	10	? later prehistoric
X East	hearth 261	C8	6	2	Probabably Romano-British
		D7	6	1	Late Iron Age/Romano-British
	channel 235	C9	1	3	Romano-British
	channel 244	B7	1	7	Middle–Late Iron Age
X West	pit 1508	F1	1	2	? later prehistoric
	pit 1514	G1	1	9	Rim — Iron Age or Saxon
	pit 1516	C18	1	2	Decorated — later prehistoric
		C18	14	23	Later prehistoric
	pit 1528	B27	1	4	Romano-British
	pit 1542	B5	2	3	Romano-British
	pit 1574	F2	4	84	Middle–Late Iron Age
	unstratified	D7	9	178	Late Iron Age/Romano-British
Total			73	411	

Vessel 1 represented by the 24 sherds and fragments of fabric D19, and the sherds and fragments recovered from sieving (not counted). Featured sherds: one thick sherd (interior surface missing, but at least 20 mm thick at the angle) from the base angle of a vessel with a rounded base which has become slightly flattened; one small body sherd with impressions (one linear c. 10 x 2 mm, two irregular in outline); two small sherds with rounded carinations, probably shoulder angles.

Vessel 2 represented by the 97 sherds and fragments (most very small) in fabric C19. Featured sherds: one small body sherd with one line of twisted cord impression; on very worn sherd probably showing one line of twisted cord impression, or possibly more.

Vessel 3 represented by two very worn body sherds with traces of incised lattice decoration.

Later Pottery
The late prehistoric, Romano-British and later pottery assemblage comprises 73 sherds (411 g), including the material recovered from sieved samples. The majority of sherds were recovered from the pits in Area X West, although small numbers of sherds were also found in Area X East and trenches B and C. Although small, the majority of sherds are in a fairly fresh, unabraded condition. A breakdown by distribution and fabric is given in Table 30.

Fabrics
Examples of each of the major fabric groups noted above occur among this material and 16 separate fabric types were identified. The majority of fabrics present conform

to those previously described from the terrace-area excavations (for fabric descriptions, see above). Additional fabric types identified are described below. Terms used to describe the frequency of inclusions are defined as follows: rare (1–3%); sparse (3–10%); moderate (10–20%); common (20–30%). Pottery fabric totals are given in Table 30.

Fabric group B: coarse sandy wares
B26 Irregularly fired, poorly-wedged fabric containing fine quartz sand.
Date range: later prehistoric — probably Late Bronze/Iron Age.
B27 Hard, sandy, fabric containing moderately coarse quartz grains and occasional pieces of grog.
Date range: uncertain — probably Romano-British.
B28 Hard, pale buff, sandy fabric; light olive green glaze on internal surface.
Date range: post-medieval.

Fabric group C: grog-tempered wares
C18 Dark brown, grog-tempered fabric; soft, soapy texture.
Date range: probably 1st century AD.

Fabric group E: shell-tempered fabrics
E2 Variably fired, iron-rich fabric containing approximately equal amounts of finely crushed shell and quartz sand with occasional limestone fragments.
Date range: ?Late Bronze Age

Fabric group F: limestone-tempered fabrics
F1 Soft, iron-rich fabric with coarse limestone and fine quartz inclusions.
Date range: uncertain — ?later prehistoric.

F2   Hard, unoxidised fabric containing approximately equal amounts of fairly coarse limestone and quartz inclusions; inclusions tend to be clustered and rather patchy.
Date range: probably Middle–Late Iron Age.

Fabric Group G: organic-tempered fabrics
G1   Hard, unoxidised, hand-made fabric containing large quantities of vegetable matter.
Date range: uncertain — could be either Iron Age or Saxon.

Forms
Although the bulk of the assemblage is composed of featureless body sherds, the form of two vessels could be determined. The first of these, a rim sherd in the vegetable-tempered fabric G1, is from a small, slack shouldered jar with a very slightly everted rim which was found in context 1525, pit 1514. The date range of this vessel is uncertain for, although similar vessels occur in fabrics containing a small proportion of organic temper as at Riseley Farm, for example (Lobb and Morris 1994, type 13, mf.21), the quantity of temper present in this sherd is more indicative of a Saxon date to which this rather unspecific vessel form would be equally appropriate. The second vessel, represented by joining body sherds in the limestone-tempered fabric F2, from contexts 1575 and 1592, pit 1574, is a small round-bodied jar which is probably of Middle–Late Iron Age date.

Surface treatments and decoration
Although some sherds show traces of rough smoothing on the external surface, such as those of fabrics F2 and G1, comparatively few signs of surface finish were observed.

The typically Roman techniques of slipping and burnishing occur on sherds of fabrics B5 and B6, while the only glazed sherd is that of post-medieval date (fabric B28) from trench B. One sherd with parallel incised grooves, in the grog-tempered fabric C18, occurred in context 1515, pit 1516.

Discussion
The quantification and distribution of the pottery recovered are summarised in Table 30; this includes the small number of sherds from other areas of the floodplain. Although the small sherd size and lack of featured sherds hamper the precise dating of the assemblage, the bulk of the material appears to be of Iron Age or Romano-British date. The wide range of fabric types present are broadly comparable with those recovered elsewhere within the Thames Valley Park development area (*see* above) as well as at other sites within the region as a whole (De Roche 1978; Lambrick 1979; Lobb and Morris 1994; Rees in prep), although the majority are probably of fairly local origin. Although the small size of this assemblage invalidates the discussion of the proportions of the various fabrics, it is interesting to note the presence of the shell- and limestone-tempered fabrics (Fabric Groups E and F — 7 sherds 88 g) at this site, as the calcareous fabrics were very poorly represented amongst the assemblage from the Late Iron Age/Romano-British enclosure on the terrace.

Other Finds, by I. Barnes and Rachael Seager Smith

A quantity of other material was recovered. This includes 3010 g of metalworking slag, all from the Late Iron Age/Romano-British pits in Area X West. This material is highly vesicular and has an agglomerated appearance caused by the presence of large lumps of unmelted metal. It is probable that it represents fragments of hearth bottom formed during iron smithing (McDonnell 1983).

Twelve pieces (1312 g) of ceramic building material, again mostly from the pits in Area X West, were recovered. Only one fragment from pit 1514, with incised keying on one surface can be definitely assigned to a Romano-British date. In addition, 448 pieces (951 g) of fired clay were recovered. These were predominantly from features in Area X West, although ten pieces (20 g) were recovered from the fill of engineer's trench 3015 in Area Y and 62 pieces (216 g) came from the river channels in Area X East. Comparison of this material with that recovered from the Iron Age and Romano-British enclosure (*see* above) shows little similarity of fabrics. Eleven pieces of daub with preserved withy impressions were recognised, one fragment from river channel 244 in Area X East, eight from pit 1542 and two from pit 1574. All these pieces occurred in the single pale brownish–buff calcareous, iron-rich fabric containing sparse (<7%) quartz sand, moderate (10–15%) limestone fragments, and occasional red iron oxides.

Two fragments (22 g), of clay pipe bowls were recovered. One (trench B) is of a DUA type 25 (Groves 1984, 2), the standard type in southern England during the first half of the 18th century, and the second (trench C), is DUA type 15 (Groves 1984, 2) dated *c.* 1660–1680.

A worked bone needle was found in pit 1542 in Area X West. It is worked on a pig fibula with a circular perforation at the proximal end and a polished shank. Such needles are not closely datable, occurring from the Late Bronze/Early Iron Age (Seager Smith in prep) into the medieval period (MacGregor 1985) at least. The presence of small quantities of Romano-British pottery in this feature may indicate a similar date for this object.

Channels and Related Features in Areas X East and Z

Small Channels

During the contractors' excavations in the northern part of Area X East, the courses of six former stream or river channels were exposed in section (Fig. 47: 224, 225, 230, 235, and 240). All were quickly recorded but it was not possible to examine them in detail. All the channels appeared to be similarly orientated from south-west to north-east, but this apparent uniformity may have been the result of their being viewed once in section only. The channels ranged in size from 1.6 m wide and 1.1 m deep (230) to over 4.4 m wide and 1.63 m deep (240), but not all were well-defined. At least one channel (230) and possibly a second (229) may have been

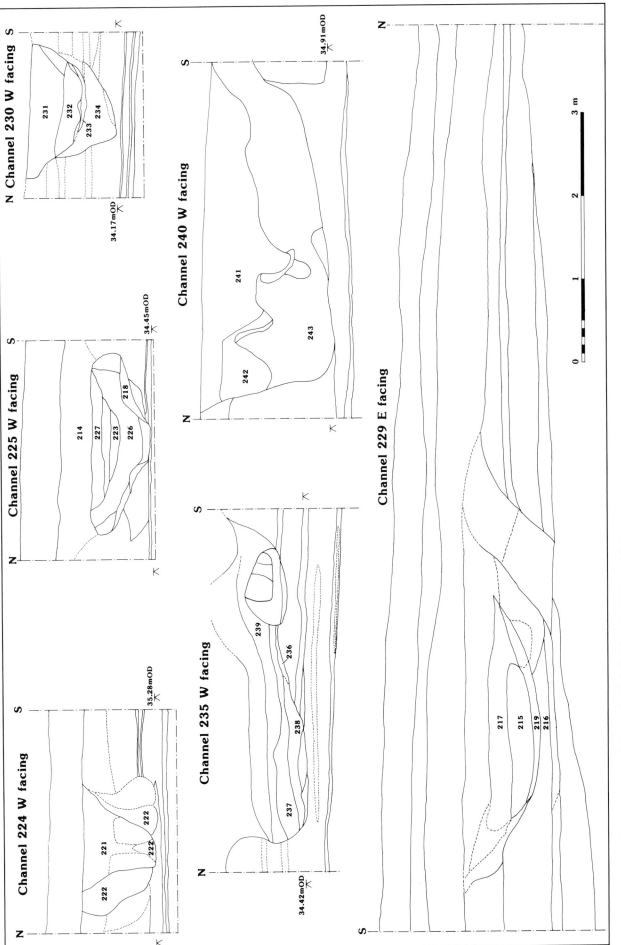

Figure 47 Area X East: sections of channels 224–5, 229–30, 235, and 240

94

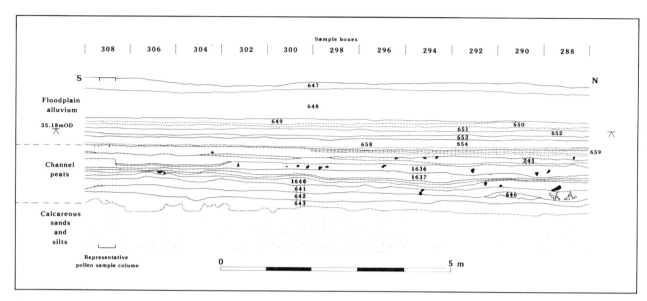

Figure 48   Channel 244: representative section

Sample boxes
| 308 | 306 | 304 | 302 | 300 | 298 | 296 | 294 | 292 | 290 | 288 |

S ... N

Floodplain alluvium — 647, 648, 649
35.18mOD
651, 653, 654, 650, 652, 658, 659
Channel peats — 245, 1636, 1637, 1640, 641, 642, 643, 646

Calcareous sands and silts

Representative pollen sample column

0 ————— 5 m

S	322	320	318	316	314	312	310	308	306	304	302	300	298	296	294	292	290	288	286	284	282	280	278	276	274	272	N
	323	321	319	317	315	313	311	309	307	305	303	301	299	297	295	293	291	289	287	285	283	281	279	277	275	273	

1m² box trenches

Key: [hatched] Unexcavated

Box no: 322	318	314	312	308	306	304	302	300	296	293	292	290
Context: 484	483	478	528	477	564	608	465	574	462	458	551	400
489	496	490	548	489	569	612	475	578	474	466	560	403
510	503	493	555	495	575	613	480	580	487	471	565	411
515	517	500	558	504	582	614	485	583	492	479	567	421
527	522	505	568	514	588	615	491	630	502	486	571	423
530	533	508	570	521	590	616	494	631	507	497	576	425
544	542	513	572	531	593	618	498	632	512	501	581	431
547	552	520	587	543	596	619	506		526	511	585	437
554	561	525	589	549	599	626	509		534	518	591	442
	563	529	592	556	603	633	516		537		594	450
	566	536	597	559	625		524		538		604	
			628	562			539		545		610	
			629				540		553		611	
							546		557		623	
							550				624	

289	288	286	285	284	283	282	278	277	275	274	273	272
379	380	381	378	577	376	377	363	369	324	1322	1321	375
383	391	388	405	579	385	384	365	374	325	1323	326	345
396	395	394	438	586	392	389	366	382	329	327	328	348
410	404	402	444	595	399	398	367	386	330	330	338	351
417	415	407	453	598	406	408	370	387	343	341	340	353
424	420	416	461	600	423	412	372	390	347	357	342	358
439	434	426	470	601	418	419	422	393	355	359	344	362
449	447	435	481	602	429	428	427	397	473	360	346	364
459	455	445	519	603	432	433	430	401	482	361	349	368
467	463	456	523	604	440	441	436	409	488		350	371
475	468	464	532	605	448	446	443	414	573		354	373
	476		535	606	454	452	451				356	
				607		457	460					
				609			469					
				620								
				621								
				622								

Located on figure 43

Figure 49   Channel 244: key to sample squares in plan and section

deliberately modified. In 230, four apparently unworked bark-covered birch twigs were recorded in the base of a possible recut, lying c. 0.1–0.15 m apart and aligned with the channel. A narrow column of light grey silt in the centre of channel 229 appeared to interrupt dark grey silty loam at either side, but it was not clear whether this was the result of deliberate interference with the channel, as could have been caused by the insertion of a post. Finds associated with the channels were few, but included a single sherd of Romano-British pottery from 235 and a turned wooden lid from 225.

A further six channels were seen in section in Area Z (Fig 44: 3000–3005). These also were not examined in detail and their apparent consistency of alignment, from south-east to north-west, was again most probably caused by the angle of the section in which they were revealed. The Area Z channels were generally larger than those in Area X East, up to 6.1 m wide in the case

of 3005 (depth not established), although the smallest, 3000, was only 0.9 m wide and 0.3 m deep. There was no evidence of any adaptation of any of the channels and no finds were recovered from them.

Other channels were noted, but not recorded, running along part of the northern edge of Area Z, in the north-west face of a temporary haul road cutting south of Area Z, and to the north of Area Y, 3013.

Channel 244

At the southern end of Area X East, excavation by the contractors exposed a major river channel, crossing the floodplain from south-west to north-east. Preservation of the channel was excellent and work in the area was suspended while part of the channel was set aside for archaeological investigation.

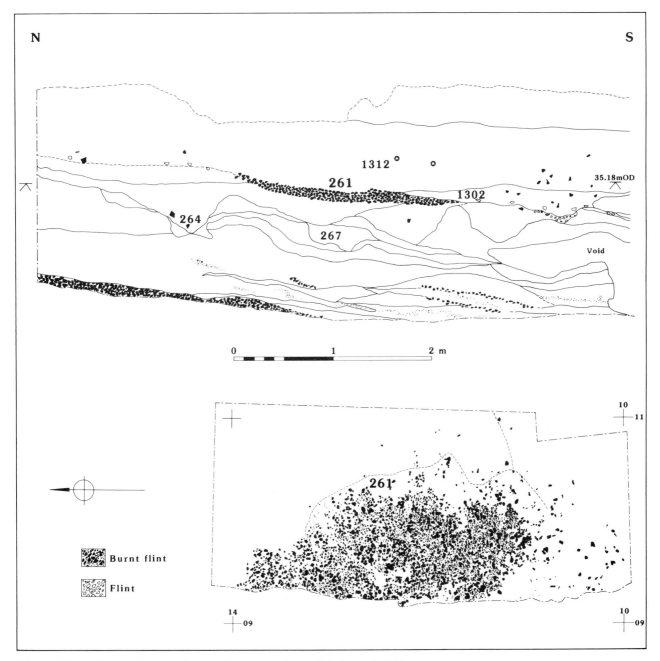

Figure 50   Channel 244: plan and section of possible hearth 261

The excavation trench provided an obliquely-angled section across the middle of the channel, at least 35 m wide at this point and 3.3 m deep (Figs 40 and 48). Up to 0.85 m of topsoil and alluvium lay above the channel, the upper third of which was filled with mainly greyish brown silts and sandy silts: the contrasting appearance of dark peaty deposits below the paler silts was the first clear sign of the channel's presence and it was to the top of these layers that much of the excavation trench was opened. Sections dug through the peaty layers, which were up to 1 m deep, disclosed the intricately-lensed blue/grey silts and greyish sands which filled the base of the channel. Well-preserved tree trunks and substantial branches had been found in the spoil removed when the machines first broke into the peat, and occasional knapped and burnt flints were noticed on the broader area subsequently exposed. None of the wood recovered from the channel during the archaeological excavation was found to have been worked (*see* below for identification). A decision was made to excavate part of the channel by hand and a strip 2 m wide and 26 m long, sub-divided into one metre squares, set out at the western side of the trench. Half of the 52 squares (Fig. 52) were excavated down through the peaty layers to the top of the 'clean' silts and sands beneath, each box being trowelled down in layers where these could be recognised, otherwise in 0.1 m spits; samples for artefact assessment were taken from each layer or spit and for pollen analysis from selected squares. For a full sediment description *see* the *Pollen* report.

A southerly extension of trenches P and Q to the west in Area Z was carried out, together with the excavation of additional trenches to the east, to define the course of the channel across the floodplain (Fig. 41). Although the channel was identified in trench P, its course was not securely established in trench Q. Its eastward course was confirmed in trench R, south of Area Y, and

suggested by observations made towards the north-eastern corner of the site. Bore-holes sunk through the fuel ash and into the underlying deposits further indicated the probable line of the channel. Once the course of the channel was known, or could at least be inferred, agreement was reached that development excavations would not encroach upon it so that it might be preserved.

At the northern edge of channel 244 was hearth 261, a series of burnt flint and charcoal deposits no more than 0.13 m deep, filling a scoop cut through the upper part of the eastern section (Fig. 50). A trench excavated down to the level of the burnt material showed that it extended in an irregular oval, *c.* 3 x 1.5 m in area (although originally larger), down the gentle slope of the channel's edge. Excavation of the burnt debris revealed that it was composed of very thin, discrete layers of charcoal, but that there was no reddening of the underlying silt to suggest that they had been burnt *in situ*. Worked flint (Table 31) was recovered from the silts directly above the burnt material and from the burnt layers themselves, as were 12 sherds (3 g) of possible Late Iron Age/Romano-British pottery. No other features were seen in the surrounding area.

Flint, by P.A. Harding

Quantities of flint recovered from channel 244 and hearth 261, as well as the rest of the floodplain with the exception of trench C, are shown in Table 31.

A diffuse spread of worked flint was found scattered within channel 244 and in and above hearth 261. This assemblage was numerically too small to allow detailed analysis, although two typologically and technologically distinct industries could be recognised (for a more detailed discussion on the characteristics of the assemblage, *see* the *Flint* report for trench C). A distinction

Table 31 quantification of worked flint from the floodplain area (except trench C)

Location	1		2	3	4	5			6			7	8	Total
	A	B				B	A	C	B	A	C			
Area X West	4	7	–	5	264	95	11	9	80	4	23	13	3	518
Area X East: channel 244	9	33	10	14	156	89	2	1	56	8	6	8	28	420
Area X East: hearth 261	–	–	–	1	44	24	2	3	19	3	7	4	2	109
Trench A	–	1	1	–	–	8	2	–	11	1	–	–	1	25
Trench B	1	1	2	–	–	10	–	–	13	4	–	1	–	32
Trench D	–	–	–	–	–	11	1	–	3	1	–	–	1	17
Trench F	–	1	–	–	–	7	–	–	5	–	–	2	–	15
Trench G	2	–	–	–	–	2	–	–	2	1	–	–	1	8
Trench H	–	–	–	–	–	2	–	2	–	–	–	–	–	4
Trench J	–	1	–	–	–	3	–	–	3	–	–	1	–	8
Trench K	1	1	–	–	–	8	3	1	9	–	1	–	–	24
Trench Y	–	–	–	–	34	1	–	–	1	–	2	1	–	39
TOTAL	17	45	13	20	498	260	21	16	202	22	39	30	36	1219

1 = cores; 2 = core fragments; 3 = debitage; 4 = chips; 5 = unbroken; 6 = broken; 7 = burnt; 8 = retouched tools
A = blade; B = flake; C = bladelets

could also be made on the basis of patination, although there was no apparent correlation between patinated/unpatinated material and the two industries.

Burnt and Foreign Stone, by Rachael Seager Smith

A total of 259 pieces (1534 g) of burnt stone was recovered. All derived from the area of the hearth associated with the upper fills of the former river channel 244 in Area X West. In addition to these, 15 pieces (1881 g) of unburnt, non-local stone were identified, none of which showed any signs of deliberate working or shaping. With the exception of one piece (37 g) from feature 3, trench C, and two pieces from pits 1574 (721 g) and 1528 (18 g), Area X West, all the stone was from the peat filled river channel 244 in Area X East. The stone types present were examined by David Beckett (Post-Graduate Research Institute for Sedimentology, Reading University). Rock types present, included Old Red Sandstone; veined quartz, probably derived from the West Country or Wales, quartzite, greensand as well as a variety of sandstones, some possibly of the Millstone Grit type. Beckett concludes that almost all the stone fragments are 'foreign' in that they do not occur naturally in the Reading area, but all are likely to have arrived by natural processes (ie carried by glaciers or river/s).

Animal Bone, by M. Iles

Ninety bones were examined from channel 244, of which 71% (64 bones) were identifiable to species. They were identified using the comparative collection at the Centre for Human Ecology, Department of Archaeology, University of Southampton.

Methods
The present ground level is at approximately 36 m O.D. and the top of channel 244 1.35 m below this (ie 34.65 m O.D.). The peat in the channel was excavated in 1 m squares and within each square by layers, where these could be distinguished, or by 0.1 m spits. In the absence of secure dating evidence, each context was correlated to the pollen and inferred dating sequence (Keith-Lucas this volume). The channel was excavated to a maximum depth of 1.5 m but no bone was recovered from a depth greater than 1.2 m. Sediments below 1.2 m were essentially calcareous sands and silts.

Bone recovered from contexts not in channel 244 are not discussed here, details can be found in archive.

Results
A summary of the assemblage retrieved from channel 244, by period, is given in Table 32. Full details can be found in archive.

Younger Dryas (Loch Lomond Stadial) (Pollen Zone TVP-2c)
The small assemblage (Table 32) from within the channel includes wild boar and *Bos* which are common in the Loch Lomond Stadial, but the presence of a sheep/goat upper molar is problematic. Sheep were not introduced

to Britain until the Neolithic in the 4th millennium BC. The possibility that the tooth comes from *Capra ibex* (ibex/goat) was considered but this is extremely unlikely due to the rarity of this taxon in the British late glacial (Grigson 1978) and to the lowland nature of this site. Moreover, distinguishing *Capra* from *Ovis* on upper molars is rarely attempted by archaeo-zoologists.

For *Sus* (pig) it was not possible to take any measurement on humerus, as described by von den Driesch, however, width and depth measurements were taken at the deltoid tuberosity. These were compared with a modern wild boar and confirm that this specimen is wild boar (*Sus scrofa ferus*) rather than domestic pig. Although this bone is considered to come from wild boar, it need not necessarily be contemporary with the date postulated for the context. Wild boar was present in Britain until the 17th century AD.

The *Bos* tibia is in an excellent state of preservation and shows no evidence of cracking indicative of shrinkage. The distal width of the *Bos* sp. tibia falls outside of the range for aurochs at Star Carr (Legge and Rowley-Conwy 1988) and modern American bison (Speth 1983) where both sexes have been measured. Instead it compares well with domestic cattle as shown by evidence from Windmill Hill (Grigson 1965).

The results from this small faunal assemblage, therefore, raise the question of the relationship between the pollen record and the faunal material excavated from that sequence in the palaeo-channel. It is possible that the peats are not as uniform as originally considered and that the sampled sequence is not fully represented here. Perhaps more likely, the integrity of the stratigraphy may require questioning. It is possible to argue that in the case of the *Ovis* and *Bos* specimens that we have intrusions from a later period. In the absence of absolute dates for these specimens, it is difficult to be certain about the true age and significance of this small sample.

Mesolithic (Pollen Zone TVP-3–TVP-4)
The majority of the assemblage (Table 32) is *Bos*, but it also includes red deer, and roe deer. Thirty five bones from one individual were recovered from trenches 304 and 306. These were in a semi-articulated state and were seen to correspond stratigraphically to the pollen assemblage zone TVP-3 which represents the transition from Late-Devensian to Flandrian and early Boreal. As such, and after consultation with the excavator, this find is considered to be of Mesolithic date. The partial skeleton (Fig. 51) is reasonably well preserved with shrinkage cracks on the ribs and vertebrae.

If the dating of the context is correct, then this individual would be expected to be aurochs (*Bos primigenius*) and not domestic cattle (*Bos taurus*). However, it is not possible to distinguish between these two species on the basis of the bones present. In order to provide some indication, the axis from the Thames Valley Park skeleton was measured and compared with specimens from Hungary and early domestic cattle from England. Even though few published measurements are recorded for axis, the specimen from Thames Valley Park is considerably smaller than the aurochs identified by Bökönyi (1972), but is larger than the range given for domestic cattle both in Hungary and Britain (Grigson

Table 32 animal bone from channel 244

Pollen Zone	Younger Dryas TVP-2c	Mesolithic TVP-3– TVP-4	Neolithic TVP-5	Bronze Age TVP-5, TVP-6b, TVP-7
Species				
Bos sp.	1	38	3	–
Cattle (*Bos taurus*	–	–	–	4
Horse (*Equus* sp.)	–	–	–	1
Pig (*Sus domesticus*)	–	–	–	1
Red deer (*Cervus elaphus*)	–	2	2	–
Roe deer (*Capreolus capreolus*)	–	1	–	–
Sheep/goat	1	–	1	8
Wild boar (*Sus scrofa ferus*)	1	–	–	–
Large mammal	1	1	1	–
Small mammal	2	1	1	2
Unidentifiable	6	10	1	–
Total	12	53	9	16

1965). Grigson (1969) gives provisional size ranges for skulls and some limb bones for both male and female aurochs in Northern Europe in post-glacial times. Sexual dimorphism is obvious in almost all measurements, with cows being smaller. There is also some overlap in size between domestic males and wild females. As the sex of this individual is unknown, it is not possible to identify it further than *Bos* sp.

The partially articulated state of the ribs and vertebrae does demonstrate that they were not redeposited within the channel by later reworking of the sediments. One rib and three vertebrae have shallow cut marks (Fig. 51) consistent with those made by a flint blade. There are no gnawing marks on these elements. The absence of the high utility limb bones suggests that this may have been a kill site; the question of which elements would be carried away from such a site was first considered by White (1952) who assumed that elements with the greatest utility or food value would be the most likely to be carried off. The presence of a few cut marks on the thoracic vertebrae suggests that this individual was indeed defleshed, although the scarcity of butchery traces indicates that processing was non-intensive. The cervical vertebrae have a slightly lower food utility than the ribs and thoracic vertebrae and average food utility values when compared to other elements in the skeleton (Speth 1983). The lack of gnaw marks may indicate that these articulated elements were rapidly buried before attracting carnivores.

One antler tine and a loose upper molar from red deer were recovered. There is evidence of deer gnawing on the tine suggesting that it comes from a shed antler.
Neolithic (Pollen Zone TVP-5)
Details of the assemblage are given in Table 32. It was not possible to measure any of the *Bos* sp. bones, but visually their size is comparable to other Neolithic domestic cattle (*Bos taurus*). One metacarpal (cattle) comes from a juvenile individual less than a year in age. Red deer is represented by one upper molar and antler

fragment. The base was missing so it was not possible to tell if the antler had been shed or was deliberately removed from a dead animal. The antler had, however, been modified, having been chopped through the beam below the ?bez tine. This is a technique commonly used in the production of antler picks at both Stonehenge and Durrington Walls (Serjeantson and Gardiner 1995) and the antler may represent waste from the production of a pick, although other uses are equally likely.

Early Bronze Age to Bronze Age/Iron Age Boundary (Pollen Zone TVP-5a, TVP-6b, and TVP-7)
Details of the assemblage are given in Table 32. Sheep/goat is the most common species in this phase and red deer is no longer represented. Horse also appears for the first time. Pollen zones TVP-5a and TVP-6b suggest that the Early Bronze Age was a period of regional woodland clearance and expansion of arable farming. TVP-7 indicates that this period of intensive agricultural activity continues until the Bronze Age/Iron Age period. Davis (1987, 180) has suggested that a decrease in hunting of wild animals 'may be linked with forest clearance, the increasing numbers of sheep, and perhaps increased farming efficiency'. The number of bones from probable Bronze Age contexts here is very small, but does not conflict with Davis' conclusion.

Conclusions
The presence of the sheep/goat tooth and the domestic cattle-sized tibia within Pollen Zone TVP-2c suggests that there was some reworking of the sediments of the palaeo-channel.

Although it is not possible to say with certainty that the partial skeleton comes from an aurochs the butchery evidence on the bones suggests that it may have been a kill site rather than that of accidental death in the palaeo-channel. It is likely that the incomplete carcase was buried rapidly and so avoided further disartic-

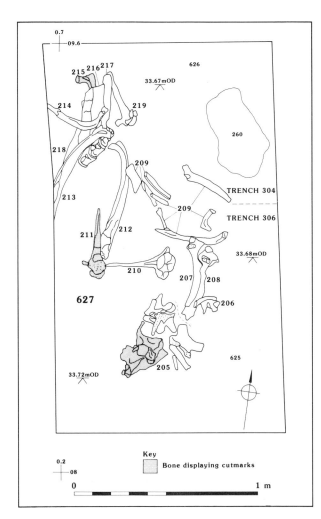

Figure 51   Channel 244: plan of semi-articulated bos sp. showing location of cut marks

ulation and gnaw damage from carnivores. It is also likely, in the absence of extensive cut marks, that there was a considerable amount of meat still left on the spinal column.

The frequent use of wild and domestic species in the Neolithic and the absence of wild species in the Bronze Age is consistent with other assemblages of this date.

Pollen, by M. Keith-Lucas (submitted October 1990)

Methods
Pollen analysis was carried out on the sediments in channel 244. Samples were collected from an exposed vertical face (Fig. 48) and prepared for pollen analysis using standard techniques (hydrofluoric acid and acetolysis).

Stratigraphy
Samples were taken to a depth of 3.6 m. From 3.6 m to 2.5 m, the sediments were essentially calcareous sands and silts. A basal clayey silt to 3.45 m, gave way to

progressively purer sand at 3.15 m, and almost pure sand from 3.15 to 2.95 m. From 2.95 m, the sediment returned to a silty sand and to a silty clay at 2.7 m. Above 2.5 m, the sediments were acid peats to 1.35 m. The basal peat was an amorphous sandy detrital peat, overlain from 2.3 m by wood peat, with branches and twigs in random orientation. At 2.12 m, a dark brown, amorphous silty peat started, penetrated by vertical root channels, and with white salts tending to crystallise out on the surface. From 1.92 m to 1.66 m, this changed to a lighter brown herbaceous silty peat with vertical orange and black roots passing through it. Worked flints were present up to 1.79 m but absent from the upper part. From 1.66 m to 1.61 m was a dark brown wood peat, and from this level to 1.44 m, a more silty light brown peat containing worked flints again. The uppermost layer of peat was a grey–brown to black amorphous silty peat containing occasional sandy lenses and animal bones. This extended to 1.35 m above which all the sediments were essentially floodplain alluvium. To 1 m, the alluvium was non-calcareous. From this level to 0.6 m, the alluvium was a calcareous grey clayey silt. An iron-rich layer began at 0.6 m and extended to about 0.2 m. The alluvium from 0.2 m to 0.1 m was gleyed, and mottled orange–brown in an otherwise grey silty clay. The top 0.1 m was a humus-rich black turf layer.

Presentation of results
The pollen diagram (Fig. 52) is presented as a 'dog tooth' diagram with open curves representing a x10 magnification of the scale. The pollen sum is total pollen and spores.

In Figure 53, some dates taken from other published sources which can be assigned to certain clearly recognisable regional vegetational changes in this pollen diagram have been plotted against the depth of the horizons to which these dates can be assigned. This gives a graph showing approximate rates of sediment accumulation in the palaeo-channel, which, although it cannot be totally accurate without a single radiocarbon date, at least shows the periods of very rapid and comparatively slow sediment accumulation.

A formal description of the local pollen assemblage zones follows, followed in turn by an interpretation of the vegetational history of the site.

Pollen assemblage zones

TVP-1 360–350 cm (Pinus–Picea)
Pinus sylvestris pollen frequencies exceed 15%. Pollen of *Juniperus communis* and *Betula nana* and Gramineae was not detected. Cyperaceae pollen frequencies exceed 25%. This zone contains the only records of *Polemonium caeruleum* and *Glaux maritima* and the only pre-clearance record of *Picea abies*.

TVP-2 350–240 cm (Juniperus–Betula nana)
Defined by the presence of *Juniperus communis* and *Betula nana* pollen, with Gramineae pollen frequencies exceeding 5%. This zone can be sub-divided into three sub-zones as follows:

TVP-2a 350–285 cm (Pinus–Cyperaceae sub-zone): *Pinus sylvestris* pollen frequencies fall below 15% but exceed 6.5% and Cyperaceae fall below 25% but exceed 13%. Pollen frequencies of Umbelliferae are also consistently high.

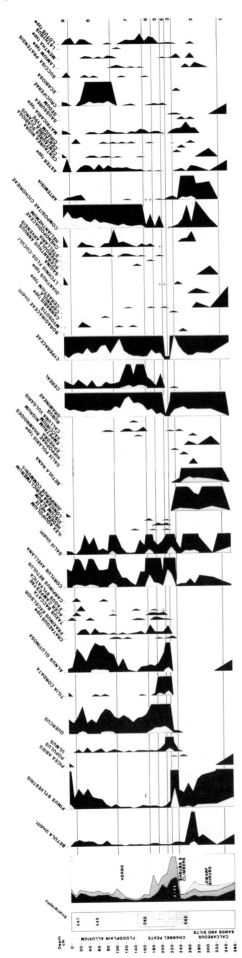

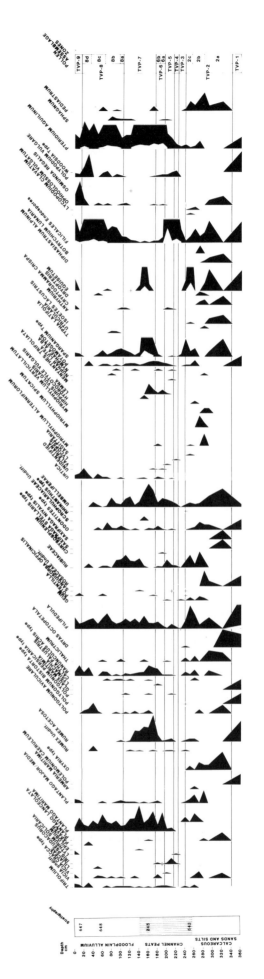

Figure 52 Channel 244: pollen diagram

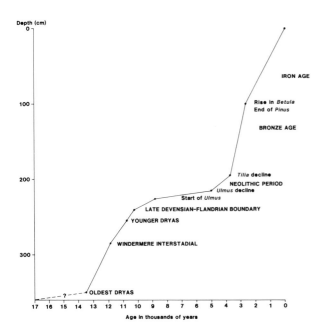

Figure 53　　Channel 244: rates of sedimentation

This sub-zone contains the only records of *Sagina*, *Saxifraga stellaris*, *S. nivalis*, and *Woodsia*-type. It also contains the only pre-clearance records of *Cerastium* and *Centaurea nigra*-type.

TVP-2b 285–255 cm (Betula–Artemisia sub-zone): *Pinus sylvestris* pollen frequencies fall to below 6.5% and *Betula* undiff. rises to more than 1.6%. *Artemisia* pollen frequencies exceed 4%, and Cyperaceae fall below 13% at the outset of this sub-zone. *Salix* undiff. pollen frequencies exceed 4%.

This sub-zone contains the only records of *Salix polaris*-type, Boraginaceae undiff., *Helianthemum*, *Saussurea*, *Centaurea* cf. *cyaneus*, *Armeria maritima*, *Hippuris vulgaris*, *Myriophyllum spicatum*, *Utricularia*, and *Botrychium lunaria*.

The following pollen spores have their last appearance during this sub-zone: *Empetrum nigrum*, *Dianthus*-type, *Rosaceae* undiff., *Myriophyllum verticillatum*, *Cryptogramma crispa* and *Diphasiastrum alpinum*. It also represents the last pre-clearance appearances of *Vaccinium*, *Lamium*-type, *Papaver*, *Polygonum aviculare*, *Nuphar lutea* and *Dryopteris*.

TVP-2c 255–240 cm (Cyperaceae–Filipendula sub-zone): *Pinus sylvestris* pollen frequencies remain at less than 6.5% while *Betula undiff.* falls to less than 1.5% and *Salix* undiff. falls to less than 4%. *Artemisia* pollen frequencies also decline to less than 4%. Cyperaceae rise in excess of 24%, and *Filipendula* above 2%.

This sub-zone contains the only records for *Ephedra*, *Campanula* and *Lycopsis* pollen. Several species missing from sub-zone TVP-2b reappear, for instance, *Polygonum bistorta* and *Dryas octopetala* at the upper zone boundary. The sub-zone ends with the last occurrences of *Juniperus communis*, *Betula nana*, *Sedum*, *Plantago maritima*, *Oxyria*-type, *Polygonum bistorta*-type, *Dryas octopetala*, *Isoetes lacustris*, *Huperzia selago*, *Lycopodium clavatum*, and *Myriophyllum alterniflorum*. It also has the last pre-clearance occurrences of *Aster* type, *Cirsium*-type, *Vicia* undiff., *Plantago media/major*, *Rumex* undiff., *Rumex acetosa*-type, *Ranunculus acris*-type, *Thalictrum*, *Potentilla*-type, *Sanguisorba*, *Odontites*-type, *Rhinanthus*-type, and *Ophioglossum vulgatum*.

TVP-3 240–225 cm (Pinus–Corylus)
Pinus sylvestris pollen percentages rise to a peak at over 45%, *Corylus avellana* to over 25% and *Salix* undiff. to over 14%.

Tilia cordata and *Alnus glutinosa* are absent from the pollen record. Pollen frequencies of Gramineae and Cyperaceae and spore frequencies of *Equisetum* decline, as do many of the tall-herb or water-edge community associates, such as *Filipendula*, Rubiaceae and Umbelliferae. Filicales endospores remain low at less than 6%. *Calluna vulgaris* makes a last pre-clearance appearance.

TVP-4 225–215 cm (Ulmus–Tilia–Alnus)
Pinus sylvestris pollen percentages fall to less than 1.5%, while *Ulmus* and *Quercus* pollen frequencies rise to more than 5%, *Tilia cordata* to more than 6%, *Alnus glutinosa* to more than 6.5%, and *Fraxinus excelsior* to more than 1.2%. *Corylus avellana* values exceed 20%, peaking at 37.5% in this zone. *Fraxinus excelsior*, *Taxus baccata*, *Ilex aquifolium*, *Hedera helix* and *Viscum album* first appear, along with Cruciferae, *Iris pseudocorus*, *Lythrum salicaria*, *Potentilla*-type and *Polypodium vulgare*. Gramineae and Cyperaceae remain low at less than 4% and 8% respectively. Filicales endospores exceed 4.6% and *Cerastium*-type reappears.

TVP-5 215–195 cm (Quercus–Tilia)
Ulmus pollen frequencies decline to less than 5%, *Fraxinus excelsior* to less than 1.2%, *Alnus glutinosa* to less than 6.5%, while *Quercus* rises to more than 12%. *Tilia cordata* frequencies remain high at more than 3.5% but *Corylus avellana* declines to less than 20%. Gramineae pollen frequencies rise to more than 4% but less than 10% and Cyperaceae rise to more than 8%, while Filicales endospore frequencies continue to rise to a peak of 34.6%.

This zone marks the only appearances of *Vicia cracca*-type and *Menyanthes trifoliata* pollen. Many species appear for the first time, namely *Fagus sylvatica*, *Acer campestre*, cereal-type (as a continuous curve), *Stellaria*, Chenopodiaceae, *Plantago lanceolata*, *Polygonum persicaria*-type, *Lemna* and *Sphagnum*.

Others reappear after disappearing at the end of zone TVP-1. These are *Aster*-type, *Trifolium*, *Rumex* undiff., *Rumex acetosa*-type, *Ranunculus acris*-type, *Thalictrum*, *Sanguisorba*, *Odontites*-type, *Nymphaea alba*, *Athryrium*, and *Ophioglossum vulgatum*.

TVP-6 195–175 cm (Quercus–Pteridium)
Tilia cordata pollen frequencies decline to less than 3.5%, dropping to zero by the end of the zone. *Quercus* remains at more than 5%. Pollen frequencies of *Fraxinus excelsior*, *Corylus avellana* and *Salix* undiff. rise to a peak at 180 cm. Gramineae rise to more than 10% but do not exceed 18%, Compositae: Cichorieae pollen frequencies do not exceed 3%, but *Plantago lanceolata* frequencies exceed 1.3%. Filicales endospore frequencies fall sharply while those of *Pteridium aquilinium* rise above 7%. This zone can be divided into two sub-zones:

TVP-6a 195–185 cm (Cyperaceae–Pteridium sub-zone): *Fraxinus excelsior*, *Corylus avellana* and *Salix* undiff. pollen frequencies remain low at less than 1.2%, 15%, and 6.5% respectively. *Quercus* pollen percentages exceed 10%, Gramineae and Cyperaceae show minor peaks, the latter exceeding 15%, and other pasture species such as Compositae, Cichorieae, *Plantago lanceolata*, *Trifolium* and *Lotus*-type also peak in this sub-zone. *Spergula arvensis* and *Chrysosplenium* are restricted to this sub-zone.

A continuous curve for Chenopodiaceae starts in this sub-zone, and *Cirsium*-type pollen reappears after an absence since the Late-Devensian (TVP-2). The decline in Filicales endospores and the rise in *Pteridium aquilinium* occurs at the outset of this sub-zone.

TVP-6b 185–175 cm (Corylus–Salix sub-zone): *Fraxinus excelsior*, *Corylus avellana* and *Salix* undiff. pollen frequencies rise to greater than 1.2%, 15%, and 6.5% respectively. *Quercus* pollen percentages fall to less than 10%. Pollen frequencies of *Gramineae* and *Cyperaceae* fall, the latter to below 15%. Cereal-type pollen increases to more than 2%, while *Compositae: Cichorieae*, *Lotus*-type, *Plantago lanceolata* and *Umbelliferae* show temporary declines.

Lysimachia and *Sagittaria* pollen is confined to this sub-zone, *Succisa pratensis* first appears in this sub-zone, *Vicia* undiff. and *Plantago media/major* reappear after an absence since TVP-2, while *Iris pseudocorus* puts in its last appearance.

TVP-7 175–105 cm (Gramineae–Cereal-type)

Quercus pollen frequencies fall below 5% except at 120 cm, *Alnus glutinosa* pollen frequencies fall below 2.2%, *Fraxinus excelsior* falls to less than 1.3%, *Corylus avellana* to less than 15% and usually less than 3.5%, and *Salix undiff.* pollen frequencies also decline. *Gramineae* rise to more than 18% and cereal-type to more than 1%. *Compositae: Cichorieae* rise to more than 4.3% but do not exceed 10%, *Aster*-type exceeds 0.4% but remains below 1%. *Cruciferae* remain at less than 6% and *Filicales* endospores at less than 1.3%. Many pollen species peak in this zone, for instance *Rumex acetosa*-type, *Ranunculus acris*-type, *Rubiaceae* and *Umbelliferae*.

This zone contains the only occurrences of *Rubus, Lathyrus, Scleranthus annuus, Hypericum, Scrophulariaceae undiff., Hydrocotyle vulgaris* and *Osmunda regalis*.

It also has the only Flandrian occurrences of *Lamium*-type and *Papaver* pollen which were present in the Late Devensian. *Myosotis* first appears in this zone, but continues beyond it, and the following reappear in this zone, after Late Devensian occurrences, and continue beyond it: *Centaurea nigra*-type, *Mentha*-type, *Polygonum aviculare* and *Caltha palustris*.

TVP-8 105–15 cm (Alnus glutinosa–Compositae: Cichorieae–Filicales)

Quercus pollen frequencies rise above 5% at the lower zone boundary, *Alnus glutinosa* rises to more than 2.2%, *Corylus avellana* to more than 3.5%, *Gramineae* fall to less than 18% and *Compositae: Cichorieae* rise to more than 10%, *Filicales* endospores rise above 1.3%. Four sub-zones were recognised in this zone, as follows:

TVP-8a 105–95 cm (Corylus–Salix–Cruciferae sub-zone): *Alnus glutinosa* pollen frequencies expand to more than 3%, *Corylus avellana* to more than 6%, and *Salix* undiff. to more than 4%. *Gramineae* decline to less than 18%, *Compositae: Cichorieae* expand to more than 10% but less than 12%, and *Cruciferae* expand to more than 6%. *Cyperaceae, Filipendula* and *Umbelliferae* show temporary declines, while *Filicales* endospore frequencies expand to a more temporary decline.

TVP-8b 95–65 cm (Quercus–Alnus–Cruciferae sub-zone): *Pinus sylvestris* pollen frequencies expand during this sub-zone but remain below 2.2%. *Quercus* percentages rise above 3%, *Alnus glutinosa* pollen frequencies rise in excess of 4%, while *Corylus avellana* pollen frequencies fall to less than 6% and *Salix* undiff. to less than 4%. *Compositae: Cichorieae* expand to more than 12%, *Cruciferae* remain high at more than 5%, *Rubiaceae and Umbelliferae* decline, *Polypodium vulgare* spores reappear in the pollen record and *Filicales* endospores expand to more than 2.4% but remain below 4%; *Pteridium aquilinium* exceeds 3.5%. *Cannabis*-type and *Typha latifolia* are restricted to this sub-zone and *Carpinus betulus* first appears.

The sub-zone marks the last occurrence of *Rumex acetosa*-type, *Caltha palustris, Nymphaea alba* and *Pediastrum*, and the reappearance, but last appearance, of *Nuphar lutea*.

TVP-8c 65–35 cm (Corylus–Salix–Cruciferae–Filicales sub-zone): *Pinus sylvestris* pollen frequencies continue to expand

in excess of 2.2%. *Quercus* percentages fall below 3%. *Alnus glutinosa* pollen frequencies fall while those of *Corylus avellana* and *Salix undiff.* rise above 6% and 4% respectively, although both fall temporarily below these levels in the middle of the sub-zone. *Fraxinus excelsior* pollen frequencies also rise and *Aster*-type and *Cruciferae* remain high at more than 0.6%. *Filicales* endospores rise in excess of 4%, while *Pteridium aquilinium* declines. *Myosotis* pollen peaks in this sub-zone, which also holds the only record for pollen of *Lilicaceae*, and marks the last appearance of *Myosotis, Stellaria, Mentha*-type, *Rumex undiff., Thalictrum, Odontites*-type, *Umbelliferae* and *Dryopteris*.

TVP-8d 35–15 cm (Quercus–Alnus–Polypodium sub-zone): *Quercus* pollen frequencies expand to more than 3%, while *Alnus glutinosa* and *Corylus avellana* have subsidiary peaks at 3% and 4% respectively. Pollen frequencies of *Gramineae* begin an upward trend while those of *Cyperaceae* decline. *Compositae: Cichorieae* rise to more than 22% but less than 30%, and *Artemisia* pollen is in excess of 0.6%. *Cruciferae* decline sharply to less than 0.6%, *Lotus*-type pollen percentages peak, *Polygonum aviculare* exceeds 0.4% and *Urtica* rises in excess of 0.6%. *Ophioglossum vulgatum* spore frequencies remain below 3%, but those of *Polypodium vulgare* rise in excess of 1.5%.

This sub-zone contains the only record of *Epilobium* pollen. It marks the last appearance of *Ulmus, Fraxinus excelsior, Acer campestre, Carpinus betulus, Myosotis, Cirsium*-type, *Polygonum aviculare, Rubiaceae, Umbelliferae,* and *Potamogeton*.

TVP-9 15–0 cm (Pinus–Ophioglossum)

Quercus pollen frequencies decline to less than 3%, *Pinus sylvestris* pollen frequencies expand, *Alnus glutinosa* falls below 3%, and *Corylus avellana* below 4%. *Compositae: Cichorieae* rise above 30% at the lower zone boundary, and *Artemisia* falls below 0.6%. *Cruciferae* rise to more than 0.6%, and *Ophioglossum vulgatum* to more than 3% at the lower zone boundary. *Polypodium vulgare* declines to less than 1.5%. *Lonicera periclymenum* pollen is confined to this zone. *Picea abies* makes its only reappearance after the Devensian (TVP-1).

Interpretation

TVP-1 360–350 cm

This zone is represented by a single sample from the basal clayey silt. The pollen concentrations were very low, and counting was made difficult by abundant derived Tertiary (Palaeocene/Eocene) pollen and spores, which could be distinguished from Quaternary pollen and spores by their darker colour. The low local pollen productivity is probably responsible for the comparatively high regional pollen component, especially of *Pinus sylvestris* and for the appearance of supposed long-distance transported species such as *Picea abies*.

Whether the palaeo-channel was filled with water to any great depth at this stage is unclear. The sediment type suggests still or comparatively slow-moving water, but the only aquatic pollen encountered was that of *Potamogeton*, which could have blown in from elsewhere. Aridity, and hence salinity of the soils, is suggested by the presence of *Glaux maritima*.

The abundant *Sedum, Polemonium caeruleum, Rumex acetosa, Polygonum bistorta*-type, *Filipendula* and Umbelliferae suggest a tall-herb community growing locally (within the channel?), while *Cerastium*-type, *Aster*-type, *Dryas octopetala, Glaux maritima, Odontites*-type and *Woodsia*-type suggest more of a dwarf arctic-alpine community perhaps in more exposed sites. It is possible that this sample dates from well into the Devensian, before the Late Devensian, but if so it is surprising that it was not subsequently re-worked. This could then be an interstadial deposit which might explain the comparatively high *Betula undiff.* (tree birch), *Pinus sylvestris,* and *Picea abies.*

TVP-2a 350–280 cm

Locally, the presence of *Pediastrum, Isoetes lacustris* microspores and *Sparganium*-type pollen indicates comparatively deep water, and the considerable input of sand, especially from 315 to 300 cm which was almost pure sand, suggests much aeolian deposition. Figure 53 shows the presumed rapid infilling of the palaeo-channel during this phase. High pollen frequencies of *Juniperus communis, Empetrum nigrum,* and *Cyperaceae* suggest a tundra heath, while *Ceratium*-type, *Sagina, Artemisia, Papaver* and *Cryptogramma* point to unstable habitats, as on the gravel banks of the probably braided river channels. *Oxyria*-type, *Thalictrum* and the *saxifrages* probably colonised damp seepage channels but otherwise there is little evidence for the more stable habitats indicated in the previous zone.

Altogether this gives a picture of a tundra landscape, and is probably referable to the whole of the earlier part (Oldest to Older Dryas) of the Late Devensian.

TVP-2b 280–255 cm

The rise in *Betula* undiff. and *Salix* undiff. and the decline of *Pinus sylvestris* pollen frequencies suggests the local establishment of sparse birch–willow woodland, resulting in increased local pollen productivity drowning the regional component *(Pinus sylvestris). Gramineae* and associated species of tall-herb communities, such as *Compositae: Cichorieae, Filipendula* and *Rubiaceae* expand, as do species of more stable *calcareous* soils such as *Helianthemum.* Most of the indicators of unstable habitats present in sub-zone 2a persist, so the gravels themselves were probably not yet stabilised. Tundra heath communities also persist, possibly on plateau gravels above the floodplain level of the River Thames. The presence of *Myriophyllum* species, *Hippuris vulgaris* and *Nuphar lutea* suggests that the water was still quite deep, but sand input declined and was replaced by a deposition of clay with a higher organic content. This sub-zone can thus be correlated with the Late Glacial Interstadial (Windermere Interstadial), in which *Betula* woodland became widely established in southern Britain.

TVP-2c 255–240 cm

The decline in *Betula* undiff. and *Salix* undiff. pollen frequencies, with the continued presence of *Juniperus communis* reflects a loss of woodland locally and a return to tundra conditions. There is a general decline in many of the herbaceous taxa such as *Compositae: Cichorieae, Artemisia, Aster*-type, *Matricaria*-type, *Plantago maritima, Plantago media / major, Oxyria*-type, and *Odontites*-type, suggesting a loss of habitat, perhaps by renewed braided channel instability and cryoturbation of soils. This sub-zone corresponds to the Younger Dryas (Loch Lomond Stadial) stage of the Late Devensian, and

its end marks the final disappearance of many of the arctic-alpine elements from the flora. Locally the increase in *Equisetum* spore and Cyperaceae pollen frequencies marks a transition to the reed-swamp community of shallower water, and the organic detritus input to the river channel increases concomitantly.

TVP-3 240–225 cm

The beginning of this zone reflects the transition from Late Devensian to Flandrian, and the outburst of *Pinus sylvestris* and *Corylus avellana* pollen frequencies marks the early Boreal climatic zone (Early Mesolithic). Very little sediment accumulation is taking place, and the whole of the early Flandrian is crammed into some 15 cm of sediment. Herb pollen is greatly reduced, except *Sparganium*-type, which includes *Typha angustifolia,* and may represent a further shallowing of the water as the *Cyperaceae* and *Equisetum* are replaced locally.

TVP-4 225–215 cm

This zone reflects the immigration of mixed oak forest trees and the regional establishment of closed deciduous woodland. The high *Ulmus* and *Tilia cordata* pollen frequencies suggest a comparatively undisturbed forest of early Atlantic climatic period. If there was any pre-Elm Decline Mesolithic activity, it was clearly minimal, and is not reflected in the pollen diagram. The sediments change markedly in character near the lower zone boundary, from a sandy detritus peat to a wood peat, with a very low mineral influx. Wood from this depth was identified as *Quercus* (7 samples); *Fraxinus excelsior* (1) and *Alnus* (2). Locally, only *Sparganium*-type pollen persists amongst the aquatica and this could derive from *Typha angustifolia* and hence a reed-swamp species. The appearance of *Cruciferae, Iris pseudocorus, Lythrum salicaria* and *Potentilla*-type (possibly *Potentilla palustris*) along with the persistence of *Filipendula, Rubiaceae* and *Umbelliferae* suggest a marshy tall-herb community possibly as marginal vegetation, though the trees clearly came right to the edge of the channel to allow large branches to fall in. The shading provided by the trees might be the cause of reduced flowering of any aquatics present, yet the high *Salix undiff.* values suggest a fen carr community, though *Salix* wood itself was not found at the sample site. All in all, the evidence therefore points to terrestrialisation of the channel basin during this zone.

TVP-5 215–195 cm

The lower boundary of this zone is placed at the Elm Decline and the upper boundary at the Lime Decline. Thus this zone spans the Neolithic period and marks the beginning of arable and pastoral activity. The peat switches at 210 cm from a wood peat to a silty herbaceous peat, reflecting the profound changes taking place locally. Local woodland of *Alnus, Corylus,* and *Salix* was cleared, though regional woodland of *Quercus* and *Tilia* appears to have persisted. Cereal crops and weeds of agriculture, as evidenced by cereal-type, *Chenopodiaceae,* and *Urtica* pollen, appeared and arable farming led to an increased silt load in the river. This siltation may have raised the land around the river channel or blocked an overflow outlet, as we see a reversion succession. *Potamogeton* pollen frequencies rise and the presence of *Menyanthes trifoliata* suggests shallow open water. Yet *Iris pseudocorus* pollen frequencies also peak in this zone and *Filipendula, Rubiaceae,* and *Umbelliferae* pollen frequencies rise again, suggesting establishment of marginal vegetation.

Floodplain meadows, much as at present, probably first started to form during this period, as the gravels now became blanketed with a layer of silt. The rise in the pollen frequencies of *Gramineae, Cyperaceae, Compositae: Cichorieae,* Lotus-type, *Plantago lanceolata,* and *Rumex acetosa*-type, which form characteristic components of the subsequent alluvial layers over the river channel, all point to the beginning of such communities in place of woodland beyond the banks of the channel. The comparatively high percentages of *Tilia cordata* pollen suggests that lime may have been dominant in the regional woodlands, as its pollen percentages are close to those of *Quercus,* yet it is both a lower producer and poorer disperser of pollen than *Quercus* (Andersen 1973). In this respect this site is similar to those in the Severn Valley studied by Brown (1982).

TVP-5a 195–185 cm
This sub-zone spans the *Tilia* decline, taken to indicate the beginning of the Bronze Age. The fact that other forest trees appear unaffected suggests a selective felling of *Tilia* in the regional woodlands. A slight expansion of *Corylus avellana* and *Salix undiff.* pollen frequencies may be a response to opening of the canopy by increased flowering of the undershrubs or more effective pollen transport as wind movements within the trunk space increased. The decrease in fern spores would be a consequence of drying out of the woodland as more openings were created, allowing fewer epiphytic and ground-living ferns.

Thus the Early Bronze Age seems to be a period of regional woodland clearance and expansion of arable farming as cereal-type and *Chenopodiaceae* pollen percentages rise. But to a much greater extent pastoral land-use expanded locally as pollen frequencies of *Gramineae, Cyperaceae, Compositae: Cichorieae,* Lotus-type, *Plantago lanceolata,* and *Umbelliferae* all increase to a peak at 190 cm before declining again in the next sub-zone. This could reflect a further extension of the floodplain meadows as increased silt deposits covered the valley gravels.

That Bronze Age activity was occurring locally is proved by the presence of worked flints in the peat. The local habitat at this time must still have been open water, as *Lemna* and *Potamogeton* pollen suggest, and the amorphous silty peat would have been laid down by this, by now acid and probably anaerobic, environment.

TVP-6b 185–175 cm
This sub-zone marks a temporary increase in many of the colonising species of tree and shrub such as *Fraxinus excelsior, Corylus avellana* and *Salix.* This appears to be at the expense of the pasture species, so it could represent a period of relaxation of grazing, allowing some re-colonisation of the floodplain meadows, or it could represent changes occurring beyond the floodplain as further mature woodland was cleared, and more colonising species took over. The second of these interpret-

ations seems more probable, because *Quercus* pollen declines markedly in this sub-zone, and this could lead to increased flowering and thus increased pollen production and dispersal of the species listed above, which in turn would artificially depress the percentages of most other species.

Hence it appears that the Early Bronze Age, from which date these sediments are presumed to derive, was a second period of intensive woodland clearance after the first in the Neolithic. The fact that pollen of cereal-type and many arable indicators does not decline at this point, suggests that arable land must have been expanding in extent, and this would also tie in with the concept of increased woodland clearance.

TVP-7 175–105 cm
Most tree and shrub pollen and fern spore frequencies decline to their lowest since these species became established. Conversely grasses, cereals, *Chenopodiaceae, Plantago lanceolata, Rumex acetosa*-type, *Ranunculus acris*-type, *Umbelliferae,* and *Pteridium aquilinium* all expand to their maximal values. This is thus a period of intensive agricultural activity, both arable and pastoral, probably from the earlier Bronze Age through to the Bronze Age/Iron Age boundary.

The sediment changes from a silty peat, through a thin wood peat layer, back to a silty peat at 161 cm. In this layer, up to depth of 144 cm, there were abundant worked flints again, indicating considerable local human activity, and this corresponds with the phase within this zone with the least tree and shrub pollen. The switch from peat to non-calcareous alluvium at 135 cm does not, however, show up as any marked change in the pollen diagram. Siltation was clearly very rapid at this time which suggests a high density of Bronze Age settlement, agricultural activity, and erosion in the catchment of the Thames.

Locally the succession proceeds from *Lemna* and *Potamogeton,* below 160 cm indicating open water, to *Sparganium*-type and *Equisetum* at 150 cm, indicating a reed-swamp community, while above this the expansion of *Cyperaceae* and *Cruciferae* at 120 cm suggests that the channel had now become infilled again and supported a marsh vegetation.

TVP-8a 105–95 cm
This sub-zone represents a short-lived regeneration of *Corylus* and *Salix* but the start of a longer regeneration cycle of *Quercus* and *Alnus.* The increase of ferns also reflects the spread of damp woodland and this appears to be at the expense of many of the marsh-land herbs such as *Cyperaceae, Filipendula,* and *Umbelliferae.* As these are essentially local components of the flora, the implication is that colonisation by trees is occurring locally on the floodplain.

This may be the result of a deteriorating climate near the Bronze Age/Iron Age transition, with less grazing pressure on the now wetter floodplain, particularly near low-lying channels. The fact that more flooding may be occurring by calcareous river water is reflected in the change from a non-calcareous to a calcareous alluvium, at 100 cm.

TVP-8b 95–65 cm
This is a period of spread of alder at the expense of hazel and willow, continuing the process of colonisation of the wetter parts of the floodplain noted in the last sub-zone. The rise in *Pinus sylvestris* is typical of Late Iron Age to Romano-British pollen spectra from south-east England, and following a decline in *Calluna vulgaris* pollen frequencies, may reflect the colonisation of regional heathlands by pine. The rise in *Quercus* may also be a regional phenomenon as more grazing land is abandoned, but the rise in *Alnus glutinosa* is almost certainly local, and closely correlated as it is with the rise of *Filicales endospores* and *Polypodium vulgare* spores, which are unlikely to travel great distances. Many of the tall herb or marshland herb species decline further, so the local habitat now appears to have reverted to a more closed alder carr, with *Cyperaceae* and ferns as the main associates. However, pollen of *Gramineae* remains in almost constant proportion, while the proportions of *Aster*-type, *Compositae: Cichorieae, Cruciferae, Plantago lanceolata, Filipendula,* and *Odontites*-type tend to rise. This suggests that the floodplain meadows still persist and may even be increasing in extent, so the colonisation by alder could be a quite small-scale local phenomenon confined to the river channel itself. There remains one problem, and that is whether differential preservation might account for some of the rise in such taxa as *Compositae: Cichorieae*, particularly in these more calcareous levels. However, the good preservation of more readily degradable taxa such as *Salix undiff.* and *Cyperaceae* argues against this.

TVP-8c 65–35 cm
This sub-zone marks another phase of woodland clearance both regionally (*Quercus*) and locally (*Alnus glutinosa*). The associated rise in the under storey or colonising species, *Fraxinus excelsior, Corylus avellana* and *Salix undiff.* is exactly as seen in earlier cycles of clearance, such as in TVP-6b, but apart from a rise in *Chenopodiaceae* and *Polygonum aviculare* pollen percentages, there is no indication here of any increase in arable farming.

What is more likely, therefore, is an extension of pastoral land use, with the clearance of alder, the decline in the tall herbs such as *Umbelliferae*, and the increase in weedy species which might colonise heavily-trampled ground such as *Polygonum aviculare* all pointing to increased grazing pressure on the floodplain meadows. The period covered by these sediments probably corresponds to the early medieval period. By this time, the rate of siltation has declined relative to that in the Bronze Age (Fig. 53) so either less arable farming was taking place, or soil conservation measures had improved, or the more erodable sediments on the hilltops and hillsides had already been eroded. During this period, the palaeo-channel, now well-blanketed with alluvial sediments, probably carried a vegetation much like that of the rest of the floodplain. The odd occurrences of the pollen of water plants could be the result of pollen inwash with sediments when the meadows were flooded or the blowing-in of pollen of wind-pollinated species from the main river channel, but their sporadic occurrences are unlikely to indicate the persistence of any open water in the palaeo-channel.

TVP-8d 35–15 cm
This sub-zone shows a general regeneration of trees (*Quercus, Alnus* and, *Corylus*) with associated ferns (*Filicales endospores* and *Polypodium vulgare*) and a decline in arable weeds (*Chenopodiaceae, Matricaria*-type, *Polygonum aviculare*) and many of the floodplain associates, for instance pollen of *Aster*-type and *Cruciferae* (which could equally derive from arable weeds), as well as the tall-herbs, such as *Succisa pratensis, Vicia undiff.* and *Umbelliferae*. In their place, lower-growing pasture plants appear to thrive: *Compositae: Cichorieae, Lotus*-type, *Trifolium, Plantago lanceolata, Ranunculus acris*-type. This suggests a regional increase in woodland, but a local increase in grazing pressure on the floodplain meadows and possibly a drying of the habitat, as *Cyperaceae* also decrease.

TVP-9 15–0 cm
This is essentially the zone in which the existing surface vegetation became established. A further decline in broad-leaved trees occurs, but new plantations of *Pinus sylvestris* to the south and west have a marked effect in the pollen diagram. It is interesting to note that the spread of beech in the Chilterns does not show up as a clear phenomenon, but this could be explained by the low pollen productivity of *Fagus sylvatica* linked with the fact that the beechwoods are largely to the north and east of the site, whereas the prevailing wind is from the south-west, from which more pine pollen would be carried. The spread of *Ophioglossum* in the damp floodplain meadows seems to be a largely recent phenomenon, though it was present in small amounts before. Generally the floristic composition of the meadows has remained remarkably constant since the Bronze Age, when they appear to have first formed. The greatest changes have been in the loss of many of the tall herb species such as *Rumex acetosa, Thalictrum, Rubiaceae, Odontites*-type and *Umbelliferae*, suggesting a greater emphasis on hay production in the past, while the shorter-growing herbs such as *Compositae: Cichorieae, Aster*-type, *Lotus*-type, *Trifolium, Plantago lanceolata* and *Ranunculus acris*-type have tended to increase, suggesting a greater emphasis on grazing at the present time. The recent rise in *Urtica* may also reflect this increased grazing pressure. These changes have not been abrupt, but have occurred gradually in a series of steps and short-term reversals.

Discussion
The Thames Valley Park sediments provide a long pollen record from the Late-Devensian to the present day.

The Late Devensian (Upper Palaeolithic) sediments which may date from the Younger Dryas alone or may span a longer period, contain pollen indicating a *Juniperus-Empetrum* heath, probably on the higher terrace gravels, and locally unstable habitats with a wide range of colonising species or 'weedy' species of such habitats. *Empetrum* heath was widespread in southern England during the Younger Dryas, for example at Elstead, Surrey (Seagrief and Godwin, 1960) and towards the end of the Windermere interstadial at Woolhampton in the Kennet Valley (Collins, 1994).

Other sites in the Thames Valley, for instance at Abingdon (Aalto *et al*, 1984) appear to have had a higher proportion of tall herbs. These differences may reflect the proximity to the various sites of gravel terraces as opposed to softer clay soils. The palaeo-channel contained open water during this period, and the sandy sediment may have been, at least in part, of aeolian origin, and the ruderal nature of the flora suggests intense cryoturbation.

The Flandrian (Post-glacial or Holocene) sequence is typical of many floodplain sequences, except that there is a hiatus in deposition, or at least very slow aggradation in the Boreal. The very open floodplain habitats virtually ceased to exist at the time of the expansion of *Pinus sylvestris*, though there is still a little *Artemisia* pollen suggesting the survival of some unstable habitats. Locally the palaeo-channel terrestrialised and became dominated by *Salix* scrub. The expansion of woodland meant that soil erosion and hence siltation virtually ceased. However, in the Kennet Valley (Holyoak, 1980; Collins, 1994), the Boreal is the period of maximum peat accumulation, possibly behind beaver dams. In many other pollen diagrams from southern Britain a similar hiatus in deposition to that in the Thames Valley Park sediments occurs. For instance, in the Ouse valley of the Sussex High Weald, Scaife and Burrin (1983) found that alluviation began in the early Flandrian (Early Mesolithic), probably as a result of natural erosion of as yet unstabilised soils.

There was then a hiatus in deposition through the Boreal and Atlantic Periods until the Neolithic, when alluviation recommenced. Scaife (1987) concluded that there was little evidence in the South East for any effects of Mesolithic man on the Atlantic Period's vegetation. In the Thames Valley Park sediments, it is only with the start of the Neolithic that rapid sediment accumulation recommenced, as soils were again destabilised by agriculture. The elm decline coincides with the establishment of floodplain pasture on these newly deposited alluvial sediments. In many published pollen diagrams of floodplain alluvial sequences, alluviation did not begin until the Bronze Age, when a massive opening up of the landscape occurred (Keatinge, 1983).

The palaeo-channel itself appears to have supported an *Alnus/Salix/Corylus* carr from the Boreal/Atlantic transition to the Bronze Age. The local occurrence of wood of *Quercus, Fraxinus* and *Tilia* within the peat suggests that these trees were growing in the pre-Elm Decline woodland on the banks of the palaeo-channel before Neolithic clearance. However, the carr growing on the palaeo-channel infill was not cleared until the Bronze Age. Although *Salix* pollen peaks on two occasions in the Iron Age, along with *Alnus* and *Corylus* in particular, there are no remains of wood in the sediments from these later periods, so the pollen could derive from isolated trees or hedgerows on the floodplain grasslands rather than from any re-establishment of carr vegetation.

Peaks of *Alnus* pollen within alluvial sequences were found on the Kennet floodplain near Burghfield (Thompson and Allen, 1992) and the Thames floodplain

at Runnymede Bridge (Greig, 1991). These could reflect periods in which grazing or hay cutting were relaxed and there was some regrowth of woodland, but in all cases the pollen of open habitats dominates, so any regrowth of woodland was probably only on a small scale.

The very high percentages of Compositae, tribe Cichorieae, *Plantago lanceolata* and *Ranunculus acris*-type are typical of floodplain alluvium in southern Britain, as noted by Keith-Lucas (1983–85) on the Kennet floodplain, for example. It has been suggested that the high percentages of pollen of Compositae might result from selective preservation, but the fact that delicate pollen grains, such as those of Cyperaceae, survive well suggest the 'bias' may be caused by summer grazing, curtailing the flowering and pollen production of the later-flowering species, and thus giving undue weight to the pollen of early-flowering species, relative to their importance in the vegetation. As far as the grassland species go, there has been comparative stability in the floodplain habitats since the alluvial sediments first started to accumulate in the Neolithic period.

Wood and Timbers, by R. Gale

Samples of waterlogged wood were examined and identified to genus using comparative analytical methods. The material comprised a mixture of stems, branch, trunk and probably some root fragments.

The majority, comprising *Quercus* (oak), Pomoideae (hawthorn, apple, whitebeam, rowan) and Salicaceae (poplar/willow), was found in the upper layers 245/246 of channel 244, equating to Pollen Zone TVP-7. A single fragment of *Fraxinus* (Ash) was found in a lower deposit (254) of the same channel in a position equating to Pollen Zone TVP-2c/3.

Fragments of *Acer* (maple), *Corylus* (hazel), *Quercus* (oak), Pomoideae and Salicaceae were also recovered from channels 225, 229, and 230, all from undated contexts.

Waterlogged Plant Remains,
by W.J. Carruthers (Submitted 1991)

During the excavations at Thames Valley Park samples were taken from a number of columns through the peat in channel 244 for plant macrofossil analysis. Six of these samples from three 1 x 1 m squares were selected for outline analysis, these are detailed in Table 33, and their positions shown on Figure 48.

Each sample consisted of a 1 litre block of peat taken from a 0.1 m deep spit. Processing of the samples was carried out by Wessex Archaeology staff using standard techniques (Allen 1992); the peat was pre-soaked in water and gently agitated to facilitate disaggregation. Unfortunately, several tubes of cleaned residue were broken in transit. The results from these samples (marked as ! in the species list) are therefore incomplete through loss of material and will also be biased depending on which mesh size residue was lost.

Table 33 location of plant macrofossil samples within channel 244 by square and context

Depth from Surface of Channel (m)	Relative Location within Channel	Square 274 Context	Square 296 Context	Square 318 Context
0.0–0.1	top	–	462	–
0.4–0.5	middle	341	–	–
0.7–0.8	–	–	526	–
0.8–0.9	bottom	361	–	–
1.0–1.1	–	–	–	566
1.3–1.4	–	–	557	–

Results

A list of taxa recorded from the samples is given in Table 34. Because of the variable quality of the data and the need for only an outline vegetational sequence, quantification of the remains was by rough frequency ratings rather than absolute counts. In total, the assemblages ranged in size from just a few seeds to several hundred.

Discussion

The principal aims of the analysis were to obtain confirmation of the palynological results (see Pollen, above) and recover evidence of anthropogenic activity in the area. Since only a small number of samples were examined, and some of these were incomplete and contained low concentrations of macrofossils, few conclusions can be drawn from these results. Lateral and vertical comparisons must be seen as extremely tentative using this small quantity of data, and comparisons with pollen evidence hold their own problems, such as differences in level of identification and seed/pollen dispersal. Whereas the pollen evidence indicates primarily regional changes in vegetation, macrofossil evidence is essentially of local significance. In addition, the pollen samples were taken from a different point in the palaeo-channel from any of the three macrofossil columns, so that the recorded depths for changes in the pollen assemblage are unlikely to correspond directly to depths in the macrofossil columns. However, a few general observations are noted below.

Habitats represented by the plant macrofossils

The predominant components of the plant macrofossil assemblages are the seeds of aquatic and semi-aquatic plants, as might be expected in a channel peat. Plants of slow-flowing to stagnant water in ponds, ditches, riverbanks or marshes are much in evidence, such as water-plantain (*Alisma plantago-aquatica*), crowfoot buttercups (*Ranunculus* subg. *Batrachium*), spike-rush (*Eleocharis* subg. *Palustres*) and duckweed (*Lemna* sp.). These taxa are possibly slightly more frequent in the top and middle samples, but the variable quality of the data makes comparisons of this kind difficult.

Other habitats represented in the seed assemblage are disturbed/cultivated soils and woodland/scrub/hedgerows. The former group contains weeds such as thistles (*Cirsium / Carduus* sp.), fumitory (*Fumaria* sp.) and sow-thistle (*Sonchus asper*). Very few seeds of these taxa were recovered from the top and middle samples and none from the bottom samples. Blackberry (*Rubus fruticosus* agg.) and elder (*Sambucus nigra*) were evidence of the latter habitat type, but again the number of seeds was small (middle and bottom samples only).

Comparisons between the seed and pollen evidence

The following paragraphs assume that the pollen and macrofossil samples can be equated horizontally across the palaeo-channel, but it should be remembered that the situation is unlikely to be so simple.

a) Bottom

The roughly equivalent pollen sample to that of the bottom macrofossil samples is of probable Bronze Age/Iron Age date and shows evidence of intensive agriculture, both arable and pastoral (Keith-Lucas, this report). No clear evidence of human activity is seen at this point in the macrofossil columns, except for the presence of elder which is often found growing in soils with a high nitrogen content and so is usually associated with human disturbance.

The aquatic pollen indicates a change from open water (*Lemna* and *Potamogeton*) in an earlier pollen zone to a reed-swamp and then marsh flora (including Cyperaceae pollen). *Lemna* sp. and *Potamogeton* sp. macrofossils are indeed absent from the bottom macrofossil samples, although they are present in the middle and top samples. Evidence for the Cyperaceae is present as a few sedge (*Carex* sp). nutlets in the bottom and middle samples.

b) Middle

The middle macrofossil samples would be equivalent to pollen zones 8b and 8c if the deposits had been laid down simultaneously, which is suggested as including the Late Iron Age to medieval periods. Slight evidence of increased human disturbance is present as spiny sow-thistle and fumitory seeds at this level, as well as the continued presence of elder. Keith-Lucas suggests that the channel had primarily dried up by this time, although some pollen of aquatics was present. The recovery of large quantities of water-plantain and crow-foot seeds from the middle of the macrofossil columns indicates the continued presence of slow to standing water in some areas. The high occurrence of moss in the samples could equate to the increase in *Sphagnum* pollen at this level, suggesting boggy patches.

c) Top

The single macrofossil sample examined from the top of the palaeo-channel contained increased quantities of spike-rush seeds as well as a high occurrence of crowfoot. Spike-rush is said to be unable to compete with tall-growing vegetation and so is often associated with grazed, wet pastures (Walters, 1949). The pollen evidence indicates an increase in grazing as opposed to hay production in the upper levels of the channel deposit.

Table 34 plant remains from channel 244

Taxa	Habitat	Context 566	462!	526	557!	341!	361
Acer pseudoplatanus L. (sycamore)	HSW	–	–	–	–	–	[**]
Alisma plantago-aquatica L. (water-plantain)	BP	–	**	***	–	–	–
Carex sp. (sedge)	BGM	*	–	**	*	**	*
Cirsium/Carduus sp. (thistle)	CDG	–	*	–	–	–	–
Eleocharis subg. *Palustres* (spike-rush)	BMP	–	***	**	–	–	–
Fumaria sp. (fumitory)	CD	–	–	–	–	*	–
Glyceria sp. (flote-grass)	BMPR	–	**	–	–	–	–
Gramineae NFI (grasses)	DG	*	–	–	–	–	–
Lemna sp. (duckweed)	P	–	–	**	–	–	–
Lycopus europaeus L. (gipsywort)	BM	*	–	–	–	–	–
Mentha sp. (mint)	BCDMP	***	–	–	**	–	–
cf. *Oenanthe aquatica* (L.) Poiret (fine-leaved water dropwort)	P	*	**	*	–	–	–
Potamogeton sp. (pondweed)	PR	–	*	–	–	–	–
Ranunculus subg. *Batrachium* (crowfoot)	BPR	**	****	****	*	–	–
Ranunculus subg. *Ranunculus* (buttercup)	DG	–	–	*	–	–	–
Rubus fruticosus agg. (blackberry)	DH	–	–	*	–	–	–
Sambucus nigra L. (elder)	DHSW	*	–	*	–	**	–
cf. *Sium latifolium* L. (greater water-parsnip)	P	–	*	–	–	–	–
Sonchus asper (L.) Hill (spiny sow-thistle)	CD	–	–	*	–	–	–
Characeae (stonewort algae)	–	–	***	–	–	–	–
Moss NFI	–	–	**	***	–	–	–
Wood frags/twigs	–	–	**	–	***	–	–
Charcoal	–	–	–	–	**	*	–
Cladoceran ephyppia	–	–	**	–	***	–	–

Frequency ratings: * = occasional; ** = several; *** = frequent; **** = numerous; [ ] = modern contaminant; ! = incomplete sample
Habitats: B = bankside; C = cultivated; D = disturbed; G = grassland; H = hedgerow; M = marsh; P = ponds/ditches; R = rivers, streams; S = scrub; W = woodland

Glyceria sp. seeds were recovered only from the top sample, perhaps indicating some reed-swamp.

Comparing the occurrence of some other taxa which provide little interpretative insight but which may be of general interest: *Rubus* pollen grains were recorded from zone 7 only (E bottom) but the genus was presented by a single blackberry seed in a middle sample. Mint (*Mentha* sp.) seeds, which were quite frequent in the bottom samples, were not present in the upper macrofossil samples but the genus was present as pollen in zones 7 to 8c (E bottom to middle).

It is notable that despite high pollen frequencies for alder throughout the (presumed) period samples for macrofossils, not a single seed or catkin was recovered. This perhaps indicates that the alder was not growing in the immediate area, as alder seeds and catkins preserve well and can be numerous in an alder carr deposit.

Other Areas

No features of archaeological origin were found in any of the other areas on the floodplain. However, a number of palaeo-channels and natural deposits were noted, from which artefacts were recovered. Where artefacts were recovered from these areas of a type found elsewhere on the floodplain, in areas of archaeological interest, these are described above in the relevant sections. Artefacts of leather were found in only one, isolated, area of the site and these are discussed below.

Leather from the Pipe Trench, by Quita Mould

Eighteen pieces of leather were found in spoil from two machine excavated pits dug to lay service pipes beneath

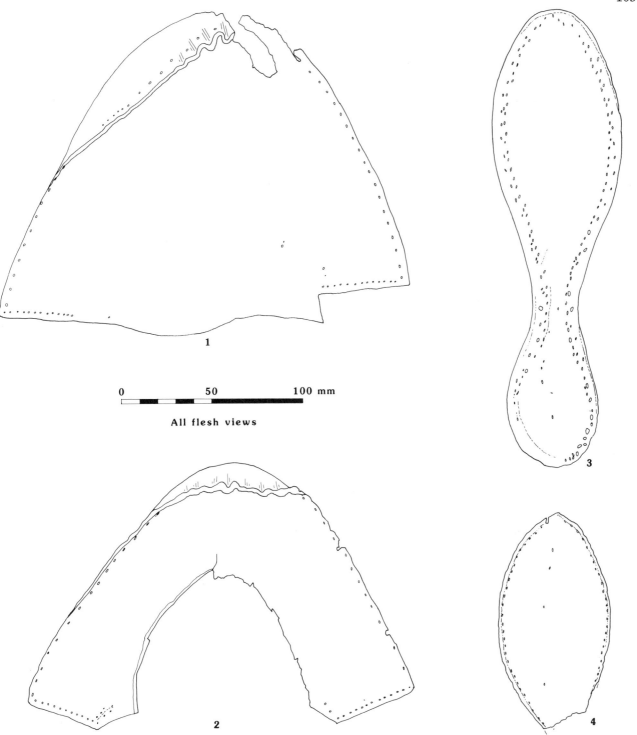

0   50   100 mm

All flesh views

1

2

3

4

Figure 54   Leather from the pipe trench

the Thames in the north-eastern part of the site (Fig. 54). The nature of the excavated silts suggested that the deposits derived from a previous alignment of the river, although the mixture of artefacts (mostly modern) did not allow its infilling to be closely dated. The leather assemblage comprises discarded welted shoe parts, shoe making waste and a fragment of lapped seam cut from a larger object.

Shoes

The diagnostic shoe components found include two vamps of cattle hide, one being accompanied by a matching fragment of two-piece quarters, a middle sole and an insole fragment, all from shoes of welted construction. The complete vamp (Fig. 54: 1) has a bluntly pointed, pleated toe and extends high up the instep into a short tongue. Its left quarter is peaked at centre back, the top edge dropping below the ankle. The second vamp (Fig. 54: 2) has a similar toe, the throat shape is unknown having been deliberately cut away before being discarded. The uppers have their side seam/throat junctions reinforced on the interior (flesh side) by the addition of a strengthening cord. Stylistically the uppers are likely to date from the late 16th to the early years of the 17th century.

The middle sole (Fig. 54: 3) and insole forepart (Fig. 54: 4) found are made straight with a bluntly pointed toe, narrow tread and waist. The narrow waist suggests a date c. 1610, but accumulating evidence suggests that it continued to be popular through James I reign (June Swann pers comm). The bottom unit shape is compatible with the upper styles recovered and it is possible that they may belong to one of the vamps, giving a shoe likely to date to the first decade of the 17th century. A small fragment of strap may possibly come from a shoe fastening, if this is the case, it belongs to a buckled shoe which, if welted, cannot date any earlier than the later part of the 17th century.

Non-shoe leather
A length of lapped seam found retains no features to suggest a date.

Waste
The small quantity of both primary and secondary waste recovered represents shoe making waste.

5. Discussion

by John W. Hawkes and C.A. Butterworth

Palaeolithic

The earliest activity on the site is represented by a single Palaeolithic hand-axe and part of a second found during the terrace excavations. Both may be considered fortuitous discoveries, however, and cannot be taken to indicate primary activity at Thames Valley Park, as shown by the rolled condition of the hand-axe. The reworking of the course of the River Thames during interglacial periods also resulted in the destruction of potential or surviving Palaeolithic sites except where beyond direct reach of the river's influence but the impact of the human population on the environment is likely to have been slight in this early period. In the area of Thames Valley Park, the gravel terrace from which the hand-axe derives, the Lynch Hill Terrace, lies not far to the east of the site. This or other similar areas of higher land nearby are likely to have provided the tundra heath habitat indicated by pollen recovered from the river channel sediments on the floodplain.

Late Mesolithic–Early Neolithic

Interpretations of this phase of the site are handicapped by a terminology which inevitably draws an over-rigid distinction between the Mesolithic and the Neolithic. The flint assemblages from the floodplain and the terrace area and, by extrapolation, the presence of colluvium containing elements of these assemblages have been considered as Mesolithic. However, the pollen sequence implies little pre-elm decline activity and no substantial clearances (such as would surely have been necessary to produce the conditions which would promote downslope movement of soil) prior to the beginnings of arable farming in the locality. It seems probable, therefore, that activities best regarded as Mesolithic in an economic (and possibly cultural) sense were taking place on the fringes of a landscape already in the process of alteration by the onset of the Neolithic, indeed, there is no reason to suppose that the Early Neolithic material recovered from the floodplain, scarce though it is, represents anything other than a continuation of the same patterns of activity.

Potentially contemporary settlement sites in the Thames and lower Kennet Valleys are not well represented, although there is a number of sites containing a range of material spanning the Mesolithic/Neolithic transition which might suggest some continuation of Mesolithic traditions in marginal, floodplain, areas. Excavations on the Taplow Terrace at Cannon Hill, Maidenhead (Bradley et al. 1976) recovered early Neolithic pottery from a pit and other features in and around which a flint assemblage with Mesolithic characteristics was also present. The possible contemporaneity of the two elements was considered but could not be determined on the basis of the available evidence. At Remen-

ham near Henley a pit containing Early Neolithic pottery was revealed in section by a pipe trench, and flintwork, including a Late Mesolithic–Early Neolithic assemblage, was recovered from the Thames floodplain nearby (Holgate and Start 1987).

Howsoever the phase is identified or defined, the artificial limits of excavation and the limited nature of the evidence itself impede a full understanding of its extent at Thames Valley Park. Here it is clear that the density of worked flints in the two areas where these were found, on the floodplain and associated with the relict channel on the terrace, is low compared to many other similar sites. Discounting the hollow (context 3) on the floodplain, there is no indication of any possible settlement features. The size, regularity of plan, and density of artefactual material in the upper fill of the hollow had initially suggested that this might have been a man-made feature, either a 'working hollow' or a structure. Such an interpretation was difficult to sustain, however: no associated structural elements (the two nearby post-holes are almost certainly later) were discovered, no hearth was present, and the poorly-defined edge was more consistent with a natural feature such as a tree hole. Some caution must be employed in assuming that the nature and location of the settlement area and its contemporary activities can be extrapolated from the topographical situation and the known distribution of artefacts: Williamson's Moor, Eskmeals, Cumbria (Bonsall et al. 1989, 181 ff), although in a coastal location, is otherwise topographically very similar to the Thames Valley Park floodplain, with an elevated (shingle) ridge situated within an alluvial plain adjacent to a stream channel. There the highest concentration of flints was to be found on the ridge, although the only potentially contemporary settlement features, perhaps surprisingly, were confined to the alluvium. The lesson for the interpretation of Thames Valley Park is that it should not automatically be assumed that occupation would have been confined to (or even present on) the seemingly attractive gravel ridge or the terrace and nor could its location necessarily have been inferred from the flint distribution, even with a fuller data set.

The flint scatter on the terrace was adjacent to and partially within a contemporary stream channel, with no indication of associated features nearby. Although only partly defined by the surface collection and excavation programme, it is likely that the limits of the scatter had already been blurred by post-depositional processes. Within the colluvial sequences (most clearly that in trench VI) indications of marling and ploughing dating to the Romano-British period or later were observed; an extension of this activity into areas with little or no colluvial capping would have dispersed the scatter, masking any patterning and resulting in some (perhaps most) of the material upslope being incorporated into upper, ploughsoil, deposits and thus embarking on an eventual downslope course. In the absence of systematic investigation of the topsoil prior to the stripping of trench 49 it is not possible to assign limits to the flint scatter with any degree of certainty.

The question remains as to whether the flint scatter should be regarded as being more or less *in situ* as recorded, or whether it is more likely that the whole or the greater part of the assemblage originated higher up the terrace slope. Despite the likelihood that the scatter was once more extensive, it must be acknowledged that flintwork was almost exclusively confined to the colluvium, throughout which deposit it was mixed with material of later date. The presence of smaller flint chips indicate that much of the material was derived from knapping waste, although these pieces of debitage are poorly represented, even from sieved contexts. This differential bias favouring the larger elements could be accounted for by a process of post-depositional sorting such as would result from downslope movement. Nevertheless, a consideration of the geological processes beneath and within the colluvium strongly suggests that some downslope movement had already occurred by the time the artefacts were being deposited.

The proximity with which conjoining flakes were recovered suggests only limited lateral movement of at least parts of the scatter subsequent to its formation, even though the debitage may not have been in a primary position. The upheavals caused by gravel flares and the subsequent disturbance from ploughing could account for vertical displacement resulting in the mixing of finds and the disappearance of smaller flint spalls from the excavated zones of the profile. Although there are few indications from the pollen sequence retrieved from the floodplain that the open conditions necessary for the promotion of colluviation existed prior to the elm decline, the degree of movement required was slight and may have been accomplished by only very localised changes.

Despite the relative scarcity of contemporary sites in the immediate vicinity of Thames Valley Park, the floodplain and terrace locations of the flint scatters echo those of known Mesolithic sites elsewhere. Clearly the discovery of sites, particularly in recent times, reflects areas of development as much as it reflects the location of sites, but a riverine location would have provided, within a quite limited area, a broad diversity of resources and opportunities.

At Thames Valley Park, the discovery of the semi-articulated aurochs skeleton displaying butchery marks in river channel peat on the floodplain may represent a possible 'kill site' or opportunistic scavenging of an animal stranded in a marsh. The find is certainly indicative of some exploitation of the floodplain zone if not directly for hunting. The flint from the terrace area suggests an industrial function at that location but episodes of activity at both sites are likely to have been short-lived and temporary in nature. In the absence of clearly defined evidence of occupation, activity or economy (the hazel nuts from the colluvial deposits at the foot of the terrace are not securely stratified), it is not possible to assess further such questions as site function, group size, or seasonality.

Late Neolithic–Bronze Age

The archaeological material from Thames Valley Park which can be associated with this period is very limited and, with the exception of the base of a Middle Bronze Age vessel from the within the Iron Age enclosure, does not extend beyond the Early Bronze Age: fragments of Collared Urn, Beaker, and a barbed-and-tanged arrowhead from the floodplain, the Beaker period 'burial' assemblage and a scatter of contemporaneous material from the terrace. The environmental evidence suggesting a sequence of regional clearance events and an expansion of floodplain pasture implies a greater amount of activity than could be reconstructed from these artefacts alone. It is possible that the floodplain and lower terrace areas remained marginal zones within an otherwise evolving landscape, providing areas suitable for seasonal grazing on land belonging to a settlement lying further afield. However, for the later Bronze Age–Early Iron Age periods the evidence for forest regeneration is fully in accord with the total absence of any archaeological activity within the limits of the areas investigated and it is clear that the site was effectively abandoned at this time.

It is perhaps surprising that activity at Thames Valley Park should have declined at a time when the confluence of the Kennet and Thames had seemingly acquired a new importance, as evidenced by the occurrence of quantities of Late Bronze Age weaponry and other metalwork from the Kennet mouth. However, as Bradley (1986, 43) has pointed out, there need be no correlation between the distribution of deliberate deposits of metalwork and the contemporaneous local settlement pattern. The role of higher-status sites in the immediate hinterland may have been a more decisive factor in regulating the location and frequency of such deposits, and it has been argued (*ibid.*, 46) that the enclosure at Marshall's Hill, only 2 km to the south of Thames Valley Park, could have functioned in this way. The location of such sites may even have had an opposite influence, perhaps acquiring or requiring a relatively sterile 'buffer zone' where intensive occupation or activity was absent or avoided. In addition, the metalwork deposits themselves need to be regarded critically: Ehrenberg (1980) has shown that it is possible that the significance of this cluster has been over-estimated. The correlation of Late Bronze Age spearheads with Neolithic axes and Saxon spearheads is particularly marked at Kennet mouth, and this may owe much to differential recovery and the practice of dredgers in attributing finds to the nearest lock, bridge, or other topographical feature, making it likely that material was retrieved from a wider area than present records would otherwise allow (*ibid.*, 5–7). In any case, a wider perspective shows that the quantities from the area of Kennet mouth are rather less than those produced from dredging below Marlow (*ibid.*, fig. 4). Nevertheless, the apparent later Bronze Age abandonment of Thames Valley Park is contrary to the pattern now established for the lower Kennet Valley, where pollen spectra from Aldermaston Wharf, Knight's Farm (both in Bradley *et al.* 1980), and Anslow's Cottages (Butterworth and Lobb 1992) show a marked shift from woodland to grassland accompanied by an intensification of settlement activity. Certain areas were particularly densely settled: at the Reading Business Park development, 6 km upstream from Thames Valley Park, at least eight Late Bronze Age settlements existed on the floodplain and gravel terraces of the Kennet within an area of 6 km^2 (Lambrick 1990), where wells, water-holes, and paddocks indicate a substantial pastoral component for the sites nearest the river. Carbonised cereals suggest a more significant arable component on better-drained soils at slightly higher elevations (Bradley *et al.* 1980) and settlement evidence of this period may simply lie beyond the area of investigation, perhaps beneath the cropmark complex just to the east of Thames Valley Park. It is, however, perhaps unsurprising that the later prehistoric settlement pattern should favour the lower Kennet over the Thames Valley. The less well-controlled Thames is prone to bursting its banks in the stretch through Reading, and seasonal flooding of the wide, marshy valley was probably the principal reason for the establishment of the later urban centre on the banks of the Kennet (Astill 1978, 75).

Iron Age–Romano-British

The stages of evaluation undertaken at Thames Valley Park had sought to avoid placing undue emphasis on the highly visible enclosure site by establishing the actual distribution of archaeological material in the immediate area prior to formulating a final excavation design. The potential pitfalls of automatically assuming that an enclosure forms the only, or the major, focus of activity are amply demonstrated by excavations in advance of the construction of the M3 motorway in Hampshire, where the examination of an Iron Age enclosure at Winnall Down (Fasham 1985) was later supplemented by investigations of an immediately adjacent 15 ha area containing evidence for well-dispersed contemporaneous or near-contemporaneous settlement and other activities (Fasham *et al* 1989). At Thames Valley Park such an approach was only partially successful since the site boundaries dictated that potentially related elements (ditched trackway and field systems visible to the east on aerial photographs) would remain unexamined. Limitations on time and the difficulties of feature recognition following stripping were not conducive to a detailed investigation of unenclosed areas and, as a consequence, attention was of necessity directed towards the enclosure ditches and the interior and it is possible that the scale and intensity of activities beyond the confines of the enclosure have been underestimated. With this caveat, later Iron Age activity was apparently almost exclusively restricted to the enclosure (Fig. 55), only isolated elements dating to the period being found outside its confines (Fig. 56). It is likely, though, that at least some elements of the associated field system also originate in this pre-Conquest period. Non-domestic Romano-British activity, principally the small cremation cemetery, extended into a wider area (Fig. 56).

Structural evidence associated with and within the enclosure was slight. The excavation has suggested that

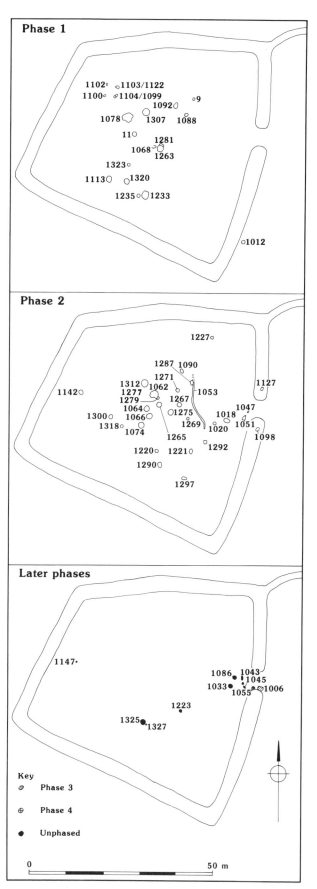

Figure 55   Development of the enclosure and its internal features

114

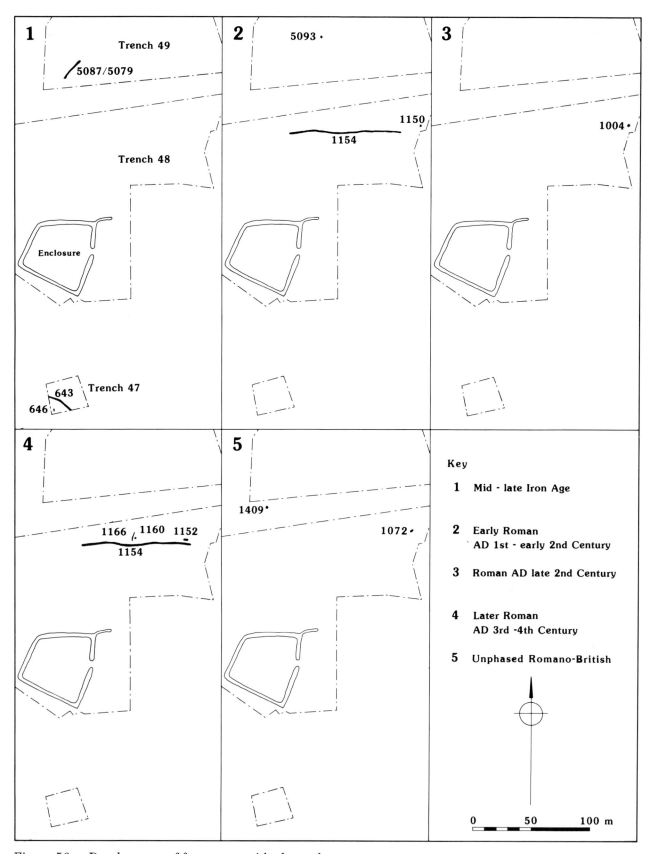

Figure 56   Development of features outside the enclosure

the enclosure may have had an internal bank, with a number of post-holes and a slot at the entrance indicating a gate. Elsewhere within the enclosure only one possible structure (a four-poster) was recognised; certainly no plan of any buildings, domestic or otherwise, could be reconstructed. Evidence for the internal organisation of the enclosure is presented on Figures 55 and 57. There was no significant difference in the pattern of features between phases 1 and 2, with most of the features occurring, as might be expected, towards the centre of the enclosed area. A slight shift towards the entrance can be seen in phase 2 but this may be more the result of differential preservation (or erosion) of relatively slight features than of any real or significant repositioning during the later phase.

The economic evidence from both plant and animal remains suggests that the enclosure may have functioned primarily as a centre for production or storage rather than consumption. Such a conclusion would help to account for the scarcity of structural features and has already been advanced to explain the paucity of carbonised grain from pits of a form conventionally interpreted as being for the storage of grain (see above). The floodplain and lower terrace areas would not, in any case, have been well suited to cereal production, indeed, the pollen evidence demonstrates the use of the former at least as meadows. It would, however, have been suitable for livestock, and better suited to cattle than to sheep. Even so it is likely that winter flooding would have required a seasonal movement of cattle to higher ground. The area to the south of the enclosure would have been suitable for such a purpose but may also have provided land for arable cultivation. In the absence of any clear evidence of settlement, the storage of large quantities of grain in an enclosure situated in an area of grass, hay, or livestock production seems unlikely and the pits may simply have been used for small quantities of foodstuffs, including cereal but perhaps also dried or smoked meat, in sufficient quantities for short-term, temporary use only. Some activity ancillary to cereal production (and storage) is indicated, although the only real evidence for the post-storage stage of grain processing, the presence of a small number of quernstones, may simply mark the preparation of flour for immediate on-site use. The animal bones present a similar picture, where the deposits from pit 1320 firmly indicate butchery but meat-yielding bones were very poorly represented; this could also be construed as indicating limited local consumption only.

Industrial or craft activities are evidenced by the presence of loomweights, smithing slag, and the ?kiln (context 1098). The latter two elements suggest a concentration of industrial activity in the vicinity of the enclosure entrance (Fig. 57). Pottery showed a similar concentration in the ditch terminals, although substantial amounts were also present in the internal pits. The location of the kiln in the southern ditch terminal may account for the presence of much pottery, including wasters, there and in the opposing terminal also. The likelihood that the kiln was used only once and the limited range of vessels associated with it again indicate temporary, short-lived use.

The animal bone came almost exclusively from the internal features with very little from the enclosure ditch, although this patterning may have been due to differential survival. Any interpretation of spatial organisation is difficult, as the bulk of the artefactual material may be accounted for by two separate events of short duration: the dumping of butchery waste in pit 1320 during the later Iron Age; and industrial activity centred on the entrance in the early 2nd century AD. The putative scrap copper alloy assemblage from the upper fills of a ditch situated to the north of the enclosure, including 3rd–4th century items (see above), suggests that some industrial function based within or adjacent to the enclosure may have taken place late in its history. However, the relatively wide date range associated with these phases of industrial activity should be emphasised and the activities are unlikely to have been continuous.

Morphologically, the Thames Valley Park enclosure corresponds with Cunliffe's (1984b) category of Late Iron Age farmstead, where 'the basic unit appears to be the enclosed settlement of single, or extended family size, 30–50 m across, beyond which exist a number of ditched paddocks used for a variety of farming operations' (ibid., 34). However, it is very doubtful whether the evidence from these excavations is sufficient to justify interpreting the enclosure as a permanent settlement. The absence of conclusive structural evidence and the low-intensity of activity, albeit over a prolonged period, are much more indicative of seasonal occupation. Such a pattern of exploitation has been suggested for sites in the Upper Thames floodplain such as Mingies Ditch and Farmoor (Hingley and Miles 1984, 57), involving either the total desertion of the settlement at certain times of the year or the concentration of the majority of activities into a short period.

The activity identified on the floodplain is not as extensive as that found centred around the enclosure on the neighbouring terrace, nor is it of a similar nature, although it is probably related. Although the pottery fabrics are slightly different from those of the enclosure, it is concluded that activity in both areas dates to the Middle–Late Iron Age/Romano-British period. The activity, represented by a series of shallow pits and a possible single rectangular building, may well constitute another area of industrial activity, again possibly associated with metal-working but perhaps of a more intensive, 'heavier' nature than that represented on the terrace: one timber-lined pit may have been a well whilst others could have been used as quenching pits, for which a location closer to the river would have been advantageous. Burnt deposits were noted, as were amounts of hearth slag from iron smithing, but little domestic material was found. It could be that the iron ploughshare tip found at the base of a pit was in the process of repair. It is likely that the activity on the floodplain represents an additional industrial element of the community whose agricultural focus was on the terrace.

It is tempting to link the origins of the enclosure on the terrace with the expansion of floodplain pasture suggested for pollen zone 8b, the balance of the (largely negative) evidence suggesting that viewing the site as a temporary base for seasonal grazing would be more appropriate than interpreting it as a permanent settlement. Intermittent occupation would also be sufficient to explain the limited amount of industrial activity

116

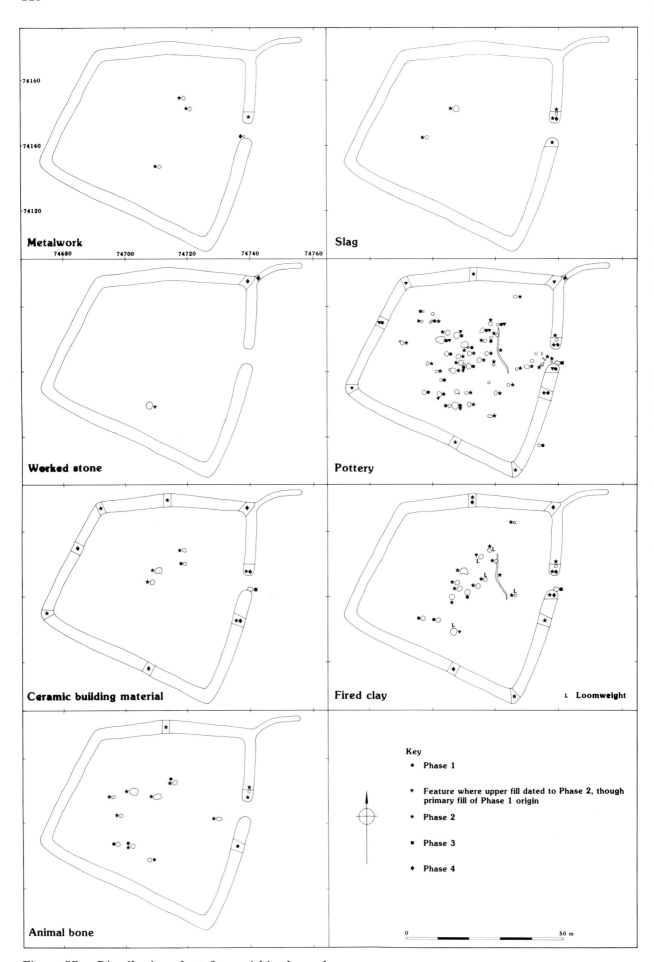

Figure 57   Distribution of artefacts within the enclosure

based on the enclosure and also on the floodplain throughout the Late Iron Age and early Romano-British periods.

In summary, evidence of an intermittent but broad temporal span of archaeological activity was recovered during the several seasons of work at Thames Valley Park. In none of the recorded archaeological phases, however, can activity be considered to have been intensive and, even within the latest and best represented of these, the Iron Age/Romano-British period, the evidence fails to point to any of this activity having been sub-stantial or long-lived. The floodplain and lower terrace areas appear always to have been marginal land, to have been used as a resource, but to have referred to a focus of activity beyond the immediate area of investigation. Lying between the River Thames and the railway line, the area has continued to be water-influenced and peripheral in nature, and to have seen only sporadic and non-intensive use into modern times. As such, it continues to provide a buffer between the river and the expanding area of Reading and its eastern satellites, Earley and Woodley.

6. Project Overview

by I. Barnes

It is not intended here to discuss the archaeological results, but rather to take an overview of the project as a response to development in an area of archaeological potential.

With the exception of the latter stages of post-excavation, funded by English Heritage, the Thames Valley Park project was funded entirely by the developer, Thames Valley Business Park Ltd, a subsidiary of Speyhawk Plc. The fieldwork, carried out between 1986 and 1988, pre-dated by a considerable period the Department of the Environment's Planning Policy Guidance Note 16, *Archaeology and Planning* (1990). The archaeological intervention was not required under national planning guidance, but rather under local regulations, namely Policy EN26 of the *Review of Berkshire Structure Plans* (1985), illustrating how Berkshire County Council led the way in formalising archaeology's place in the planning process.

It has become traditional at this point in a report to qualify the success, or otherwise, of the initial site evaluation. Here, the first evaluation, a combination of machine trenching (c. 1% of the terrace with a much smaller sample of the floodplain), hand excavation of test pits, and augering, indicated the presence of the Iron Age enclosure and identified a series of possible ditches containing Neolithic flintwork towards the northern extreme of the site on the terrace. In addition, a Palaeolithic hand-axe was recovered, as were Bronze Age and Romano-British pottery, some of which was associated with features. A second stage evaluation, including geophysical survey, failed to further define the putative Neolithic ditches but did uncover a Romano-British cremation burial.

The subsequent excavation corroborated, with one major exception, the evaluation results. On the terrace, the enclosure was duly uncovered and confirmed to date to the Iron Age/Romano-British period, other Romano-British finds were made, as were a low level of Bronze Age discoveries. The major difference was that the Neolithic ditch sequence was reinterpreted as the course of a stream channel into which Mesolithic flintwork (the date of the assemblage having been reconsidered) had settled. How can this shift in interpretation be explained? The evaluation had looked only at a few machine sections of the feature and there was much discussion at the time over whether the feature was natural. The argument in favour of its being a man-made ditch was encouraged both by the presence of artefacts deep within the channel fills and by a geologist's opinion that the fills were not of a type normally found in natural, undisturbed channel contexts. Once the site had been stripped, however, it became readily apparent from the meandering plan view that this was not a ditch sequence but rather a series of natural channels. The view of the geologist also changed on

inspection of further sections and the presence of the flintwork was reinterpreted.

A second problem was the lack of information gathered on the floodplain area of the development, a shortfall which had repercussions later in the project. In defence of the evaluation strategy, the original development plan would have resulted in little disturbance to the floodplain, hence little in the way of evaluation was required in that area. The change in policy to allow the burial of pulverised fuel ash on the floodplain dramatically altered the situation. This decision, taken shortly after construction work had started, allowed no time for further evaluation to be undertaken, which meant that all archaeological actions had to be reactive in an area of high potential, not an ideal situation. Much information was retrieved on the floodplain nevertheless, but, had the 1986 evaluation more fully covered the area, it is probable that a more coherent strategy could have been formulated.

Between the second stage evaluation and the excavation, several pre-excavation surveys were undertaken in an attempt to enhance the results already gathered. The grid of hand-excavated test pits was completed over the terrace, the soil from some of the pits being sieved for artefacts, whilst a number of phosphate sample transects and a gridded sample were taken. None of this work produced results of any significance, however. The main virtue of the continued test-pitting was not the additional information it produced, which was minimal, but rather the validity the sieved results gave to the artefact recovery rate from the evaluation. The phosphate sampling was probably too ambitious in intent, the area covered and the density of the grid, at 25 m spacing, being such that it was impossible to pick up significant changes. It might have been better to concentrate the survey in areas such as the enclosure at a much higher density, perhaps 1 m intervals, which could perhaps have allowed interpretation of activity within specific areas to be made.

As with all excavations, hindsight is a wonderful thing and certain aspects of the work might have been better if differently conducted. The stripping of approximately 6 ha of trench on the terrace was undertaken using box-scrapers since it was considered too time consuming to use tracked excavators and dumper trucks. Though confident that no significant discoveries were missed as all stripping was closely monitored, the box-scrapers did not allow enough control over the level of the strip. In places, where more control was required, such as over the enclosure and channels, further machining with JCB excavators was necessary, reducing the amount of time available for examination of the deposits.

On a more certain point, it would have been better to have excavated the area of the enclosure ditch terminals more extensively. The plotting of artefact distributions showed this area to have the highest density of finds recorded anywhere on the site and it would have been interesting to have further defined the patterns for comparison with the distribution of finds within the enclosure. It might have been possible to determine whether the increased densities were connected solely with the industrial activity discovered in the terminals or with a wider set of activities.

Finally, it would have been better if this report could have been written as a chronological summary, rather than as two individual, overlapping, excavation reports. Unfortunately, the terrace report had been largely completed before the commencement of the unexpected floodplain excavation. Integration of the two pieces of work would have greatly increased the post-excavation costs.

A thought for the future concerns the site and its context. The Iron Age/Romano-British remains found were not of high density and would seem to be peripheral to a centre of activity beyond the development area. A glance at Figure 3 shows that it is likely that this centre is on the hill top to the east. Possible future excavation, whether in advance of development or research, may place the evidence from Thames Valley Park better into context.

Viewed in retrospect, the Thames Valley Park project can be seen as a success. The local planning authorities highlighted the archaeological potential of the site, which backed by local legislation, the developer had evaluated with largely successful, informative, results. Information from the evaluation allowed for mitigation of the effects of the development by large-scale excavation of the terrace area. The watching brief proposed for the floodplain was adapted as circumstances changed during the construction programme to result in a second large-scale excavation. Post-excavation work ran smoothly until the developer encountered financial difficulties, at which stage English Heritage stepped in to ensure that the results could be brought to press. It would seem not unreasonable to suggest that the Thames Valley Park project has shown, once again, that local authorities, developers, archaeologists, and national bodies can work together to a common goal.

Bibliography

Aalto, M.M., Coope, G.R. and Gibbard, P.L., 1984, 'Late Devensian river deposits beneath the floodplain terrace of the River Thames at Abingdon, Berkshire, England', *Proc. Geol. Assoc.* 95, 65–79

Abercromby, J., 1912, *Bronze Age Pottery*, Oxford.

Allen, M.J., 1992, *Environmental and Artefact Sampling policy*, Salisbury, unpubl. Wessex Archaeology Guideline 15.

Ames, R.E., 1991–3, 'A Mesolithic assemblage from Moor Farm, Holyport, near Maidenhead, Berkshire', *Berkshire Archaeol. J.* 74, 1–8.

Andersen, S.T., 1973, 'The differential pollen productivity of trees and its significance for the interpretation of a pollen diagram from a forested region', in Birks, H.J.B. and West, R.G. (eds), *Quaternary Plant Ecology*, Oxford, 14th Symposium of the British Ecological Society, 109–15.

Andrews, A.H. and Noddle, B.A., 1975, 'Absence of premolar teeth from ruminant mandibles found at archaeological sites', *J. Archaeol. Sci.* 2, 137–44.

Armitage, P.L. and Clutton-Brock, J., 1976, 'A system for classification and description of the horn cores of cattle from archaeological sites', *J. Archaeol. Sci.* 3, 329–48.

Astill, G.G., 1978, *Historic Towns in Berkshire: an Archaeological Appraisal*, Reading, Berkshire Archaeol. Comm. Public. 2.

Atkinson, R.J.C. and Evans, J.G., 1978, 'Recent excavations at Stonehenge', *Antiquity* 206, 235–6.

Barton, R.N.E. and Bergman, C., 1982, 'Hunters at Hengistbury: some evidence from experimental archaeology', *World Archaeol.* 14 (2), 237–248.

Bateman, T., 1861, *Ten Years' Diggings in Celtic and Saxon Grave Hills*.

Binford, L., 1981, *Bones: ancient men and modern myths*, New York.

Bökönyi, S., 1972, 'Aurochs (*Bos primigenius* Boj.) Remains from the rjég peat-bogs between the Danube and the Tisza rivers', *Cumania 1. Archeologia*, 17–54.

Bonsall, C., Sutherland, D., Tipping, R. and Cherry, J., 1989, 'The Eskmeals Project: Late Mesolithic settlement and environment in north-west England', In Bonsall, C. (ed.), *The Mesolithic in Europe: Papers Presented at the Third International Symposium, Edinburgh 1985*, Edinburgh, John Donald.

Bradley, R., 1986, 'The Bronze Age in the Oxford area — its local and regional significance', in Briggs, G., Cook, J. and Rowley, T. (eds), *The Archaeology of the Oxford Region*, Oxford, 38–48.

——, Lobb, S.J., Richards, J.C. and Robinson, M., 1980, 'Two Late Bronze Age settlements on the Kennet gravels: excavations at Aldermaston Wharf and Knight's Farm, Burghfield, Berkshire', *Proc. Prehist. Soc.* 46, 217–95.

——, Over, L., Startin, D.W.A. and Weng, R., 1976, 'The excavation of a Neolithic site at Cannon Hill, Maidenhead, Berkshire 1974–5', *Berkshire Archaeol. J.* 68, 5–20.

Brown, A.G., 1982, 'Human impact on the former floodplain woodlands of the Severn', in Bell, M. and Limbrey, S.,(eds), *Archaeological Aspects of Woodland Ecology,* Oxford, Brit. Archaeol. Rep. 146, 93–104.

Butcher, S., 1982, 'The brooches', in Leech, R., *Excavations at Catsgore 1970–1973*, Bristol, Western Archaeol. Trust Monog. 2, 105–11.

Butterworth, C.A. and Lobb, S.J., 1992, *Excavations in the Burghfield Area, Berkshire: Developments in the Bronze Age and Saxon Landscapes,* Salisbury, Wessex Archaeol. Rep. 1.

—— and Hawkes, J.W., 1990, *Reading Cross-Town Route: archaeological evaluation at Broken Brow 1990, with a consideration of the Dreadnought Anglo-Saxon Cemetery*, Salisbury, unpubl. Wessex Archaeology rep.

Carruthers, W.J.C., 1991, 'The carbonised and mineralised plant remains', in Bellamy, P., 'The investigation of the prehistoric landscape along the route of the A303 road improvement between Andover, Hampshire, and Amesbury, Wiltshire 1984–1987', *Proc. Hampshire Fld Club Archaeol. Soc.* 47, 36–41.

——, 1995, 'Plant remains', in Fasham, P.J. and Keevil, G. with Coe, D., *Brighton Hill South (Hatch Warren): an Iron Age Farmstead and Deserted Medieval Village in Hampshire,* Salisbury, Wessex Archaeol. Rep. 7, 56–60.

Castle, S.A., 1976, 'Roman pottery from Brockley Hill, Middlesex, 1966 and 1972–4', *Trans. London Middlesex Archaeol. Soc.* 27, 206–27.

Charles, D., 1979, *Aspects of the chronology and distribution of Silchester ware Roman pottery*, unpubl. undergrad. dissert. , Univ. Reading.

Clark, J.G.D., 1934, 'The classification of a microlith culture: the Tardenoisian of Horsham', *Archaeol. J.* 90, 52–77.

—— and Rankine, W.F., 1939, 'Excavations at Farnham, Surrey (1937–38): the Horsham Culture and the question of Mesolithic dwellings', *Proc. Prehist. Soc.* 5, 61–118.

Cleal, R.M.J., 1991–3, 'The pottery' in Healy, F.1991–3, 'The excavation of a ring-ditch at Englefield, Berkshire, by John Wymer and Paul Ashbee, 1963', *Berkshire Archaeol. J.* 74, 18–21.

Collins, P.E.F., 1994, *Floodplain Environmental Change Since the Last Glacial Maximum in the Lower Kennet Valley, South–Central England,* unpubl. Ph.D thesis, Univ. Reading.

Corder, P., 1941, 'A Roman pottery of the Hadrianic–Antonine period at Verulamium', *Antiq. J.* 21, 271–98

Cowell, R.W., Fulford, M.G. and Lobb, S., 1978, 'Excavations of prehistoric and Roman settlement at Aldermaston Wharf 1976–77', *Berkshire Archaeol. J.* 69, 1–35.

Crummy, N., 1983. *The Roman Small Finds from Excavations in Colchester 1971–9,* Colchester, Colchester Archaeol. Rep. 2.

Cunliffe, B.W., 1978, *Iron Age Communities in Britain,* London, Routledge (2nd ed.).

—— 1984a, *Danebury, an Iron Age Hillfort in Hampshire: Vol I The Excavations; Vol II The Finds,* London, Counc. Brit. Archaeol. Res. Rep. 52.

—— 1984b, 'Iron Age Wessex: continuity and change', in Cunliffe, B.W. and Miles, D. (eds), 1984, 12–45.

—— and Miles, D. (eds), 1984, *Aspects of the Iron Age in Central Southern Britain,* Oxford, Univ. Oxford Comm. Archaeol. Monog. 2.

—— and Poole, C., 1991, *Danebury, an Iron Age Hillfort in Hampshire: Vol V, the Excavations 1979–8: the Finds,* London, Brit. Archaeol. Res. Rep. 73.

Davis, S., 1987, *The Archaeology of Animals,* London, Batsford.

DeRoche, C.D., 1978, 'The Iron Age pottery' in Parrington, M., *The Excavation of an Iron Age Settlement, Bronze Age Ring-Ditches, and Roman Features at Ashville Trading Estate, Abingdon (Oxfordshire) 1974–76,* London, Counc. Brit. Archaeol. Res. Rep. 28, 40–74.

Dudley, D., 1968, 'Excavations on Nor'Nour in the Isles of Scilly, 1962–6', *Archaeol. J.* 124, 1–64.

Ehrenberg, M., 1980, 'The occurrence of Bronze Age metalwork in the Thames: an investigation', *Trans. London Middlesex Archaeol. Soc.* 31, 1–15.

Fasham, P.J., 1985, *The Prehistoric Settlement at Winnall Down, Winchester: Excavations of MARC3 site R17 in 1976 and 1977,* Gloucester, Hampshire Fld Club Archaeol. Soc. Monog. 2.

——, Farwell, D.E. and Whinney, R.J.B., 1989, *The Archaeological Site of Easton Lane, Winchester,* Gloucester, Hampshire Fld Club Archaeol. Soc. Monog. 6.

Flanagan, L.N.W., 1970, 'A flint hoard from Ballyclare, Co. Antrim', *Ulster J. Archaeol.* 33, 15–22.

Foch, J., 1966, 'Metriche Untersuchungen an Metapodien einiger europaischer Rinderrassen', unpubl. undergrad. diss. , Univ. Munich.

Ford, S., 1987a, 'Flint scatters and prehistoric settlement patterns in south Oxfordshire and east Berkshire', in Brown, A.G. and Edmonds, M.R. (eds), *Lithic Analysis and Later British Prehistory,* Oxford, Brit. Archaeol. Rep. 162, 101–136.

——, 1987b, *East Berkshire Archaeological Survey,* Reading, Berkshire County Council.

Fox, C., 1943, 'A Bronze Age barrow (Sutton 268) in Llandow parish, Glamorganshire', *Archaeologia* 89, 89–126.

Frere, S., 1984, *Verulamium Excavations III,* Oxford, Oxford Univ. Comm. Archaeol. Monog. 1.

Froom, F.R., 1972, 'A Mesolithic site at Wawcott, Kintbury', *Berkshire Archaeol. J.* 66, 23–44.

——, 1976, *Wawcott III: a stratified Mesolithic succession,* Oxford, Brit. Archaeol. Rep. 27.

Fulford, M.G., 1975a, *New Forest Roman Pottery,* Oxford, Brit. Archaeol Rep. 17.

——, 1975b, 'The pottery', in Cunliffe, B.W., *Excavations at Portchester Castle: I Roman,* Rep. Res. Comm. Soc. Antiq. 32, 275–367.

Gingell, C.J. and Harding, P.A., 1979, A method of analysing the technology of flaking in Neolithic and Bronze Age flint assemblages', *Staringia* 6, Maastricht, Nederlandse Geologische Vereniging, 73–6.

Grant, A., 1982, 'The use of tooth wear as a guide to the age of domestic ungulates', in Wilson, B., Grigson, C. and Payne, S. (eds), *Ageing and Sexing Animal Bones from Archaeological Sites,* Oxford, Brit. Archaeol Rep. 109, 297–314.

Green, H.S., 1980, *The Flint Arrowheads of the British Isles,* Oxford, Brit. Arch. Rep. 75.

Green, C.S., 1987, *Excavations at Poundbury Vol. I: the Settlements,* Dorset Natur. Hist. Archaeol. Soc. Monog. 7

Greene, K., 1979, *Report on the Excavations at Usk 1965–1976: the Pre-Flavian Fine Wares,* Cardiff, Nat. Mus. Wales.

Greig, J., 1991, 'The botanical remains', in Needham, S.P., *Excavation and Salvage at Runnymede Bridge, 1978: the Late Bronze Age Waterfront Site,* London, Brit. Mus. Press, 234–62.

Grigson, C., 1965, 'Faunal remains: 3 measurements of bones, horncores, antlers, and teeth', in Smith, I., *Windmill Hill and Avebury: Excavations by Alexander Keiller 1925/1939,* Oxford, Univ. Press, 145–67.

——, 1969, 'The uses and limitations of differences in absloute size in the distinction between the bones of aurochs (*Bos primigenius*) and domestic cattle (*Bos taurus*)', in Ucko, P.J. and Dimbleby, G.W. (eds), *The Domestication and Exploitation of Plants and Animals*, London, Duckworth, 277–94.

——, 1978, 'The Late Glacial and Early Flandrian ungulates of England and Wales — interim review', in Limbrey, S. Evans, J.G. (eds), *The Effect of Man on the Landscape: the Lowland Zone*, London, Counc. Brit. Archaeol. Res. Rep. 21, 46–56.

——, 1982, 'Sex and age determination of some bones and teeth of domestic cattle: a review of the literature' in Wilson *et al.*, 1982, 7–24.

Groves, J., 1984, *Guide to the DUA Clay Tobacco Pipe Type Series*, London.

Guido, M., 1978, *Glass Beads of the Prehistoric and Roman Periods in Britain and Ireland*, London, Rep. Res. Comm. Soc. Antiq. London 35.

Harding, D.W., 1974, *The Iron Age in Lowland Britain*

Harding, P.A. and Richards, J.C., 1991–93, 'Sample excavation of a Mesolithic flint scatter at Whistley Court Farm', *Berkshire Archaeol. J.* 74, 45.

Hawkes, S.C. and Dunning, G.C., 1961, 'Soldiers and settlers in Britain: with a catalogue of ornamental buckles and related belt fittings', *Medieval Archaeol.* 5, 1–70.

Hawkes, C.F.C. and Hull, M.R., 1947, *Camulodunum*, London, Rep. Res. Comm. Soc. Antiq. 14.

Hingley, R. and Miles, D., 1984, 'Aspects of Iron Age Settlement in the Upper Thames Valley', in Cunliffe, B.W. and Miles, D. (eds), 1984, 52–71.

Holgate, R. and Start, D., 1987, 'A Neolithic pit at Remenham, near Henley-on-Thames, Berkshire', *Berkshire Archaeol. J.* 72, 1–8.

Holyoak, D.T., 1980, *Late Pleistocene sediments and biostratigraphy of the Kennet Valley, England*, unpubl. Ph.D thesis, Univ. Reading.

Isaac, C.L.I., 1977, *Olorgesailie. Archaeological Studies of a Middle Pleistocene Lake Basin in Kenya*, Chicago, Univ. Press.

James, S.E., 1982, *Some Late Bronze Age / Early Iron Age pottery from Reading Museum*, unpubl. undergrad. dissert. , Univ. Reading.

Jones, M.U. and Jones, W.T., 1975, 'The cropmark sites at Mucking, Essex, England', in Bruce-Mitford, R. (ed.), *Recent Archaeological Excavations in Europe*, Oxford, 133–87.

Jones, M., 1979, 'The plant remains' in Parrington, M., *The Excavation of an Iron Age Settlement, Bronze Age Ring-Ditches and Roman Features at Ashville Trading Estate, Abingdon (Oxfordshire) 1974–76*, London, Counc. Brit. Archaeol. Res. Rep. 28, 93–100.

——,1984, 'The plant remains' in Cunliffe 1984a, 483–95.

——,1985, 'Archaeology beyond subsistence reconstruction' in Barker, G. and Gamble, C. (eds), *Beyond Domestication in Prehistoric Europe. Studies in Archaeology*, 107–28.

Kay, Q.O.N., 1971, '*Anthemis cotula* L.', *J. Ecol.* 59, 623–36.

Keatinge, T.H., 1983, 'Development of pollen assemblage zones in south-eastern England', *Boreas* 12, 1–2

Keith-Lucas, M., 1983–85, 'Pollen', in Johnson, J., 'Excavations at Pingewood', *Berkshire Archaeol. J.* 72, 49–51

Lambrick, G., 1979, 'The Iron Age pottery' in Lambrick, G. and Robinson, M., *Iron Age and Riverside Settlements at Farmoor, Oxfordshire*, London, Counc. Brit. Archaeol. Res. Rep. 32, 35–46.

——, 1990, 'Farmers and shepherds in the Bronze and Iron Ages', *Current Archaeol.* 121, 14–18.

Legge, A.J. and Rowley-Conwy, P.A., 1988, *Star Carr Revisited,* Oxford.

Lobb, S.J. and Morris, E.L., 1994, 'Investigation of Bronze Age and Iron Age features at Riseley Farm, Swallowfield, Berkshire', *Berkshire Archaeol. J.* 74, 37–69.

—— and Rose, P.G, 1996, *An Archaeological Survey of the Lower Kennet Valley, Berkshire*, Salisbury, Wessex Archaeol. Rep. 9.

Lyne, M.A.B. and Jefferies, R.S., 1979, *The Alice Holt / Farnham Roman Pottery Industry,* London, Counc. Brit. Archaeol. Res. Rep. 30.

MacGregor, A., 1985, *Bone, Antler, Ivory and Horn: the technology of skeletal materials since the Roman period*, London, Croom Helm.

Maltby, J.M., nd, *The animal bones from the excavations at Owslebury, Hampshire: an Iron Age and Romano-British Settlement*, unpubl. Ancient Monuments Lab. Rep. 6/87.

Manning, W.H., 1974, 'Excavations on Late Iron Age, Roman and Saxon sites at Ufton Nervet, Berkshire, in 1961–1963', *Berkshire Archaeol. J.* 67, 1–61.

——, 1985, *Catalogue of the Romano-British Iron Tools and Fittings in the British Museum*, London, Brit. Mus. Press.

McDonnell, G., 1983, 'Tap slags and hearth bottoms, or how to identify slags', *Current Archaeol.* 86, 81–83.

McKinley, J.I., 1984, *Cremated remains from the Wallington Road cemetery, Baldock*, unpubl. rep. for Letchworth Mus.

——, 1993, 'Bone fragment size and weight of bone from modern British cremations and its implications for the interpretation of archaeological cremations', *Int. J. Osteoarchaeol.* 3, 283–7.

——, 1994, 'Bone fragment size in British cremation burials and its implications for pyre technology and ritual', *J. Archaeol. Sci.* 21, 339–42.

Mepham, L.N., 1992, 'The pottery', in Butterworth and Lobb 1992, 108-14

Millett, M., 1979, 'The dating of Farnham (Alice Holt) pottery', *Britannia* 10, 121–137.

——, and Graham, D., 1986, *Excavations on the Romano-British Small Town at Neatham, Hampshire 1969–1979,* Gloucester, Hampshire Fld Club Archaeol. Soc. Monog. 3.

—— and Russell, D., 1984, 'An Iron Age and Romano-British site at Viables Farm, Basingstoke', *Proc. Hampshire Fld Club* Archaeol. Soc. 40, 49–60.

Monk, M.A. and Fasham, P.J., 1980, 'Carbonised plant remains from two Iron Age Sites in Central Hampshire', *Proc. Prehist. Soc.* 46, 321–44.

Morris, E.L., 1991, 'Ceramic analysis and the pottery from Potterne' in Middleton, A. and Freestone, I. (eds), *Recent Developments in ceramic Petrology,* London, Brit. Museum Occ. Pap. 81, 277–87.

Neal, D.S., 1974, *The Excavation of the Roman Villa in Gadebridge Park, Hemel Hempstead, 1963–8,* London, Britannia Monog. 6.

Newcomer, M.H. and Sieveking, G. de G., 1980, 'Experimental flake scatter-patterns: a new interpretative technique', *J. Fld Archaeol.* 7, 345–52.

Ohnuma, K. and Bergman, C., 1984, 'Experimental studies in the determination of flaking mode', *Bull. Inst. Archaeol.* 19 (1982), 161–70.

Peacock, D.P.S., 1987, 'Iron Age and Roman quern production at Lodsworth, West Sussex', *Antiq. J.* 67, 61–85.

—— and Williams, D.F., 1986, *Amphorae and the Roman Economy, an Introductory Guide,* London.

Piggott, S., 1962, *The West Kennet Long Barrow Excavations 1955–56,* London.

—— and Seaby, W.A., 1937, 'Early Iron Age site at Southcote, Reading', *Proc. Prehist. Soc.* 4, 43–57.

Poole, C., 1984, 'The structural use of daub, clay and timber', in Cunliffe 1984a, 110–23.

Rankine, W.F. and Dimbleby, G.W., 1961, 'Further excavations at Oakhanger, Selborne, Hampshire. Site VIII', *Wealden Mesolithic Res. Bull.* 1–8, Privately printed.

Rashbrook, C., 1983, A discussion of the pottery found at Hamstead Marshall, near Newbury, Berkshire, unpubl. undergrad. dissert. , Univ. Reading.

Rees, S., 1981, *Ancient Agricultural Implements,* Aylesbury, Shire.

Rees, H., 1995, 'Iron Age and Roman pottery', in Fasham *et al.* 1995, 35–46

Reynolds, P., 1974, 'Experimental Iron Age storage pits', *Proc. Prehist. Soc.* 40, 118–31.

Rye, O.S., 1981, *Pottery Technology,* Washington.

Scaife, R.G., 1987, 'A review of later Quaternary plant microfossil and macrofossil research in southern England; with special reference to environmental archaeology', in Keeley, H.C.M. (ed.), *Environmental Archaeology: A Regional Review,* London, Hist. Build. Monu. Comm. England, Pap. 1, Vol. 12

—— and Burrin, P.J., 1983, Floodplain development in, and the vegetational history of, the Sussex High Weald and some archaeological implications', *Sussex Archaeol. Collect.* 121, 1–10.

Seager Smith, R.H. and Davies, S.M., 1993, 'Roman pottery', in Woodward, P.J., Davies, S.M. and Graham, A.H., *Excavations at Greyhound Yard, Dorchester 1981–4,* Dorchester, Dorset Natur. Hist. Archaeol. Soc. Monog. 12, 202–89

Seagrief, S.C. and Godwin, H., 1960, Pollen diagrams from southern England: Elstead, Surrey', *New Phytologist* 59, 84–91.

Sellwood, L., 1984, 'Objects of iron', in Cunliffe 1984a, 346–71.

Serjeantson, D. and Gardiner, J., 1995, 'Antler implements and ox scapulae shovels', in Cleal, R.M.J., Walker, K.E. and Montague, R., *Stonehenge in its Landscape: Twentieth-Century Excavations,* London, Eng. Herit. Archaeol. Rep. 10, 414–29.

Shaw, M., 1979, 'Romano-British pottery kilns on Camp Hill, Northampton', *Northamptonshire Archaeol.* 14, 17–30.

Smith, I.F., 1965, *Windmill Hill and Avebury: Excavations by A. Keiller 1925–39,* Oxford, Clarendon.

Smith, K., 1977, 'The excavation of Winklebury Camp, Basingstoke, Hampshire' *Proc. Prehist. Soc.* 43, 31–130.

Speth, J.D., 1983, *Bison Kills and Bone Counts,* Chicago, Univ. Press.

Stead, I.M. and Rigby, V., 1986, *Baldock: the Excavation of a Roman and Pre-Roman Settlement, 1968–72,* London, Britannia Monog. 7.

Swan, V.G., 1984, *The Pottery Kilns of Roman Britain,* London, Roy. Comm. Hist. Monu. Supp. Ser. 5.

Thompson, B., and Allen, M.J., 1992, 'Pollen', in Butterworth and Lobb 1992, 159–65.

Thompson, I., 1982, *Grog-Tempered 'Belgic' Pottery of South-Eastern England,* Oxford, Brit. Archaeol. Rep. 108.

Timby, J., 1985, 'The pottery' in Fulford, M., *Guide to the Silchester Excavations: the Forum Basilica 1982–84,* unpubl., Dept. Archaeol. Univ. Reading.

Walters, S.M., 1949, 'Eleocharis L', *J. Ecol.* 37, 196–198.

White, H.J.O., 1907, *The Geology of the Country Around Hungerford and Newbury.*

White, T.E., 1952, 'Observations on the butchery techniques of some aboriginal peoples', *American Antiquity* 17, 337–38

124

Williams, A., 1944, 'Excavations in Barrow Hills Field, Radley, Berkshire, 1944', *Oxoniensia* 13, 1–9.

Williams, D.P.S. and Peacock, D.F., 1983, 'The importation of olive oil into Roman Britain', in Blázquez, J.M. and Remesal, J. (eds), *Production y comercio del Aceite en la Antigüedad. II Congresso,* Madrid, 263–80.

Wilson, D.G., 1984, 'The carbonisation of weed seeds and their representation in macrofossil assemblages' in Balkema, A.A. (ed.), *Plants and Ancient Man,* 201–6.

Wood, E.S., 1971, 'The excavation of a Bronze Age Barrow: Green Howe, North Deighton, Yorkshire', *Yorkshire Archaeol. J.* 43, 2–32.

Wymer, J.J., 1966, 'Excavations of the Lambourn long barrow 1964', *Berkshire Archaeol. J.* 62, 4.

——, 1968, *Lower Palaeolithic Archaeology in Britain,* London, Duckworth.

Young, C.J., 1977, *Oxfordshire Roman Pottery,* Oxford, Brit. Archaeol. Rep. 43.

Index

By Lesley and Roy Adkins

IA is used as an abbreviation for Iron Age, and RB for Romano-British. Chronological order takes precedence over alphabetical order. For example, under animal bones, Mesolithic and Neolithic appear before Bronze Age and Iron Age.

Wessex Archaeology Reports

All reports are available, post free, from Oxbow Books, Park End Place, Oxford OX1 1HN

No. 1 *Excavations in the Burghfield Area, Berkshire: Developments in the Bronze Age and Saxon Landscapes,* C.A. Butterworth & S.J. Lobb 1992, ISBN 1 874350 01 9, £20.00

No. 2 *Excavations in the Town Centre of Trowbridge, 1977 & 1986–88,* Alan H. Graham & Susan M. Davies 1993, ISBN 1 874350 02 7, £18.00

No. 3 *Jennings Yard, Windsor: a Closed Shaft Garderobe and Associated Medieval Structures,* John W. Hawkes & Michael J. Heaton 1993, ISBN 1 874350 05 1, £15.00

No. 4 *Excavations at County Hall, Dorchester, Dorset, 1988: in the North-West Quarter of Durnovaria,* Roland J.C. Smith 1993, ISBN 1 874350 08 6, £15.00

No. 6 *Early Settlement in Berkshire: Mesolithic–Roman Occupation Sites in the Thames and Kennet Valleys,* I. Barnes, W.A. Boismier, R.M.J. Cleal, A.P. Fitzpatrick, and M.R. Roberts 1995, ISBN 1 874530 12 4, £18.00

No. 7 *Brighton Hill South (Hatch Warren): an Iron Age Farmstead and Deserted Medieval Village in Hampshire,* P.J. Fasham and G. Keevill with D. Coe 1995, ISBN 1 874350 13 2, £20.00

No. 8 *Archaeology in the Avebury Area, Wiltshire: Recent Discoveries Along the Line of the Kennet Valley Foul Sewer Pipeline, 1993,* Andrew B. Powell, Michael J. Allen, and I. Barnes 1996, ISBN 1 874350 15 9, £10.00

No. 9 *Archaeological Survey of the Lower Kennet Valley, Berkshire,* S.J. Lobb and P.G. Rose 1996, ISBN 1 874350 14 0, £20.00,

No. 10 *Three Excavations Along the Thames and its Tributaries, 1994: Neolithic to Saxon Settlement and Burial in the Thames, Colne, and Kennet Valleys,* Phil Andrews and Andrew Crockett 1996, ISBN 1 874350 18 3, £10.00

No. 11 *Excavations along the Route of the Dorchester By-pass, Dorset, 1986-8,* Roland J.C. Smith, Frances Healy, Michael J. Allen, Elaine L. Morris, I. Barnes, and P J. Woodward 1997 ISBN 1 874350 10 8; £36.00

No. 12 *Archaeology on the Route of the Westhampnett Bypass, West Sussex, 1992: the Cemeteries,* A.P Fitzpatrick 1997 ISBN 1 874350 20 5; £25.00

No. 13 *Excavations in Newbury, Berkshire, 1979–1990,* A.G. Vince, S.J. Lobb, J.C. Richards, and Lorraine Mepham 1997, ISBN 1 874350 21 3; £16.00

Also available: *The English Palaeolithic Reviewed* ed. C. Gamble & A.J. Lawson 1996, ISBN 1 874350 17 5; £10